ELIZABETH F. KUNIHOLM
ATTORNEY AT LAW
4101 LAKE BOONE TRAIL
SUITE 504
RALEIGH, NC 27607

1070

JURY

PERSUASION:

psychological strategies & trial techniques

JURY
PERSUASION:
psychological strategies & trial techniques

BY DR. DONALD E. VINSON

 PRENTICE HALL LAW & BUSINESS

Requests for permission to make copies of any part of the work should be mailed to:

Permissions
Prentice Hall Law & Business
270 Sylvan Avenue
Englewood Cliffs, NJ 07632

Printed in the United States of America.

Portions of certain chapters of this book previously appeared in *Jury Trials* (Michie 1986).

Library of Congress Cataloging-in-Publication Data

Vinson, Donald E.
    Jury persuasion : psychological strategies and trial techniques / Donald E. Vinson.
        p.   cm.
    Includes bibliographical references and index.
    ISBN 0-13-328287-2
        1. Jury — United States.   2. Trial practice — United States.
    3. Persuasion (Psychology)   I. Title.
KF8972.V56   1993
347. 73'752 — dc20
[347.307752]   93-18912
                                           CIP

This book is dedicated

to

VIRGINIA VINSON

*Whose love, patience, and devotion
enable me to pursue the work
I so greatly enjoy.*

Table of Contents

Acknowledgments

The development of this book involved the assistance of many people. I would like to acknowledge the significant contributions of Dr. David S. Davis, Dr. Ross P. Laguzza, and Dr. Philip K. Anthony of DecisionQuest, Inc. Their editorial input and redrafting efforts in the early stages of the manuscript were enormously helpful and enhanced the book in many ways. It has been a privilege to work with these bright and talented friends on this project and on many cases over the years. I am also grateful to the trial lawyers who have taken time from busy schedules to share their comments, observations, and courtroom experiences throughout the book. Their contributions have added a dimension of relevance and practical insight that I am confident the reader will find interesting and enjoyable. They have been identified in the **Contributing Lawyers** section at the beginning of the book. I would also like to thank my publishers, Lynn and Steve Glasser, and Dan Mangan, Vice President, Editorial, at Prentice Hall Law & Business. I also gratefully acknowledge Noah J. Gordon, Managing Editor, for his editorial expertise and contributions. Finally, I would like to thank Rita Plantamura, my executive assistant, for the tremendous assistance she provided over the course of this project. Her patience, superb organizational skills, and facility with word processing were invaluable.

About the Author

DR. DONALD E. VINSON

Dr. Donald E. Vinson is recognized as the country's leading authority in the field of jury behavior and trial strategy. He is frequently interviewed by and quoted in major media, including the *Wall Street Journal, New York Times, International Herald Tribune, Los Angeles Times, Forbes, The Economist, Time Magazine, CBS Evening News, NBC Nightly News,* and *Nightline.* Vinson is an author or contributor to ten books and more than 40 articles on the role of behavioral and social science research in the litigation arena. He is a member of the Editorial Advisory Board of *Inside Litigation,* and is the Co-Editor of the *Litigation Series* at Prentice Hall.

With a B.A. in Economics, an M.S. in Marketing Research, an M.A. in Sociology and a Ph.D. in Marketing and Consumer Behavior, Dr. Vinson taught courses in consumer behavior and marketing research at LSU, UCLA, and was Chairman of the Marketing Department at the University of Southern California. During his tenure in academia, Vinson fashioned the principles which led to the development of behavioral science consulting for litigation. Over the last 17 years, he has worked with hundreds of attorneys throughout the country in a majority of the high profile cases that have gone to trial. Dr. Vinson founded Litigation Sciences, Inc., and was Chief Executive Officer until he left the firm in 1989.

Contributing Authors

DR. DAVID S. DAVIS

Dr. David Scott Davis has written and lectured extensively on jury behavior and has advised lawyers on jury persuasion strategies in hundreds of cases. He received his AB degree from Rutgers, MSC from the London School of Economics, and Ph.D. in Sociology from Princeton. Dr. Davis is the Managing Partner of DecisionQuest's office in Boston and has worked at the Department of Justice and as a Post-doctoral fellow at UCLA.

DR. ROSS P. LAGUZZA

Ross Laguzza began studying juror psychology in 1981, and over the years has consulted with attorneys in over 500 major trials in 36 states and Puerto Rico. He is a frequent lecturer on the principles of jury decision making and strategies for persuasion in the courtroom. Dr. Laguzza received his Ph.D. in Applied Social Psychology from the University of Nebraska-Lincoln. He is the Managing Partner of DecisionQuest's Houston office.

DR. PHILIP K. ANTHONY

Dr. Anthony has been a leading figure in the field of jury psychology and trial consulting for more than 12 years and has authored numerous publications on the subject of jury persuasion. He received his Ph.D. from the University of Southern California in Communication Sciences and Social Psychology and is the President and CEO of DecisionQuest, Inc., which is headquartered in Los Angeles.

Contributing Lawyers

Lane D. Bauer
Shook, Hardy & Bacon
Kansas City

Robert T. Berendt
Monsanto Company
St. Louis

Robert A. Boas
The Coca-Cola Company
Atlanta

Jack E. Brown
Brown & Bain
Phoenix

James A. Bruen
Landels, Ripley & Diamond
San Francisco

Robert A. Clifford
Robert Clifford & Associates,
*   P.C.*
Chicago

James W. Creamer, Jr.
Creamer and Seaman, P.C.
Denver

Donald D. Eckhardt
A.O. Smith Corporation
Milwaukee

Charles J. Faruki
Faruki Gilliam & Ireland
Dayton

William A. Gordon
Mayer, Brown & Platt
Chicago

Edwin W. Green
Bronson, Bronson & McKinnon
Los Angeles

Andrew C. Hartzell, Jr.
Debevoise & Plimpton
New York

Richard A. Hibey
Andeson, Hibey, Nauheim &
*   Blair*
Washington, DC

Bud G. Holman
Kelley Drye & Warren
New York

John A. Irvine
Thelen, Marrin, Johnson &
*   Bridges*
Houston

Michael B. Keating
Foley, Hoag & Eliot
Boston

Diann H. Kim
Tuttle & Taylor
Los Angeles

William H. King, Jr.
McGuire, Wood, Battle &
*   Boothe*
Richmond

George S. Leisure, Jr.
Donovan Leisure Newton &
*   Irvine*
New York

Warren Bricken Lightfoot
Lightfoot, Franklin, White &
*   Lucas*
Birmingham

Patrick Lynch
O'Melveny & Myers
Los Angeles

Edward F. Mannino
Mannino, Walsh & Griffith, P.C.
Philadelphia

John S. Martel
Farrela, Braun and Martel
San Francisco

Thomas J. McDermott, Jr.
Bryan Cave
Los Angeles

Frederick W. Morris
Leonard, Street & Deinard
Minneapolis

R. John Nyhan
Pillsbury, Madison & Sutro
Los Angeles

Eugene G. Partain
King & Spalding
Atlanta

Charles F. Preuss
Bronson, Bronson & McKinnon
San Francisco

James W. Quinn
Weil, Gotshal & Manges
New York

Alan H. Silberman
Sonnenschein Carlin Nath &
*   Rosenthal*
Chicago

Franklin M. Tatum III
Wright, Robinson, McCammon,
*   Osthimer & Tatum*
Richmond

Gerald Walpin
Rosenman & Colin
New York

H. James Wulfsberg
Lempres and Wulfsberg
Oakland

Introduction

On a late winter evening in 1976, I received a phone call that inalterably changed my life in so many ways that, looking back today, I still find somewhat startling. I was a college professor at the University of Southern California and I was happily engaged in things professors do — teaching, research, and writing academic articles that no one, other than a handful of other professors, would ever read. I loved what I was doing. Teaching was enormously fun and I was becoming more and more intrigued with my research on the ways in which the values, attitudes, and beliefs people held influenced the decisions they made. This, of course, had obvious implications for advertising, marketing, politics, and communication in general. If we understood the decision making process, we could then design persuasive strategies to influence these decisions.

Fate was an implacable strategist. But for the intervention of the IBM antitrust litigation and the creative genius of Tom Barr and David Boise at Cravath, Swaine & Moore, and Nick Katzenbach at IBM, I would have undoubtedly remained sanguinely cloistered on a college campus in downtown Los Angeles. This was not to be. With the fateful phone call, I was retained to undertake a study (later referred to as the "shadow jury"* project by the media) that, for all practical purposes, initiated the field of jury research. IBM was preparing for trial in a case that involved extremely complex computer technology, sophisticated economic analysis, and a variety of challenging antitrust concepts for non-lawyers. The Cravath team wondered what preconceived ideas about these issues the jurors would carry with them into the courtroom. How would their attitudes, opinions, and personal experiences influence the ways in which they might evaluate the evidence in the case? And of course, most importantly, how could the IBM team enhance the effective-

---

* *Shadow Jury* is a registered trademark of Litigation Sciences, Inc.

ness of its communication with the jury during the course of the trial? IBM won the case with a directed verdict after the plaintiff's case-in-chief, but the attendant publicity that this initial jury research project received after the case concluded elicited the interest of other litigants preparing for trial. Jury research was born. Over the years, the novel concept of studying jury behavior has become recognized as a standard component of trial preparation.

Since leaving the university, I have had the unique opportunity of working with hundreds of trial lawyers to develop persuasive trial strategies and tactics based on applied psychology, sociology, and communication research. A large number of these people have become good friends to whom I am deeply indebted. Their trust, loyalty, and receptiveness to new ideas has provided me with an exhilarating and rewarding professional life vastly beyond the expectations of a USC professor in 1976.

This book has been written for trial lawyers or those who are interested in what trial lawyers do. With this in mind, I have relied heavily upon personal experiences and insights where the applications of the behavioral sciences have practical implications to courtroom persuasion. A book of this nature clearly represents many compromises. One could argue that various theoretical constructs or research findings that could contribute to our understanding of persuasion are absent from this book. Additionally, some of the material that is included has received limited coverage. This is certainly true. The role of Freudian psychology in persuasion theory, as one example, could easily consume multiple volumes rather than the brief attention devoted here. Thus, it is important to state at the outset that this is not a book on the theory of persuasion nor is it a review of the contemporary literature on the subject from an academic perspective. Rather, it was written to provide busy people with an overview of selected topics from psychology, sociology, and communication science which are particularly relevant to persuasion in the courtroom. The book has been designed to explain many of the important elements of the psychology of persuasion and then provide recommendations or examples of how the information can be effectively used. It is meant to be a practical and pragmatic treatment of ideas and techniques of persuasion that lawyers can employ to enhance their trial advocacy skills. Hopefully, the reader will find it interesting, provocative, and a useful tool in preparing cases for trial.

Organization of the Book

As stated earlier, this book is focused on the presentation of various theories, concepts, and observations on psychological strategies and techniques for jury persuasion. Wherever possible, highly specific suggestions for their implementation are provided. Occasionally, there will be do's and don'ts for attorneys to consider, but overall, the point of the book is to acquaint the reader with ideas and insights developed by social scientists which can be productively used in any area of litigation irrespective of the facts associated with a particular case.

This can be illustrated with a few simple observations. In trying to persuade a jury in any case, it is very important for attorneys, for example, to try to discover something about a juror's verdict preference in voir dire, or even prior to voir dire. Psychologists have shown that people decide between alternative explanations of someone else's behavior by using attitudes already in place. These attitudes concern the behavior under evaluation and the person being judged. This psychological insight about the importance of prior attitudes is the basis for trial strategy in general and for specific persuasion strategies and techniques in each in- dividual case.

A second example concerns memory and retention. Communication psychologists have established that people tend to remember the information they hear first longer than information that comes later. This gives rise to the general proposition, long confirmed by many findings, that jurors tend to retain information which is presented at the beginning and at the end much better than other information they receive during the middle of the trial.

The ability to formulate persuasion strategies based on such psychological principles gives attorneys a powerful tool. The framework of legal issues upon which any case is adjudicated is certainly critical and must obviously remain primary. But beyond that, jurors invariably find many other aspects of human behavior and character relevant.

The ability to accurately evaluate these aspects of human psychology is critical to our effectiveness in persuading other people of our ideas, positions, or arguments inside the courtroom. This is also equally true in any other environment in which lawyers need to be persuasive.

Chapter 1 begins with a general discussion of persuasion and reviews the topic from the perspective of philosophers, psychologists, and famous trial lawyers. Thoughts about rhetoric or persuasive oratory are reviewed, as are the scientific foundations of the study of persuasion within a more global communications context.

Juror attitudes and opinions, in the form of beliefs, values, and sometimes prejudice and bias, are the framework jurors use to interpret facts in a case. The ways in which these attitudes are formed and subsequently held by jurors is the starting point in formulating strategies for effective jury persuasion. Once we understand what jurors think, know, and believe, we can design presentations to be consistent with their attitudes, reinforce attitudes positively associated with our case, or attempt to change negative attitudes that could be injurious to our position. This subject is discussed in length in **Chapter 2.** The communication process and the attributes of persuasion are the subject of **Chapter 3.** Here, a detailed explanation of credibility—for both lawyers and witnesses—is provided along with strategic recommendations for dealing with credibility problems. Persuasion techniques involving the use of emotional messages, rhetorical questions, repetition, and the appropriate organization of a persuasive presentation are described. In **Chapter 4,** we examine how jurors use the information lawyers and witnesses give them. Contrary to the "rational" process that lawyers may expect, jurors, like other human beings, frequently rely upon heuristics or simplifying rules to interpret and make sense out of information available to them. **Chapter 5** is devoted to an examination of how jurors learn new ideas, concepts, or information. Central to this important issue is the issue of voluntary vs. involuntary learning, and various reinforcement techniques that the trial lawyer can utilize to enhance the juror learning process. Memory and the concepts of retention and forgetting are reviewed along with explanations of how jurors attribute innocence or blame to the parties involved in litigation.

The next three chapters deal with persuasion strategies at important stages of the trial process. **Chapter 6** is focused on persuasion in voir dire. This includes a discussion of juror bias, methods of detecting bias, and various techniques for seizing an advantage when questioning the jury panel. The chapter concludes with a number of amusing juror selection myths trial lawyers have been known to employ when making their peremptory strikes. Based on the knowledge about the jury panel obtained from the voir dire process, **Chapter 7** examines strategies for jury selection. In actuality, the lawyer eliminates jurors rather than "selects" them, and a sophisticated approach to these decisions involves an appreciation of juror motivations, personality, social influence, and how leadership works in a small group. The opening statement is the *sin-*

que-non of jury persuasion. **Chapter 8** analyzes why this element of the trial is so critically important and what specific steps the trial lawyer can take to maximize its persuasive impact. This includes a discussion of the primacy-recency concept, the role of thematic anchors, and recommendations for the structure, organization, and delivery of opening statements.

Recognizing that persuasion in the courtroom involves visual as well as oral communication skills, **Chapter 9** deals with the psychology of demonstrative evidence. In order to persuade with visual evidence, the jury must first perceive the lawyer or witness' efforts. To effectively manage this process, we must understand the way jurors see—that is, the psychology of perception. After describing how jurors see, we then deal with the physiology of perception and the contribution of Gestalt principles in the design and preparation of demonstrative evidence. The latest technologies for the presentation of courtroom exhibits are described and their persuasive impact on the jury is examined.

More and more frequently, the risks associated with taking a case to trial for defendants involves serious consideration of the possibility of punitive damages. The specter of punitive damages is thus an enticement to proceed to trial or the frightening inclination to avoid it. Understanding punitive jurors and the motivation to award punitive damages is the topic of **Chapter 10.** Here we examine the psychological and sociological factors associated with punitive verdicts and identify a number of juror characteristics generally associated with the desire to punish. Based on this knowledge, strategic recommendations are provided to deal with this issue. Ironically, while the prospect of punitive damages fills defendants with fear and loathing, they are, in reality, relatively easy to detect with well designed pre-trial jury research. In **Chapter 11** we review a number of research methods and techniques available from the social sciences to analyze juror behavior. In order to effectively construct and implement persuasive strategies based on our knowledge of persuasion, it is important that the input or advice the lawyer receives is valid and reliable. This chapter discusses the requirements for scientific rigor in the field of jury research, describes frequently utilized methods for analyzing juror behavior, and provides a brief, non-mathematical summary of appropriate data analysis procedures.

The final chapter of this book, **Chapter 12,** provides a case example of jury persuasion strategies and techniques that were devised and presented by two teams of the country's most prominent trial lawyers. The reader is presented with a behind-the-scenes view of the ABA's famous mock trial, *The United States of America v. Lee Harvey Oswald,* which has been the subject of numerous articles, television coverage, and professional legal education and training programs. The strategies and tactics utilized by the lawyers are described, the reactions of the jury are analyzed, and an interpretation of the verdict is presented.

Jury persuasion strategies do not offer attorneys magic formulas for winning cases. They are based on painstaking pre-trial preparations which fundamentally consist of empirical research on scientific principles. There are intuitive as well as artistic elements in developing a strategy of this kind, and its success is dependent upon the skill of the practitioners, both with regard to its formulation and its use.

The effective use of jury persuasion strategies and techniques can provide trial lawyers with enormous benefits if they are willing to approach the subject with an open mind and to blend their legal orientation with one based on a sophisticated appreciation of human behavior. It is hoped that this book will further these efforts.

DONALD E. VINSON
Los Angeles
January, 1993

CHAPTER 1

Persuasion in the Courtroom

Understanding Jurors

This book is as much about lawyers as it is about jurors. True, jurors are clearly the recipients of persuasive communication in the courtroom, but it is the lawyer who initiates the process or "puts the ball into play." The act of persuasion is an effort to reinforce, change, or create some specific attitude, opinion, or behavior in another individual or group of people. It is a dynamic process involving the relationship between those who attempt to persuade and their intended audience. The phrase dynamic process is a critical one. It implies that for the lawyer to be persuasive, he must adjust his strategies and tactics to the characteristics of the jury.

Jurors are not passive receptors of the lawyers' arguments, witness testimony, or admitted evidence. They do not, with total objectivity and neutrality process and store information, first from one side and then the other, and then later retrieve and methodically analyze it to arrive at a reasoned conclusion after days, weeks, or even months of trial. Unlike computers, human beings are incapable of performing such difficult information processing tasks. The cumulative knowledge from the social and behavioral sciences regarding the ways in which people evaluate information and make decisions reinforces the common sense notion that this is simply not the way jurors arrive at verdicts. What jurors hear and see in a courtroom is a function of (1) what they are given to hear and

1

see, and (2) an extremely complex psychological process of attaching meaning and relevance to the messages provided.

The Art of Persuasion

Recognizing this fact, the key to courtroom persuasion is understanding what jurors feel, what they know, what they believe and then providing them with messages consistent with these predispositions. Thus, jury persuasion is really a strategic activity—one which is dependent upon the trial lawyer's ability to conceive, craft, and articulate messages with which the jury will agree. To be effective, it demands sophisticated insight into the complexities of human psychology combined with sound instincts, good judgement and well developed oratory skills. The late Bob Hanley, a truly gifted trial lawyer, argued that jury persuasion represents a subtle combination of art and science. Hanley believed that the art was associated with presentation skills which could be taught. But more importantly, he also believed that it involved the ability to develop strategies, themes, and courtroom tactics that would convince the jury of the correctness of the lawyer's positions in the case. This component of the advocate's persuasive skill is dependent upon an understanding of human behavior which can be greatly assisted by the social sciences. It is interesting to note that not unlike Hanley, other nationally prominent trial lawyers such as Phil Corboy, Harry Reasoner, Jim Neal, Bob Warren, Jim Brosnahan, Bob Fisk, Fred Bartlit, and Pat McCartan to name a few, frequently employ behavioral science expertise to help them develop and test the persuasive effectiveness of their courtroom presentations.

It was once said of William Jennings Bryan, "One could drive a prairie schooner through any part of his argument and never scrape against a fact." Bryan was one of the most accomplished orators and persuaders of the past 200 years, yet his success was not seen as a result of his simple and logical presentation of facts. It was generally accepted that he possessed other qualities along with unique courtroom techniques which may have had as much to do with his persuasive abilities as his mastery of the facts.

Persuasion involves the presentation of facts, arguments, and information calculated to change another person's attitudes. However, the process is more than a straightforward communication of objective facts and information. Steve Susman, a trial lawyer with considerable success in persuading jurors, believes that he is personally more effective in the courtroom when he is less detailed in his presentations. He believes that lawyers frequently get into trouble when they attempt to communicate too many facts and too much detail in a case. To paraphrase Susman, to give the jury everything is to give them very little. Persuasion is more than just simply relating facts in an attempt to influence other people. If persuasion were that simplistic, we would not need courtrooms or jurors. A computer program could be written to easily determine decisions once the facts had been entered as data. Clearly then, there must be other aspects of the phenomenon of persuasion that lawyers must consider beyond the mere articulation of facts.

For scholars and social observers in disciplines such as political science, communications, and consumer behavior, the notion of persuasion has been an elusive and intriguing concept. Addressing the complexity involved in persuasion, advertising experts have long believed that no successful advertising campaign can ignore the attitudes of the consuming public. Since attitudes affect the way a product is seen and affect the very perception of facts, facts alone cannot combat hostile attitudes. A particularly illustrative incident occurred when the Red Cross asked the American public for blood donations. At first, the Red Cross had used an appeal to patriotism to enlist donors. Their patriotism campaign proved to be a dismal failure. By employing an abstract principle, they were unsuccessful in motivating concrete action: donating blood. Survey research was later conducted to learn why their campaign had failed. The findings were surprising and appeared to defy logic or even rationality. It was learned that giving blood arouses many anxieties, especially among men. Donating blood was equated with giving away part of their virility, strength, and masculinity. Once the anxiety over the basic issue of virility had been aroused, the potential donors were incapable of "hearing" factual information provided by the Red Cross about rapid blood regeneration or the importance of responding to national emergencies. It was determined that to get men to donate blood, it would be necessary to make them feel virile and more masculine in the process. The persuasion strategy that was developed consisted of focusing on the brave and masculine aspects of giving blood, for example giving out pins that displayed a symbolic drop of "blood" attesting to the donor's bravery. Also emphasized in the campaign was the idea that truly masculine men have so much masculinity that they could afford to give a little away. The revised campaign worked quite well as evidenced by the dramatic increase in blood donations to the Red Cross immediately after its implementation. By identifying the underlying prejudicial attitudes and developing a strategy to circumvent them, the campaign successfully persuaded men to become donors.

Classical Persuasion: The Art of Rhetoric

Plato has given us some of the earliest writings about rhetoric. He attributed rhetoric's proliferation as an art, to the founding of democracy at Syracuse in the 5th century BC. At Syracuse, the tyrant Thrasybulus had confiscated all personal property. When his despotic government was overthrown, and a democratic one established in its place, exiles began to return to their homelands. At that time, there were no written records regarding land ownership. The returning exiles were required by the new government to plead their own cases in court to obtain the return of their property. In order to successfully argue in their own defense, these citizens had to become proficient in the art of persuasion. Indeed, the word rhetoric is derived from the Greek "rhetor," meaning "speaker in the assembly." Thus, in ancient times, rhetoric was concerned with the practice of oratory, or formal public speaking. In preparing for their day in court, these early litigants frequently sought instruction from specialists called "Sophists," or "wise men." Sophists were professional educators and lecturers who had turned their attention from the study of science and philosophy to the more practical matters of rhetoric, politics, and the law. Although they had not formulated theories of persuasion, they were quite successful in aiding their fellow citizens in becoming more proficient at oratory. In fact, the sophists developed a reputation of becoming so skilled in persuasion that they could effectively argue any side of an argument. Regrettably, these abilities so enraged their neighbors that sophists were often put to death.

Persuasion was considered an important topic by early Greek writers. An ability to persuade others was considered a valued art and they attempted to formalize "theories" of persuasion. The concept of *arete*, that embodied the ancient Greek cultural ideals of excellence, often incorporated the virtue of persuasion. It was considered more noble to verbally persuade another person than to use brute force to convince him. Because some sort of public performance or oration was regarded as the greatest attainment an educated man could achieve, rhetoric discipline was at the center of the educational process in Western Europe for two thousand years.

Through the writings of Socrates' student Plato, we are presented with the first discussions concerning the importance of rhetoric. In his *Phaedrus*, Plato represented Socrates as saying, "Is not rhetoric, taken generally, a universal art of enchanting the mind by arguments, which is practiced not only in courts of law and in public assemblies, but in private houses also, having to do with all matters, great as well as small?" Plato was principally concerned with the ethics, or proper use of rhetoric. He was not concerned with the mechanisms of *how* rhetoric persuades the listener. Interestingly, Plato believed that rhetoric would invariably be used for evil purposes, which seems ironic in that he himself used it to his own advantage when presenting his ideas. Plato's concerns about the ethics of persuasion are with us to some extent today: The physicist, Robert Oppenheimer, once remarked that the acquisition of knowledge by psychologists opens up the most terrifying prospects of controlling what people do, how they think, how they behave, and how they feel. His statement, made only a few decades ago, reflects Plato's concerns espoused in the fifth century B.C. Contemporary journalists unfamiliar with the concept of trial advocacy, and, more surprising, by some attorneys, still raise questions regarding the ethical propriety of conducting jury research to help develop effective persuasive strategies for the courtroom.

The philosopher who had the most notable influence upon the study of rhetoric and persuasion was Aristotle. He considered rhetoric a useful tool for human interaction irrespective of good or evil intentions and was not particularly concerned with the ethics of persuasion. Aristotle's *Rhetoric*, the oldest and most complete text on the subject of persuasion, contains the concepts and principles used by educators in the fields of rhetoric and oratory for over two thousand years. While his initial ideas were altered somewhat by his followers, he originally proposed a number of basic tenets which are considered to be truisms even today. For example, he held that the speaker must know his audience and will be most effective when he uses the same reasoning accepted by the audience. In addition, to be effective in the art of persuasion, the speaker was instructed to appeal to the motives that typically move—"motivate"—the audience. Most importantly, Aristotle identified three "means" of persuasion: the appeal to reason (logos), the emotional appeal (pathos) and finally, the appeal of the speaker's character (ethos).

Aristotle's early ideas touched upon developments in persuasion theory which would not be understood for another two thousand years. However, his contemporaries and the philosophers who followed him altered his theories by shifting the emphasis away from the audience, back again to the speaker. An elaborately detailed structure developed from his teachings which divided the study of rhetoric into five parts: (1) invention, the process of finding arguments for the speech; (2) arrangement, the organization of the speech; (3) style, concerned with the language itself; (4) memory, which focused on the techniques for memorizing the speech; and (5) delivery, which taught techniques for managing the voice and gesture, or nonverbal behaviors, during the speech. By emphasizing these five aspects of the delivery, Aristotle's followers had de-emphasized his audience-centered ideas. They would not surface again until the nineteenth century.

Aristotle identified three types of rhetoric: forensic, deliberative and epideictic. The forensic, or legal, was used in defense of individual freedoms. The deliberative was concerned with the public forum and addressed issues of domestic and foreign affairs of the government. The epideictic, or oratory of ceremony, was used to eulogize an individual, a cause or a movement. Daniel Webster, the great American statesman and orator, was known to excel in all three forms of oratory. Webster brought more than 150 pleas before the United States Supreme Court. He debated in the United States Senate against Robert Young Hayne and John Calhoun on the issues of federal versus state's rights, slavery and free trade. He also delivered moving eulogies for Thomas Jefferson and John Adams. Aristotle's identification of these three rhetoric types was useful as a descriptive tool. Even though his content classification was embraced by later philosophers in its entirety, it nevertheless contributed little towards an understanding of *how* persuasion could be accomplished.

Greece was not alone in the premium it placed on the art of persuasion. The Roman philosophers Cicero and Quintillion also addressed the importance of rhetoric. Like Aristotle, they were neither interested in the ethics nor the "how-to" of persuasion. They were more concerned about describing the orator and focusing on his personal qualities. By observing persuasive speakers, Cicero came to describe what constituted a good persuasive presentation. Among his generalizations were the assertions that a speaker's character persuades a listener and a good orator presents the strongest arguments first and last. Quintillion admonished that it was never effective to attack an argument which one's opponent has not mentioned, and he noted that any statement may be punctuated and emphasized by a "pause" for effect. They both agreed that in order to be a successful orator, one must acquire a broad liberal education. Again, their views were generally descriptive observations of what good orators did, and were not concerned with how persuasion occurred.

The Beginnings of Modern Thought

The 2,000 year-old classical tradition, begun by Aristotle, ended with the publication of George Campbell's, *The Philosophy of Rhetoric*. Published in 1776, it resembled a true theory more than any work published before. It differed from the classical approach in that speeches were no longer classified in terms of their content, i.e. deliberative, forensic, or epideictic. Instead, the focus was upon how the logical and emotional elements of the speech as well as the characteristics of the speaker functioned to persuade. The motivations of the audience became an important consideration with this approach. Unlike preceding views, the speaker's character was seen as determined by how the *audience* observed and evaluated him, not by anything intrinsic in his personality. Persuasive oratory began to reflect not only the speaker's beliefs, but more profound ideals that were felt and accepted by the majority of listeners. Today, most of us would agree that the same speaker may be evaluated differently depending upon the particular motivations held by disparate audiences.

During the nineteenth century, the British Parliament, an institution not noted for its progressive reforms, displayed a trend toward common speech and away from the allusions to ancient Greek and Roman thought. Oratorical greatness was identified with strong emotional phrasing and delivery. Both reason and emotion were essential. The ideal orator was personal in his appeals and strong in his ethical proofs. He was neither objective nor detached from his audience.

The Scientific Study of Persuasion

The impetus for the study of attitudes and how to persuasively change them came as a result of the Second World War. The method for studying persuasion was strongly influenced by the rise of logical positivism, a philosophy that insisted that all statements be verified by observation or experiment. The war and the experimental method fostered intense interest on the study of communication in general and the attributes of persuasion in particular. Many practical issues needed to be addressed by wartime governments that were dependent upon the ability to persuasively communicate with their citizens. These included, for example, the need for changing attitudes of bomber crews, determining the persuasive effects of training films on enlisted men, or convincing housewives to change the food habits of their families. The philosophical climate of the time required less speculation and more empirical evidence. It was an ideal time for the development of an extensive body of knowledge about communication and persuasion. It is interesting to note that both Hitler and Churchill relied heavily upon the use of persuasion strategies to achieve their war time objectives. Having very different intentions, they both used persuasive oratory with enormous skill and success. Hitler mobilized the defeated and divided Germany into a country bent upon conquest, while Churchill inspired England to meet Hitler's challenge with opposition. How different history might have been had Churchill not possessed persuasive abilities equivalent to those of Hitler.

Shortly after the war, Professor Carl Hovland, who had worked in mass communications research while in the army, headed the newly formed Attitude Change Center at Yale University. Hovland and his colleagues were interested in determining what variables could increase the persuasiveness of a given communication and what underlying psychological mechanisms and processes might influence the "persuasibility" of an individual. In the 1950's, the Yale researchers identified three basic elements which are common to all persuasion situations and which induce attitude change. These were: (1) the source or speaker; (2) the message; and (3) the receiver. Among the elements which were found to be important for the source were perceived credibility (trustworthiness and expertise), similarity to listener, and the speaker's attractiveness to listener. The important message elements that were identified were rate of speech, use of rhetorical summary, drawing conclusions for the listener, one- versus two-sided messages, order in which the arguments are presented, and appeals to the listener's fears. The characteristics of the audience that were found to be important in the early Yale studies were intelligence, gender, and initial attitudes. All of these early findings reflected a common theme: *The receiver of the message determined the persuasive effects of the communication.* For example, the impact of how fast the speaker talked was dependent upon whether the listener believed he was trying to hide something. Or, the credibility of the speaker was not simply a function of his academic credentials, but of how credible he appeared to the audience. Hence, the most notable change from the classical Greek approach to the study of persuasion to the scientific approach was the shift in prominence from the speaker to the listener, and in particular, to the listener's attitudes.

Since the Yale research in the 1940's, there has been a burgeoning level of interest in the field of persuasion. Most of the academic research conducted has occurred primarily in the area of social psychology and has been involved with theories of attitude formation and change. This topic will be examined in detail in Chapter 2.

Communication Psychology

Beginning in the 1920's, there has also been an interest in the various forms of communication technologies and how they might influence or persuade people. In the 1960's, a Canadian educator, Marshall McLuhan, presented the idea that "the medium is the message." He was convinced that the impact of the visual media of film and TV was so tremendous that it outweighed the influence of any other communication form, including speech. McLuhan and other communication specialists of his era warned that a visual medium was far more powerful in its potential for persuasion.

Lawyers in the courtroom have traditionally used verbal arguments to persuade jurors. But most trial lawyers agree that the use of demonstrative exhibits can significantly enhance their ability to communicate effectively with a jury. This view is predicated on the belief that the learning process for most people involves sight as well as sound. Well designed exhibits can make a strong impression on the jury and will affect deliberations because jurors can carry them into the jury room. As we shall see in Chapter 9, there has been a recent expansion in the scope of visual technology available to the lawyer. The laser disc medium and video depositions, as well as computer animation and simulations, are now economically feasible and easily accessible to trial lawyers. Contemporary researchers have begun to explore the effect these media have on jurors. In general, McLuhan's concerns have not materialized. Jurors see the new technology as similar to their everyday experiences with TV, video, and even Nintendo games. In fact, this technology is so common-place for many jurors that some lawyers believe that it may be expected in courtroom presentations in the not-so-distant future. When asked what effect movies and TV lawyer shows such as LA Law have on jurors' perceptions of the courtroom and new courtroom technology, some attorneys believe that it has changed juror's *expectations* about how lawyers should conduct themselves during the trial. This suggests that in American society today, part of a jury's expectations may be based on these entertainment experiences and that while the attorney does not have to necessarily meet these expectations, he had better be prepared to accept the consequences of his approach if he fails to do so. This issue will be examined and discussed in detail later in Chapter 12 when we review juror reactions to the state-of-the-art technology utilized in the JFK/Oswald Trial.

Conclusion

As we have seen, persuasion has been the favorite topic of social psychologists for decades as well as an important subject to philosophers for centuries. Classical theories about rhetoric, oratory, and persuasion focused upon the speaker. Intrinsic qualities of the speaker were regarded as consequential while the part played by the audience was considered unimportant. The classical tradition was entrenched from the fifth century B.C. until the middle of the twentieth century. However, persuasion is more than the simple listing of facts in order to change another's attitudes. Since World War II, a large body of scientific evidence has been generated by social psychologists, anthropologists, communications specialists, and consumer researchers. The findings from this research, which has been ongoing for the past four decades, have enabled communication experts today to make accurate and scientific interpretations about how persuasion is achieved. The material which is presented in the following chapters of this book describes how our knowledge of persuasion and the use of persuasion strategies can be employed to assist trial lawyers make informed decisions on how to influence jurors and their verdicts.

Legal battles in the courtroom and the opportunity to persuade juries represent the essence of democracy and individual freedom. Persuasion equated with freedom? Superficially, the two ideas seem mutually exclusive or at least antagonistic. There are generally negative connotations connected with strong attempts to persuade. Most people prefer to decide "on their own" rather than by being persuaded by someone else. Nevertheless, political historians and social critics are quick to note that since Plato's time, there is a correlative, if not causal, relationship between the art of persuasion and the existence of democracy.

This view is resonated in attitudes held by many trial lawyers. The belief that democratic governments should encourage and support the responsibility of trial lawyers to argue cases and persuade juries on behalf of their clients is a fundamental premise upon which the concept of trial advocacy is based. Regrettably, access to trial by one's peers, and the ability to persuasively prosecute or defend an issue in dispute, is severely limited in many places of the world today. Europeans marvel at the American legal system because it is available to everyone. Many Americans fail to understand that the reason there are so few lawsuits in Europe or Japan is because ordinary people do not have access to the courts. Throughout the world, trial by jury is limited. In the twentieth century, jury trials have been abandoned or eliminated in most civil-law countries. More than 90% of all jury trials are held in the United States. The privilege to argue for our rights and to persuade others that we are correct is considered by many as a bastion of individual freedom. And although there are those who fail to recognize the point, it is the trial lawyer's obligation to be his client's advocate. This includes knowing and using every bit of information available about the basis of persuasion and the effective implementation of persuasive techniques in the courtroom.

CHAPTER 2

The Key to Persuasion: Juror Attitudes and Beliefs

Cognitions

Consistent with what many trial lawyers suspect, jurors do not typically come to conclusions by an inductive process of carefully weighing and sifting evidence. Inductive thinking is thinking which begins with the collection and interpretation of specific information and then the forming of opinions and conclusions. It is a mental calculation in which the sum of factual information yields general conclusions. In a jury context, inductive thinking represents the balancing of evidence for first one side and then the other and then making inferences and verdict decisions.

Many people, however, do not reach conclusions inductively. They make immediate judgements and then seek support for their view from available information. Most jurors, for example, typically reason deductively. They latch onto a few fundamental premises and fit the facts to these premises as they are received. Philosophers call deductive thinking reasoning from the general to the particular.

The ideas or premises jurors bring with them into the courtroom constitute what psychologists call cognitive structures. Cognitions pertain to what we know. Cognitive structures are made up of what we *think* we know. While cognitive structures enable us to learn things that are new, they tend to perpetuate themselves by screening out information that is inconsistent with what is already believed. Occasionally, we encounter people who are flexible and "objective," but this is frequently the result of some special training or higher education. Such people do, on occasion, become jurors. For the most part, however, lawyers encounter a great deal of cognitive inflexibility among jurors. Their cognitive structures act as a mechanism through which they admit information consistent with what is already there. Hence, most jurors strive to reach verdicts which do not conflict strongly with cognitions in place at the beginning of the trial. As Bud Holman[*] points out, this comes forth in post-trial juror interviews again and again. In one case, after a major industry-wide antitrust trial, a juror confessed that during a courtroom recess she broke away from the other jurors when she saw trial counsel in the courthouse lobby. She told him that she never would believe his client would do anything wrong and wanted him to know that. She was quite proud of her effort. Fortunately, nobody heard her comments, although her report was later confirmed by recollections of other jurors that she had indeed bolted from the group at lunch-time for a moment before returning. That defendant's case was well on the way to being decided by that juror long before any significant evidence was in!

Cognitions are frequently associated with such words as beliefs, attitudes, opinions, or values. They can often be inferred from what an individual says or does. However, these cognitions differ in several important respects. The most important differences relate to their duration and intensity. Our opinions are usually related to current questions and tend to be temporary. Our beliefs and attitudes are more deep-seated and lasting. Although no hard-and-fast rule says that we must describe differences in these terms, we can think of opinions as impressions, attitudes as convictions, and beliefs as values. Because attitudes represent an individual's convictions, they play a central role in evaluating alternatives and in making decisions.

Based upon our educational training in the behavioral sciences and our observations of jurors in hundreds of cases throughout the country, we have consistently emphasized a fundamental message to trial lawyers: jurors' perceptions of the trial process and their ultimate decisions are largely determined by their pre-existing cognitions which act as screens or filters to interpret, distort, or reinforce information presented during the

---

[*]   Bud G. Holman, *Kelley Drye & Warren, New York.*

trial. This basic psychological principle, when strategically applied, is one of the trial lawyer's most potent and persuasive advocacy tools. Attorneys who understand the jurors' cognitive and emotional perspective as manifested in attitudes and values will have a distinct advantage in presenting their case, as well as in influencing the outcome of the jury's verdict.

Belief Systems

The predispositions that jurors bring with them into the courtroom are organized into what psychologists call belief systems. Belief systems are made up of attitudes and values which define how a person understands the world. While values represent a person's general ideals and principles, attitudes relate to how these ideals are expressed in the evaluation of specific objects, people, and situations. For example, a person who strongly believes in equality (a general value), may strongly favor capital gains taxes (a specific attitude), not because of the merits of this particular form of revenue generation for the government, but rather as a means for distributing wealth. Attempts to persuade this person to change his mind about this approach to taxation using cogent economic, financial, or business arguments may have little effect if they are not seen by the individual as relevant to the underlying value. Further, and extremely frustrating to the advocate, "logical" arguments or objective facts related to this issue may be totally rejected or distorted in order for the individual to maintain a consistent belief system.

Attitudes and values contained in a belief system are closely tied to an individual's self-concept. People are generally more comfortable when they encounter information, people, and events which are consistent with their belief system because these experiences affirm their own concept of who they are and what they stand for. In fact, a person's belief system tends to persist even in the face of inconsistent information, and people often will take extraordinary steps to protect their view of the world (and their own self-concept). When core beliefs are threatened by contrary information, reality becomes highly malleable if not altogether disposable. Ed Mannino[*] provides an interesting example. In a case alleging that a terminated employee had not been fairly compensated, the jurors found

---

[*] Edward F. Mannino, *Mannino Walsh & Griffith, P.C., Philadelphia.*

for the plaintiff even though the defense brought out that he had been paid more in compensation in his last year than the president of the corporation. The jurors used this fact against the defendant, a financial institution, by concluding that the president must have been jealous of the plaintiff, and should have paid him even more.

Since attitudes are directly tied to a person's key values, they play a significant role in shaping how a person reacts to events both inside and outside of the courtroom. These reactions include how jurors think and feel about the entire trial experience and ultimately the decisions they make. Bud Holman recalls an incredible case in which a convicted drug user and small-time dealer, suffering from HIV positive anxieties, was working with counsel on his appeal. He could not, no matter the effort, the approach, or the time devoted to logic and indisputable history, be distracted from his contention that the HIV virus was (1) developed by Adolf Hitler's physician as a war weapon, (2) taken over by the U.S. Army after World War II and (3) thereafter employed to keep the size of the U.S. Black and Hispanic population controlled. This belief, incredible as it was, was so imbedded in the defendant's mind that he was of no help to himself at his trial or on his appeal. That was the only issue he saw and there was no way to enlarge his vision that either set of his lawyers could devise.

Freedom of Choice v. Large Salaries

It is the essence of good trial strategy to build your case around a few—even one or two—belief systems, i.e., some fundamental principle about which most people feel very strongly. For example, in a recent antitrust jury trial brought by a group of professional football players against the National Football League, the plaintiff football players built their entire case around one essential concept: freedom. These players were challenging a system of rules created by the NFL member teams which prevented them from freely negotiating with other teams after their current player contracts had expired. Their essential position was that all people, no matter how highly compensated, should have the right to choose where and for whom they would like to work.

(continued)

(continued)

The defendants, the NFL and its member clubs, sought, on the other hand, to focus their defense around another strongly felt jury attitude, i.e., that professional athletes are highly paid and, therefore, that limiting their freedom of choice was acceptable because of the business needs of professional sports leagues. In the end, the jury rejected this notion of acceptable restrictions because of the jurors' strong feelings about individual freedom of choice. The NFL defendants' emphasis on the large salaries received by professional football players did, however, have an impact on the willingness of these same jurors to award damages to each of the plaintiff players. As a result, the jury carefully reviewed the record evidence on damages and awarded damages to some but not all of the plaintiffs. Again, this emphasis on belief systems and fundamental attitudes was critical in the development of the trial strategy of both sides.

James W. Quinn
Weil Gotshal & Manges, New York

Attitudes and Decisions

Most attitudes are developed over a lifetime of personal experience with parents, friends, colleagues, teachers, books, television, and a large number of other direct and indirect sources. Attitudes vary in the intensity with which they are held, depending how closely related they are to some underlying core value. For instance, we would not expect a favorable attitude toward number two pencils to be as strong as a favorable attitude toward honoring contractual obligations, assuming, of course, that the latter is more closely tied to one's self concept and belief system. In any event, both of these attitudes could be measured and used as a basis to predict how a person will make decisions in the future. Psychologists have learned that attitudes that are closely tied to core values are the best predictors of behavior, because people are motivated to act in ways that are consistent with their values. Research has also shown that weakly held attitudes are more vulnerable to social pressures toward attitude change.

By the time jurors come into the courtroom, they have well-established belief systems that operate very efficiently in shaping their perceptions of what happens at trial and ultimately, their decisions. It is easy to understand, then, that pre-trial research into juror attitudes is one of the most important strategic applications of social science to the law. The main objective of juror attitude research is to identify the attitudes and values that determine which case facts or issues jurors will find most salient, how they will perceive the evidence on those issues, and how those perceptions are likely to influence their decisions about the case.

The crucial role of juror attitudes was underscored in a patent dispute in which an American company attempted to prove that a Japanese company's patent was invalid because of prior art. The plaintiff was able to present innumerable instances of what it alleged was prior art. However, the defense prevailed. Post-trial juror interviews revealed that among the jury panel, there was a very strong pre-existing belief that the Japanese are extremely innovative—this attitude was determinative of the verdict. The plaintiff's evidence was perceived as of minimal importance.

Attitude Sets

An attitude does not generally exist in isolation from other attitudes. Attitude components tend to be consistent and correspond to other attitudes within attitude sets. For example, a juror's attitudes about sports may tend to relate to attitudes about entertainment or relaxation. As Bud Holman humorously notes, a juror who bets on out-of-town baseball games will not hear the experts who say a scoreboard was up to the contract requirements when it does not provide out-of-town scores. Thus, attitudes as a whole tend to form clusters with other attitudes within a person's total attitudinal system. Although complete harmony need not exist, it would be expected that attitudes making up cognitive structure would be fairly consistent. Thus, for example, an individual is not likely to accept the findings of the Surgeon General's report concerning cigarette smoking and believe at the same time that cigarette smoking is harmless. Yet, as Ed Mannino suggests, a former smoker who quit because of his belief that smoking was harmful to his health may reject the claim of a plaintiff who sues a tobacco company for causing her lung cancer. The former smoker may fault the plaintiff for not quitting herself, and reject her claims of addiction based upon his personal success in having stopped smoking.   Hence, it would be expected that attitudes comprising an attitude cluster set would tend towards consistency, although this is not always the case. If a juror is a staunch Republican and possesses pro-business attitudes, he would not be expected to vote for the award of large punitive damages unless, of course, other attitudinal clusters were more relevant.   These might include his attitudes toward corporate responsibility or competition in the marketplace.

Juror attitudes do not come into play in a trial randomly. Trial content and the issues involved will mobilize juror attitudes in clusters or constellations. These constellations or attitude sets are related to specific trial content. Often there will be aspects of the trial with which jurors have had previous experience. In product liability cases, they may have used similar products. In securities litigation, they may have made or lost money investing in the stock market. Attitude sets which grow out of these experiences are behavioral based attitudes. Jack Brown,[*] in agreement with this proposition, indicates that the basic thesis that juror attitudes that are closely tied to core values are the best predictors of behavior is consistent with conventional wisdom; those who have studied the art of persuasion have long taught speakers to tailor their arguments to appeal to the deepest-held beliefs of the audience. Brown believes nevertheless, it is hard for trial lawyers to accept how limited their power is to move any juror to accept an outcome that the juror perceives as running counter to the juror's attitudinal set.

Attitudes can also form clusters in accord with demographic factors. A person's level of education, age, income, sex, or religious and political preferences can all partially determine what attitudes he will hold.

Research findings based on relationships between specific political attitudes and verdicts have been reported for jurors who favor capital punishment and severe sentences. In the American Bar Association's mock trial of Lee Harvey Oswald for the murder of John F. Kennedy, 80% of the jurors who voted for conviction revealed positive attitudes toward the death penalty in pre-trial questionnaires. Hence, not only was this attitude highly correlated with the verdict, but it could also have been a very useful predictor variable for jury selection. This would be true even if these jurors had indicated that they could "set these attitudes aside!" Jurors who favor capital punishment are more likely to vote for

---

[*] Jack E. Brown, *Brown & Bain, Phoenix.*

conviction in a murder trial, and jurors with positive attitudes toward law
and order favor severe sentences. Attitudes toward the crime itself are
also probably important determinants of a verdict. Jurors who do not
favor particular statutes, like those which pertain to victimless crimes, for
example, will show a tendency to favor the defendant. Attitudes toward
the specific circumstances of the crime can also be significant in certain
instances. Bias in rape cases is commonplace because of attitudes toward
the circumstances of the crime, the physical location, the kind of clothing
worn by the victim, the time of day, and so forth. John Irvine[*] recalls
that during trial preparation of a rape case in which the defense was
consent, the prosecutor examined the physical evidence and was surprised
to see that the expression, "Love is where you find it" was displayed
prominently on the front of the victim's red panties. The prosecutor
quickly negotiated a settlement favorable to the state before counsel for
the defense asked to see the physical evidence. While the other physical
evidence, including slight trauma to the victim, was generally supportive
of her claim of rape, it was not overwhelming. According to Irvine, the
prosecutor concluded, probably correctly, that the jurors' perception of the
alleged victim and her claim would be adversely impacted by her choice
of attire. Today, with the rise of feminist consciousness and a general
change in how male-female relationships are viewed, attitudes toward
rape as a serious crime have changed as well. Data suggests that over the
decade 1970-1980, rapists were judged more harshly as time went on.

Attitude Components

Most psychologists agree that attitudes consist of three components:
affect, cognition, and behavior. Affect refers to our emotions, feelings,
and "gut instincts" about something. Cognition refers to perceiving,
thinking, and interpreting information related to an object, person, or
event. Behavior refers to our intention to act in ways that are consistent
with an attitude. These three components are closely related and each
component is always present in any attitude, no matter how strongly held.
To change or reinforce an attitude, then, the trial attorney must understand the nature of each of the components of the attitude he is attempt-

---

[*] John A. Irvine, *Thelen Marrin Johnson & Bridges, Houston.*

ing to influence and then must design the appropriate communication strategy.

For example, jurors in a toxic tort case might come into the courtroom holding a negative attitude toward large chemical companies. They may be angry about and afraid of the effects of chemical contaminants upon the environment (emotion component), believe that most chemical companies openly engage in wrongful dumping (cognitive), and would like to find a way to punish these companies (behavioral). The attorney could try to weaken or change this attitude by reassuring jurors that this company cares about the environment, by proving that toxic materials were handled in ways above and beyond what is required, and/or by arguing that the company's unsolicited remedial activities make punitive damages unnecessary. Successfully engaging one component can make it easier to engage the other components. That is, jurors who are made to feel less emotional about an issue may be more able to consider evidence that changes the way they think as well.

Attitude Formation

Attitudes are acquired over time in three principle ways. They are either learned from others, developed through firsthand experience, or are the product of self-observation. Understanding how attitudes are acquired is a significant step toward becoming more effective in dealing with them in the courtroom.

Social Learning

Starting almost immediately, a newborn infant's preferences, and later, as he gets older, his opinions and values, are conditioned by his parents. The young child is both subtly and overtly rewarded for sharing the parents' view of the world. Unconsciously, parents model their attitudes in the way they talk and behave in the presence of certain people and things. When children begin school, their span of influence is increased to include teachers, textbooks, and, of course, other children. There are also the influences of religion, social groups and the media—television in particular. At adolescence, children tend to establish their own world view, but it is quite difficult for anyone to completely rid himself of his early training. In fact, later in life, many people come to understand that their adult view of the world is quite similar, at least at a fundamental level, to that held by their parents. Although attitudes and values continue to develop throughout life, it is very unusual for people to adopt attitudes that are inconsistent with their core belief system.

Direct Experience

Another key source of attitudes is the experiences people encounter in daily living. When we are in new situations, we learn new information about other people and things. These experiences provide a convenient and efficient guide for processing subsequent and similar experiences. For example, if a person has dealings with an unscrupulous lawyer, that person may form a negative attitude toward all attorneys and think that "all lawyers are crooks!" This attitude may be perpetuated indefinitely if the person is determined to avoid all attorneys in the future.

Personal experience is a very powerful source of our attitudes. Irrespective of education or intellect, people tend not to process their personal experiences in a very scientific manner. We tend to grossly overestimate the representativeness of something that we experience, despite the fact that our experience may have been quite limited. More simply, our attitudes become efficient, but not always accurate, short-cuts for evaluating new information.

Self-Perception

Another important way that we come to know our attitudes is by making inferences about what we believe based on observations of our own behavior. In other words, we watch ourselves behave and then develop an attitude-based explanation for what we observe. For example, a college student may enroll in a history course, purchase the required texts, start attending classes and then conclude that he likes history. Or an executive may commute two hours a day to work in Los Angeles and decide that he enjoys the time alone in traffic, or that he likes to drive. In both cases, the attitude was formed *after* the behavior was performed. Surprisingly, if you asked the student or the employee whether the behavior or the attitude came first, he would say that he held the attitude in question all along. Careful research, however, has shown that in many cases, the behavior comes first.

In a trial situation, attorneys can use the theory of self-perception to heighten jurors' awareness of their own behavior which supports a favorable attitude. Referring back to the previous example involving the chemical company, jurors with negative predispositions toward chemical companies in general could be subtly reminded of the various ways they use and benefit from chemical products at home and at work. By raising jurors' awareness of their own behavior, the lawyer increases the chances that attitudes that are favorable toward the client will be formed. In this case, jurors can be made aware of behavior that is inconsistent with the general predisposition to believing that all chemical companies are evil. Since it is unlikely that jurors will conclude that they themselves are bad people, this process may lead jurors to conclude that chemicals are necessary and/or that some chemical companies do make valuable contributions to society.

Attitude Activation

As we have indicated earlier, juror attitudes are not evoked randomly during a trial. Perceptions of the litigants, witness testimony, and comments from both the lawyers and the judge will activate related juror attitudes. Many times, the case will address issues that jurors have formed attitudes about when they were quite young; for example, attitudes toward individual responsibility, or the status and authority of physicians. Often there will be aspects of the trial with which jurors have had previous experience. In product liability cases, they may have used similar products. In securities litigation, they may have made or lost money investing in the stock market. Alternatively, jurors may have read or heard something generally or specifically related to the issues at trial.

What tends to surprise lawyers is that the attitudes that are activated in their cases may be quite different than the lawyer's logic-based predictions. For example, in a contract dispute between two large companies over the representations made in an agreement covering the sale of a subsidiary, the lawyers were concerned about how jurors would interpret key contract provisions relating to the subsequent sale. The main case strategy was based on arguing the merits of certain technical contract interpretations. However, it was determined through pre-trial research that jurors were really concerned about the economic impact and loss of jobs due to the sale of the subsidiary operation. Jurors were upset because it seemed that neither litigant had done a good job in protecting employees even though this was not an issue in the case. Despite the absence of any legal relevance, pre-trial research showed that once activated, these attitudes influenced the way jurors perceived and decided the case. It is often difficult for even the most experienced lawyers or psychologists to accurately predict which attitudes will be activated by a case without conducting empirical research.

Attitude-Behavior Inconsistencies

Psychologists have known for a long time that people's overt behavior is not always consistent with their underlying attitudes. People who hold racist beliefs do not always discriminate. People who believe strongly in altruism sometimes ignore those in obvious need of their help. Defense-oriented jurors often go along with a plaintiff verdict. Why does this happen? Are attitudes poor predictors of behavior after all? Fortunately for social scientists and anyone else who makes his living understanding and predicting human behavior, the answer to this question is no. The following attempts to explain this interesting phenomenon.

Discrepancies between attitudes and behavior occur because people do not only hold attitudes toward other people and objects, they hold attitudes toward the *situations* in which those people and objects are encountered. For example, the eldest son in a conservative family may be known around school for his liberal and rather non-traditional views. However, at home, where negative parental reaction is a certainty, these ideas are suppressed. Similarly, the racist may fear costly legal action and the altruist may be concerned about his or her own safety. In other words, people evaluate the potential consequences of attitude expression in different circumstances and alter their behavior accordingly. In a breach of contract case brought by an employee who claimed certain oral promises of compensation were made to him by a large corporation, Ed Mannino found that jurors credited the plaintiff's testimony despite proof that the plaintiff had repeatedly lied on his job application and at his deposition about his educational achievements and work record. While the jurors did not condone lying, their negative attitude toward it was overcome by stronger attitudes that the corporation had unfairly dealt with its employees, terminating many of them abruptly in an economic downturn. This corporate behavior led the jurors to excuse plaintiff's repeated episodes of lying as youthful indiscretions. Their behavior *was* consistent with an attitude toward the situation, which at the moment was more salient.

In the context of juror behavior, attitude-behavior discrepancies are most readily observed during voir dire. Prospective jurors know that society expects jurors to be fair and impartial. Traditional voir dire questions are usually quite transparent in their objective and it is easy to identify the "socially correct response." Seeking to avoid any social disapproval, people readily offer acceptable voir dire answers that do not accurately reflect their underlying values. In the majority of cases, the prospective jurors are not trying to mislead the lawyers or the court, but are attempting to maintain their self-esteem by creating a desirable impression. This is one of the reasons why traditional voir dire is highly ineffective in producing information that leads to the efficient use of peremptory strikes. This topic is more fully discussed in Chapter 6.

During deliberations, if not before, other jurors apply varying amounts of pressure toward individual jurors to get them to conform to the majority view. Many people are susceptible to this type of pressure and will even moderate their own true feelings about the case in order to garner some social approval from the group. Alternatively, deliberations often provide a more receptive environment for the expression of attitudes that could not be expressed during voir dire. In both cases, an attitude-behavior discrepancy would be present.

When it comes to understanding and predicting juror behavior, it is critical to understand the attitudes and values that are relevant to the behavior and the social setting in which the behavior will occur.

Attitude Change

It is possible to infer from what has been said so far that attitudes and beliefs are rigid and immutable. This is not entirely so. One course of action open to jurors who suffer the collision of new information with basic attitudes is to change these attitudes. Attitude change is a change from a disposition to act in one direction to a disposition to act in the opposite direction (from disliking to liking an object, person or event). Often, without intending to, lawyers find themselves asking jurors to do this. The attorney's world of logical argument involves the construction of the unshakable edifice of proof based upon the careful piling-up of fact upon fact. While such an approach may be effective in attitude change with some jurors, it is not likely to work with the vast majority of people who serve on juries. In order to change attitudes, attorneys must carry out a direct emotional assault on the attitudes or beliefs in question.

Most attempts to effect change in juror attitudes rely upon persuasive information, and the cognitive component of the attitude is the most frequent target of attitude change. Attorneys rely upon the communication of information to bring about changes in beliefs which will hopefully lead to changes in attitude. Although this is the most logical means of attitude change open to the attorney, its relative success is not particularly great.

Successful persuasion strategies will be discussed extensively in Chapter 4. For now, it is important to point out that in trial, attorneys can deal with juror attitudes in three basic ways. When favorable attitudes are encountered, communication strategies can be designed to *reinforce* those attitudes. When unfavorable attitudes are present, attempts to weaken or *change* these attitudes can be employed. Finally, when no attitudes exist on a particular subject, the attorney can provide information in an attempt to *create* a new attitude. However, it is always easier to design communication strategies that are consistent with jurors' pre-existing attitudes, or to create new attitudes, than it is to motivate jurors to completely change their views on an issue.

Reinforcing Conflicting Juror Attitudes

In some cases conflicting juror attitudes can arise. For example, it is not difficult to picture a situation in which a major chemical company would be sued by a large number of people for allegedly exposing that group to toxic substances which resulted in serious illnesses or fear of contracting serious illnesses in the future. The case arises in a reasonably small community where media coverage for years has conditioned the community to believe that the chemical company's operations have been poisoning its neighbors and that the company is a nemesis to the community.

The company is unable to obtain a change of venue and the case is tried in the very community where there has been all this media coverage. During voir dire the prospective jurors either

(continued)

(continued)

profess ignorance of the press coverage or, if they admit to being aware of it, state that they can put it out of their minds and reach a fair and impartial verdict based only on the evidence presented at trial. The judge decides that rather than having a "bellwether" trial of a few plaintiffs' cases he will try all 250 plaintiffs at once.

This would seemingly be a very bad and ominous situation for the defendant for several reasons. The defendant is a large corporation and surveys usually show a very unfavorable juror attitude toward large corporations. This large corporation is a chemical company and surveys also usually show a particularly unfavorable juror attitude toward large corporations that manufacture and sell chemicals. The trial setting is in a community in which the citizens have been conditioned for years by the media to believe that this particular chemical company has been poisoning its neighbors by exposing them to toxic substances. Clearly, these circumstances all contribute heavily to a very unfavorable juror attitude toward the chemical company defendant.

However, there are countervailing juror attitudes at work in this case. These jurors are honest, hard-working citizens who believe in fair play and that people are not entitled to be compensated when they are not injured. Indeed, these jurors would have a disgust for people and their lawyers if they believed they were taking the jurors' time and energy to feign injury or fear of injury in order to be unjustly enriched at the expense of the company, regardless of how much the jurors dislike chemical companies in general.

The trial takes place. Plaintiffs proceed to put on their case by parading all 250 plaintiffs to the witness stand. The entire process of plaintiffs' testimony takes four trial weeks. The plaintiffs

(continued)

(continued)

do not appear to be sick. There are no wheel chairs or casts healing broken bones. There are no canes or scars. There is just a display of person after person taking the witness stand looking no different than the jurors themselves and complaining about headaches, sleepless nights, nervousness and other discomforts that the jurors and everyone else in the courtroom may also experience with some regularity. In those rare instances where a plaintiff actually has a serious illness, it is clearly attributable to another cause or at least clearly not attributable to exposure to toxic substances emanating from the defendant's operations.

The plaintiffs are followed to the stand by three experts who testify on behalf of the plaintiffs. Each of these experts expresses his or her opinion that the plaintiffs have been injured by this toxic exposure on the grossest of generalizations. Cross-examination shows these experts to be uncommonly biased toward the plaintiffs with no reasonable basis in science or medicine to back their opinions.

The defense puts on credible experts who are able to convincingly show either that the plaintiffs are not ill or, if they are, it is not due to exposure to toxic substances.

During the course of trial, juror attitudes seem to change. While they were very favorably disposed toward the plaintiffs going into the trial because of all the surrounding circumstances, they ultimately come in with a verdict for the defendant. In fact, the jury's attitude (or attitudes) did not change. What happened was the evidence tapped into the already established juror attitudes that it is not fair to the defendant (no matter what they may think of the defendant) to make that company compensate people whom the jury does not believe are injured.

Robert T. Berendt
Monsanto Company, St. Louis

Attitude Salience

Jurors hold thousands of attitudes. Some are highly salient, important, and centrally held while others are of less significance. Salience refers to the strength with which attitudes are held. Salience tends to be situation specific, however. An attitude can be very strongly held in one psychological context and of less significance in another. For example, a juror's attitude toward the safety features of a particular automobile may be less salient in a purchase situation than say, attitudes towards styling, speed, prestige, or economy. However, if the same individual were a juror evaluating the same automobile in a products liability case in which a small child was seriously injured, attitudes toward the product's safety may now become significantly more salient. Hence, while it is important for trial lawyers to understand the attitudes that jurors are likely to bring with them into the courtroom, it is *critical* that they understand the salience of attitudes which are likely to be associated with issues or factors in their case.

The only way to really understand what attitudes jurors hold and the salience of these attitudes is to undertake carefully designed pre-trial research studies. When properly conducted, these studies focus on what kinds of jurors hold which attitudes, the structural composition of these attitudes, and the salience with which they are held.

In a major antitrust case, jurors were questioned by the judge during voir dire as to their attitudes toward the defendant in the case. Not surprisingly, and indeed totally consistent with pre-trial research, almost every juror expressed negative opinions toward the defendant and its level of service in the community. While these responses may have otherwise provided the trial attorneys with a great deal of discomfort, pre-trial research had also revealed that these attitudes, while widely held, would not be salient in the specific context of this case. Rather, attitudes toward technology, innovation, and scientific expertise were more determinant and correlated with verdict preference. Hence, the strategy in this particular case was designed to focus on those attitudes which were positively associated with the defendant rather than attempting to change negative ones without high salience or importance.

Complex Attitude Clusters and Juror Decision Making

Since human beings are complicated creatures, it is not surprising that the way in which their attitudes combine to influence their behavior is also quite complex. In most of our research on juror decision making, we have found that jurors' decisions tend to be determined by groups or clusters of attitudes that are correlated with each other and with the decision. When behavior is studied in this way, it is not uncommon to find some unexpected relationships between attitudes and behavior.

Case Example

In a case in which the plaintiff claimed he was wrongfully terminated from a foreign car dealership by the manufacturer, the defense found interesting attitude clusters which were used to develop case strategies, factual themes, and profiles for jury selection.

In this case, the former dealer, who had been a long-term employee with a góod performance record, claimed that the car company misrepresented the terms of his employment and induced him into investing his own money in a new dealership they never intended to support. This lack of support led to financial problems at the dealership and his eventual termination. Further, he argued that the car company had been looking for a good reason to terminate him because of his flamboyant lifestyle, of which the company did not approve. In fact, the former dealer had engaged in some questionable practices, but the evidence was unclear as to just how serious his indiscretions were.

The defendant undertook a major research effort aimed at identifying reactions to case issues and the development of juror types who would be favorably or unfavorably predisposed to the client. After extensive qualitative research on issue identification was completed, a large scale juror classification analysis was conducted.

The large study incorporated two kinds of questions: a list of proposed voir dire questions, and key attitude-based questions which came out of an analysis of small group research. This small group work had indicated that three general attitudinal and experiential areas should be explored in the survey. These were:

1. General attitudes toward employee rights.
2. Knowledge, feelings about, and experience with jobs that were highly formalized with an emphasis on written rules and procedures.
3. Attitudes about how power and recognition are distributed in large companies.

While juror profiles based on demographic variables like sex, income, age, education, religion, and political preference are deemed desirable because they are readily observable factors, we continue to find that attitudinal and personality variables are much better predictors of juror behavior. *As a general rule, the juror characteristics that are easiest to observe are the least helpful in predicting juror behavior.* However, on occasion, sophisticated statistical analyses will reveal complex interrelationships between demographic factors and certain attitudes and behavior.

In one survey, prospective jurors indicated whether or not they favored the plaintiff or the defendant. An analysis was then undertaken to determine if these verdict preferences were meaningfully related to answers to other survey questions. While no one answer alone predicted verdict preference reliably, it was found that clusters of answers would do so. Each of these clusters was based on several different answers.

The first cluster was related to concerns people had about the rights of the employees. They believed that employees in good standing should be given every opportunity to correct any performance problems before they are terminated. People that held these attitudes tended to be middle-aged, had worked for the same company for more than ten years, and considered themselves valuable and loyal employees. They felt that they were special because of their long-term devotion to their employer, and deserved special treatment. They also placed a high degree of trust and confidence in their own employer. More importantly, the thought of losing their job was very frightening. They saw themselves as economically and professionally vulnerable because at their age and career level, it would be very difficult to seek new employment opportunities.

On the surface, these people appeared to be loyal company men and women. They certainly "looked" like defense jurors. However, people who fit into this cluster were favorable to the plaintiff case. They were angry that the company did not give more leeway to a long-term employee in good standing. They saw the company's actions as a violation of trust. Psychologically, these people were motivated to protect their view of the world: good employees should be accorded some special recognition, loyalty, or preferential treatment. This group had a tendency to award high punitive damages as well.

The second attitude cluster was based on perceptions of rules and formal structure. The people in this category placed great value on organization and routine in their lives. Many of these people liked working in jobs which rewarded following specific instructions and written rules. Psychologically, these individuals needed unambiguous structure around which to organize their lives. They saw rules as necessary for the proper functioning of society, their organization, and themselves. Some of these people worked with inventory, with contracts, in the lower levels of government bureaucracies, accounting, and in law-enforcement. Others were housewives and administrative assistants. The common thread was not type of occupation per se, but rather the fact that their roles required an emphasis on rules and order. As one would expect, these people had very little tolerance for those who deviated from the rules or accepted standards of performance.

These jurors were highly critical of both litigants because neither party was seen to have followed the rules. The plaintiff failed to perform some obligations, but at the same time, the defendant did not honor its promises. However, since they were not inclined to award significant damages, and because the verdict form and instructions were seen as favoring the defendant (these jurors could be counted on to follow and enforce the judge's instructions), they were not classified as pro-plaintiff.

The third group was the most dangerous for the plaintiff. The relevant attitude cluster consisted of several highly negative predispositions against employers. These people believed that employers regularly exploit employees, do not give them fair recognition for achievement, and in general do not treat employees with fairness and dignity. They were highly cynical and distrustful of management and believed that it was acceptable for an employee to do whatever was necessary to get ahead. Unfortunately for the plaintiff however, these cynical attitudes toward employers were also applied to the plaintiff. These potential jurors believed that *this plaintiff* was not only as corrupt as his employer, but also incredibly stupid for engaging in obvious indiscretions. In this particular case, they had little sympathy for what they saw as a story about a corrupt employee outsmarted by a corrupt employer. On the surface, these jurors looked very menacing to the defendant, but through intensive research, it was discovered that in fact, not a significant threat occurred. They *looked* like they could be strong plaintiff jurors when in reality they had little empathy for the plaintiff lawyer's client.

Once the attitudinal and behavioral clusters for favorable and unfavorable jurors had been discovered, it was possible to: 1) develop key case strategies for presenting the case, and 2) devise a method for scoring prospective jurors on each cluster based on their answers to voir dire questions. Unfortunately, it is not always possible to score people on every dimension. Data will be incomplete, or there will be inconsistent responses within a particular content area. Fortunately, in this case, the clusters were independent of each other and reliable decisions could be made about the best use of peremptory challenges.

Conclusions

As we have seen, jurors may not follow the web of inference into which attorneys seek to draw them. In fact, jurors, because they are people, frequently do not attend to the vast majority of "information" presented in the courtroom. Indeed, they cannot. Unlike computers, human beings have a limited capacity to perceive, interpret, and store information. Post-trial interviews consistently reveal that jurors tend to forget a large number of details in any trial. For example, key witnesses are sometimes forgotten or misidentified. Telling pieces of demonstrative evidence, often obtained at great expense, may be simply forgotten. Juror decision making is a psychological process in which an attorney's theory of the case is evaluated in terms of its "fit" with jurors' pre-existing attitudes and beliefs. Hence, the need to identify attitudes and attitudinal configurations is a basic strategic consideration in any trial. It begins with the premise that people enter the courtroom with an array of attitudes and beliefs already in place which are based on previous experience and knowledge. Jurors are frequently in a stressful position, and new information which is not consistent with these attitudes will only increase their discomfort. As a result, they may engage in a variety of coping behaviors to avoid changing existing beliefs. They may distort evidence, and they will frequently overlook evidence altogether. Always, the information they receive will be interpreted in ways which are consistent with what jurors want or need to believe. While frustrating, these are facts that trial lawyers have to contend with when developing strategies designed to influence the jury decision-making process.

CHAPTER 3

Communication and Techniques of Persuasion

In the late 1970's, when Pat Lynch[*] and Joe Cotchett were representing the NFL in the *Los Angeles Memorial Coliseum Commission v. NFL* case, Al Davis, the charismatic owner of the Oakland Raiders, testified to a packed courtroom. Recalling that incident, Lynch reflects: "We are told that cases are decided in the opening statement. This may be so. In the six-week trial to determine whether the antitrust laws barred the National Football League from restricting a franchise from moving to a different city, Al Davis was a particularly persuasive witness. Midway through his cross-examination, Joe Cotchett leaned over to me and said:

'Life is a moving stream, and juror No. 5 just swam out of our pool and into the plaintiff's pool.' "

That juror never swam back.

The psychology of communication is another domain of the behavioral sciences which can play an important role in the development of trial strategy and tactics. Social psychologists have conducted research into the way in which one person is persuaded by the messages or communications of another for many years. Much of this work was

---

[*] Patrick Lynch, *O'Melveny & Myers, Los Angeles.*

conducted at Yale University in the 1940's and remains the foundation of communication theory today.

Effective communication can occur only when the context of the message processed by the receiver closely corresponds to that which was transmitted. The words and symbols used in the message must be oriented as closely as possible to the background, interests, needs, and predispositions of the receivers of the message. At the lowest level of intellectual abstraction, words paint pictures for people. In a courtroom, it is critically important that the lawyer clearly understands the word-driven visual images he is sending to jurors. Because of the common phenomena of selective attention, comprehension, and retention, any attempt to persuade without regard to jurors' psychological influences is doomed to failure unless the communicator has phenomenal luck.

Attributes of Persuasion

From the first moment jurors encounter an attorney in voir dire or observe a witness entering the courtroom or taking the stand, they are evaluating his or her ability to persuade. They are making decisions about that individual as a reliable source of information, as one who can be believed. The advantages that accrue to those who are able to establish persuasive powers early in the trial are obviously considerable. By the same token, certain omissions, lack of preparation, or an inappropriate approach, even during the opening moments of voir dire, can be seriously compromising and hamper a lawyer's or witness' attempts to persuade. Jerry Walpin[*] recalls an incident during cross examination in which his adversary walked back and forth handing documents to the witness. The lawyer had loud squeaky shoes, probably due to leather heels or soles. Everyone in the courtroom except Walpin's adversary could see the grimacing of the jurors as this repeated squeaki-ness grated on their ears. Whatever points he made during cross examination had little, if any, impact on the jurors, whose minds were diverted from the substance to the noise.

What makes a person persuasive? Communication psychologists indicate that two critical variables underlying the persuasiveness of a message sender are the *credibility* and *likability* of the speaker. Research has demonstrated that the credibility component of persuasion in the

---

[*] Gerald Walpin, *Rosenman & Colin, New York.*

courtroom is predicated on two qualities. The first of these is expertise or competence. Second, the speaker must be seen as trustworthy. In the case of a witness, he must demonstrate a lack of bias toward either party.

Credibility

Competence suggests a command of the subject matter at hand and involves an assessment or evaluation of not only the communicator's knowledge of the subject or expertise, but also his manner of delivery. A smooth, assured delivery, with the proper amount of eye contact, good diction, rounded sentence structure, and so forth, will be interpreted as a sign of competence. Groping of any kind, signs of disorganization, or possessing incomplete information, missing parts of which have to be obtained or looked up at another time, are all signs that jurors will interpret as incompetence or lack of expertise.

Expertise in the area of testimony is the easiest to evaluate. For most juries, it tends to be something which is both social and pragmatic. It is often related to higher education and formal credentials, but it may also be related to the witness' experience and whether or not the witness is "in a position to know." Under most circumstances, testimony about the safety of a drug from a local pharmacist will not be very credible. However, a research chemist for the FDA might be "in a position to know" even though he may have had little or no direct experience with the drug. In an airline disaster case, a member of the FAA might have credibility on the grounds of expertise, despite a lack of formal education in the field of aeronautical engineering.

How jurors will rank the importance of formal credentials vis-à-vis practical experience, or being in the right place to have gained critical knowledge, will be a function of the jurors' own educational background and personal experience. Lawyers rarely have problems establishing the requisite level of witness expertise for most jurors.

Trustworthiness is a second important sender credibility factor. Trustworthiness is closely related to a jury's conviction that an attorney or witness will only speak the truth and make assertions based on valid information. When jurors suspect that the source of the communication is being insincere or making statements that he himself only partially believes, the message sender is compromised as a trustworthy source. This is why exposing the patent untruth of something an opposing attorney has said, sometimes without even being aware that he was misinformed, can be a powerful courtroom tactic. Once trustworthiness has been lost in court, it can very rarely be regained. Related to trustworthiness is what some experts refer to as the "safety factor." Jurors can be said to feel safe with someone when he or she is perceived to be honest and well-intentioned. The safety to which we refer in this context is mainly a matter of feeling that it is safe to believe what the attorney or witness says and that there is no "risk" in doing so.

The extent to which the witness has a perceived commitment to one side or the other will have an obvious bearing on trustworthiness. As an example, testimony from corporate personnel may be discounted by jurors because of the attribution of personal vested interest. Even though jurors are very sensitive to this issue, many corporate defendants tend to rely upon their own in-house technical experts rather than retaining independent, outside experts. While technical experts from the company may, in fact, be the world's leading authorities on some subject, their credibility is normally an issue with jurors. In post-trial interviews, jurors have expressed skepticism concerning the capacity of company witnesses to be truly independent, impartial, and free of bias. Indeed, many company witnesses have confessed concerns regarding the impact of their performance as a witness on their careers.

Fact witnesses will often be seen as more credible if their testimony is not totally consistent or runs somewhat counter to what the jurors expect their position to be. Jurors are likely to believe that such a witness must be telling the truth, otherwise why would he advocate a counter intuitive position. The witness will be seen as especially competent and trustworthy. In a case involving personal injuries allegedly caused by a defective medical device, we found the most difficult witness for the defense was a physician still employed by the manufacturer of the device who testified about adverse reactions associated with the product in certain clinical settings. Company witnesses who may normally be viewed as biased because of their position can decrease that perception by conceding non-critical points rather than defensively attempting to refute or justify every issue raised by the opposition. Unfortunately in this case, the doctor did just the opposite.

Likability

The second component of persuasion is likability. As one would expect, studies have shown that a communicator who is liked will be more persuasive than one who is not liked or toward whom feelings are neutral. Such feelings of affiliation or liking can often follow from a sense of similarity with the attorney, based on common values and supposed common background. Liking or positive affect for another person can sometimes also be established by a sense of co-orientation. That is, the feeling that the message sender and jurors are coming at matters from the same perspective or the feeling that this person is "one of us"; that the individual possesses a shared cultural identity.

In a recent product liability case, the plaintiff brought in a witness at great expense to testify about the alleged metallurgical defects in a product. Defendant's counter testimony came from an engineer who had lived and worked for many years in the same community from which the jurors were drawn. When interviewed after the trial, it was difficult for the jurors to articulate the precise reasons why they found the credibility of the local engineer impeccable but were dubious about the plaintiff's witness. When this issue was probed further, it was discovered that jurors had taken a jaundiced view of the plaintiff's witness because he had come from a foreign country. They were also put off by his accent and the fact that he failed to use analogies or examples consistent with the jury's own experiences.

In the case of the local engineer in the above example, co-orientation was imputed to the witness on the basis of his local identity. In another recent case, an expert identified with a local university was perceived to be more credible than another internationally recognized expert with a more impressive background but with no local identity. Frequently a professor from the local state university will have greater jury appeal than a leading expert in the same field from a more prominent or prestigious institution located in another part of the country.

Another important factor that is frequently associated with likability is physical attractiveness. Human beings like physically attractive people and this makes these people more influential—hence the use of models and entertainment figures in consumer marketing and advertising. Nevertheless, physical attractiveness in and of itself is not always a salient factor. In a products liability case, post-trial interviews revealed that the jurors were extremely taken with the plaintiff's expert witness. He was described as very good looking, charming, and bright. However, they were persuaded by the engineer retained by defense even though he was seen as gruff, distant, and unfriendly. That was because jurors thought the defense expert's position at the State University was more impressive than the plaintiff expert's experience as a former employee of a government regulatory agency, and because the professor was seen as being more precise with his facts. How well the witness is liked also becomes less important when the jury is very involved in the issue being discussed in the testimony. This occurs because the jury will be paying more attention to the context of the message and less to peripheral cues such as the message sender. It is important to remember that credibility is more important than likability unless the message is rejected and focus is placed instead on the speaker. Messages are most frequently rejected because of problems with comprehension or lack of consistency with basic values, attitudes, and beliefs. This is true for lawyers as well as witnesses.

Embracing the Prosecution's Claim—A Defense Strategy

In a white collar criminal case, the critical issue often turns on the question of the defendant's lack of intent to lie at the time of the conduct of which he has been accused. The precision of the focus on intent is greatest in cases of perjury or false statement. Such a case gives ample opportunity to practice the psychology of persuasion. The attributes of credibility and likability must merge into a persuasive defense focusing on the defendant's lack of intent to lie.

In order to appreciate the gravity of this observation, one must first turn to other elements of the offense. Those elements identify the statement defendant allegedly made, its materiality to the proceeding, its falsity at the time of its making, defendant's knowledge that it was false at the time it was made, and his intent to make it nevertheless.

(continued)

(continued)

If the facts permit, it is not unexpected that a defense would be that defendant's statement was true, or that it was not material. This would give rise to the development of facts which focus on the event about which defendant is testifying or the nature of the testimonial proceeding itself.

However, the more difficult situation arises in cases where the defendant says he did not know his statement was false and did not intend to lie when he made it. Here guilty knowledge (scienter) and intent are pivotal to the case. It should come as no surprise that the challenge to be persuasive (i.e., credible and likable) is greatest in this context.

An approach to be considered, which is logical to the point of being obvious but with which defendants themselves often have difficulty, is to embrace the statement as the prosecutor has characterized it. In so doing, a defendant is saying to the jury, "I made this statement; it was material to the proceeding in question, it was a false statement; but I did not know it or intend to deceive anyone when I made it."

With such an approach, the processing function of the jury, if it tends toward more cognitive behavior, is immediately simplified. The sting of proving the falsity of the statement is blunted by an admission that it indeed was false. Positive emotional enforcement is generated because the jury sees a person poised to admit that, indeed, something was wrong, and the defendant has candidly admitted it.

The simplicity of the message permits its repetition thematically throughout the case. Thus, in opening statement, the alleged offending statement can be characterized as an honest mistake, a negligent comment, a cautious remark, but certainly not an intentional lie. During cross-examination of prosecution witnesses, the point can be repeatedly made that the facts also admit of

(continued)

(continued)

these less than criminal implications. Throughout the evidence, the constancy of such a theme does not require precise neutralization of each fact pointing to the falsity of the statement since at all points the jury will analytically be asking itself (rhetorically, of course), "Could this have been a mistake? Was the carelessness of the respondent enough to criminalize his conduct?"

Embracing the statement is the quintessential two-sided communication. It opens the possibility of finding an alternative to criminality. It is the path to reasonable doubt. It permits the theme to develop at the expense of the prosecution's evidence. It obviously permeates the defendant's case as he personalizes the theme that he did not know or intend his testimony to be false. It allows him to humanize his predicament by explaining that he accepts that his testimony was false but his knowledge was otherwise at the time he gave it.

Embracing the statement enhances the prospect of jury nullification. The law recognizes that nullification of a verdict in the face of evidence of guilt beyond a reasonable doubt is the right of every jury which ever convened in Anglo-Saxon jurisprudence. The courts have spoken almost as one that while recognizing that this right exists, the judges shall never tell the jury that it has it. To do so, say the judges, would promote anarchy. Without analyzing the proposition, embracing the statement provides a fertile gorund for a jury to accept enough of the positive emotional appeal of a statement admitting the falsity of the defendant's statement without going to that final step of criminalizing his conduct, even though he might very well have been lying.

(continued)

(continued)

> *Embracing the statement calls for a strategy in which a carefully articulated message is credibly communicated to a discerning jury through a frame of reference which is easily understandable, emotionally forceful, and contextually balanced. It is one of the best examples of how to marshall the facts, from opening statement through closing argument, to include many of the elements and techniques of the psychology of persuasion.*
>
> *Richard A. Hibey*
> *Anderson Hibey Nauheim & Blair, Washington, D.C.*

Witness Credibility

Trial lawyers are always concerned about the persuasive impact of their witnesses. In a large antitrust case, an expert economist was testifying about the existence and nature of monopoly power in a relevant sub-market. The defendant had been accused of Sherman Act violations, and the expert witness was someone on whom the plaintiff was counting heavily to make a substantial contribution to the case. Plaintiff's counsel were jubilant after this witness had completed his testimony. They were convinced that this testimony had provided a key element in their case. In fact, they felt that this witness had been so persuasive that he had virtually sold the jurors on their side of the issue.

At the conclusion of the trial, extensive interviews were conducted with each member of the jury. Among many other questions, they were specifically asked what they thought of plaintiff's expert witness. To the attorneys' surprise, this witness had not been persuasive, nor had he produced much of an appreciable effect at all. In fact, jurors viewed him rather negatively. They thought he was condescending. He used arcane and technical vocabulary, and, in their view, was trying to talk down to them. In short, he lacked credibility and had not been persuasive.

Why do witnesses fail in this way? The reasons can be complex, but in many instances attorneys lose perspective and do not adequately prepare their witnesses *for jurors*. Trial lawyers normally devote a great deal of time to their witnesses, but they often fail to view witnesses in terms of their possible impact upon jurors from a communications or credibility point of view. George Leisure Jr.[*] gives a humorous example from his first experience with depositions which were videotaped. He was planning to take the videotaped deposition of a senior executive of a major international corporation. While setting up the equipment, the young technicians gave him the following advice: "Do not take off your suit coat while questioning the witness, and do not smoke!" Their idea was that either action could make a bad impression on a jury if the tape were shown. The witness came into the room, a big burly fellow, was sworn, and soon asked if he could remove his coat. Leisure said, "Please do, sir." He then asked if it was all right to smoke. Leisure obliged with "Go right ahead, sir."

Since the case was settled, George never learned whether this witness had destroyed himself, but he was quite pleased with his "credibility strategy" nonetheless.

A serious problem for trial lawyers is that they may, in a very short period of time, begin to adopt the communication style of the witness in talking about the subject. Frequently, they pride themselves upon having become experts of a sort on certain technical aspects of the case. Through their interaction, attorney and witness become so familiar with the case, with technical language and vocabulary, and with each other, that an ironic transference takes place. The lawyer becomes an expert. His sophisticated technical knowledge carries over into the courtroom and can make the witness' testimony incomprehensible to many jurors.

Thus, it is easy for attorneys to overlook the fact that witnesses, first and foremost, must communicate effectively with jurors. The power to persuade and convince jurors, using certain technical information, resides in the witness' ability to make this information credible and comprehensible.

In trial after trial, one can point to examples of witness testimony which seem to contain relevant and persuasive evidence but which are nevertheless undermined because of the witness' low personal credibility. Post-trial interviews often reveal that jurors believed that what a certain witness had to say may have had an important bearing on the case, but that it was discounted because of a lack of credibility.

---

[*] George S. Leisure, Jr., *Donovan Leisure Newton & Irvine, New York.*

In any courtroom situation there are many things a juror could watch as he listens to testimony. He could watch the witness, he could watch the witness's hands, he could watch the witness's eyes, or he could watch someone in the audience who appears odd or conspicuous at that particular moment. When the lawyer leaves the decision about what the juror watches up to the juror, the juror's preexisting attitudes and beliefs will come into play to determine what gets noticed; this may or may not be what the lawyer wants the juror to notice.

The Credible Executive Witness

A contract case in which two opposing corporate executives testified illustrates an example of how the perception of bias can adversely affect factually correct testimony. The issue was whether a series of meetings and telephone conversations between the executives, together with exchanges of correspondence, constituted an enforceable contract for the sale of a large industrial property. Some of the correspondence was ambiguous and in part contradictory.

The executive of the purported purchases was an articulate witness, precise and definite as to his interpretation of the discussions and correspondence. His testimony was entirely consistent in describing the meetings and generally consistent with a literal reading of the correspondence. But he was a cold personality, appearing somewhat aloof, perhaps too definite in his position, and suggesting by his attitude that he sought to make every fact square with the conclusion that an enforceable contract had been made.

(continued)

(continued)

The other executive, testifying for the company that owned the property and claimed that no contract of sale had been agreed on, was also definite as to the facts. But he exhibited an outgoing and hearty personality more "co-oriented" with the jurors. His testimony gave the impression that he was intent on stating the facts correctly rather than on convincing the jury as to the ultimate conclusion as to whether a contract had been made. By this combination of personality, precision, and focus on factual accuracy, he was more credible and appeared less biased than the equally precise but aloof opposing executive.

Andrew C. Hartzell, Jr.
Debevoise & Plimpton, New York

Strategies to Enhance Credibility

It is possible, of course, that jurors may understand the message but fail to be persuaded by it. It can be maintained, however, that barring some gratuitous outcome, understanding the message will be a necessary prerequisite to being convinced by it (although as we note later, persuasion of another sort can occur without understanding). In the criminal trial of automobile manufacturer John Z. DeLorean, a government witness was supposed to have been the key to the prosecution of the case. Unfortunately for the government, the jury did not believe this witness. In fact, his lack of credibility was a critical element in the defendant's acquittal.

One way to enhance the credibility of witnesses is to utilize our understanding of the ways in which jurors process information and make decisions. We will examine this issue in great detail in Chapter 4. For now, it is important to remember that some jurors will respond most favorably to witnesses who are logical and straightforward in their testimony and who present facts in a detailed, structured, and logical manner. Supporting this testimony with charts, graphs, and technical exhibits is very desirable for these people. When it is necessary to present technical testimony to jurors who are less cognitively structured, it is helpful to employ concrete examples and analogies which will be familiar to jurors. Presenting technical data in an abstract form will normally be counterproductive.

Order of presentation can also be employed to make witnesses more effective. Witnesses placed first and last will be better remembered than those in the middle. Since jurors are more likely to be inattentive during the long periods of protracted witness testimony, it is important to place the most important witnesses, and the most appealing and articulate, first or at the very end of a series of witnesses.

Sometimes our selectivity of witnesses will be limited. There may be only a single witness who can supply an important piece of the evidentiary puzzle. When this is the case, we must go with whom we have. We must manage the impact of this witness' credibility, whatever it might be. One of the ways we can do this is by taking advantage of the "sleeper effect."

The sleeper effect refers to the increase or decrease in the credibility of a message, or the amount of belief induced by the message, which occurs after a lapse of time. Such a delayed effect is directly related to the credibility of the source of the communication. By positioning the witness either early or late in the trial, it is possible to exercise some influence over the impact made by the witness' personal credibility.

There are many examples of the sleeper effect in everyday life. Advertisers often depend upon this phenomenon to realize benefits from their expenditures. Their audience may not believe claims about an advertised product when they first see and hear a televised advertisement. Two weeks later, however, they may purchase the product because they remember its alleged benefits without recalling the original source of their information. As an example, many television viewers may dislike the Charmin bathroom tissue ads but actually purchase the product because it is the brand name recognized on the supermarket shelf at the time of purchase. Recall of the specific ad has probably dissipated at that particular moment in time. The consumer remembers the product and its benefits without remembering the source of the information.

The sleeper effect may also occur because the message is disassociated from a source of questionable credibility. This has strategic implications for trial attorneys. In the case of a witness with low credibility, testimony may be viewed more favorably by jurors after a lapse of some days or weeks, than immediately following the witness' appearance on the stand. Thus, when a witness of questionable credibility must be used, that witness should be questioned early in the trial. With this approach, jurors will have time to separate the message from a source they may consider dubious.

What if we have a high credibility witness? In this case, it is desirable that jurors continually associate the message with the source. If we use a high credibility witness early in the proceedings, his effectiveness will be reduced. Valuable and important expert witnesses may lose much of their impact if a substantial period of time lapses between their testimony and the jury's deliberation.

Sometimes our hand is forced in the positioning of a witness, and our high credibility witness must testify at the beginning of the trial. In this case, it may be possible to overcome the sleeper effect. One way to do this is to make sure there is as much repetition as possible in the witness' direct testimony. Research on persuasion indicates that repetition is useful in two situations. The first is when a message is hard to understand. The second is when it is necessary to maintain opinion change when there is a lapse of time between the presentation of the message and the listener's decision, reaction, or overt behavior. Continual references back to the witness' testimony throughout the trial will be extremely helpful in this situation as well.

Repetition of a Key Point

Continual references may also be of major importance when a single document, or a single sentence in a particular document, highlights one side's entire position. In an antitrust case the issue was whether one of two companies competing to acquire a third company was motivated by the desire to obtain a quasi monopoly position in a particular product market. There were voluminous documents relevant to the acquisition and to the purposes of the two competing prospective purchasers. One document, however, which was a memo to the Board of Directors of one of the companies, expressly stated that the company sought by the acquisition to obtain a dominant product-line position.

This single statement was quoted repeatedly by opposing counsel during the course of the trial and its full setting and imp-

(continued)

(continued)

lications constantly explained. Counsel emphasized that while various company officials may have stated reasons for the acquisition, all of those reasons were refined and honed down for final and decisive presentation to the Board of Directors. The Board of Directors was the ultimate decision maker and the reasons presented to them were the real, primary reasons for the acquisition. It was especially significant, therefore, that the anti-competitive motive appeared in a memo to the Board of Directors. By placing the statement in its most meaningful context and by repeatedly emphasizing that context throughout the trial, the single statement became the dominant theme of the opposing counsel's position.

Andrew C. Hartzell, Jr.
Debevoise & Plimpton, New York

There is also a possible defensive strategy in regard to the sleeper effect. Suppose our opponent has used a low credibility witness early who delivered a somewhat believable message. In this situation, the concern is that jurors will only remember the message and forget their reservations about the witness. Throughout the remainder of the trial, we can refer to this witness explicitly, causing jurors to renew the association in their minds between the message and its source. Thus, our strategy with regard to witness testimony is to remind jurors of the identity of our own high credibility witnesses and of our opponent's low credibility witnesses whenever possible.

Persuasive Messages

A persuasive communication is a communication aimed at influencing attitudes and beliefs. It may have the objective of changing pre-existing beliefs and attitudes or reinforcing attitudes which are in place. Persuasive messages may also be directed at bringing about some action or change in behavior. The messages delivered in an attorney's case presentation serve all of the above objectives at one time or another. Ultimately, these messages are directed at bringing about a specific juror action: the rendering of a particular verdict.

Communication psychologists have studied the question of the context of a persuasive communication. Among the questions which have been investigated are the way in which such a message should be organized, the order of arguments, and the advantages and disadvantages of using certain kinds of content, as well as certain general factors in the communication which make it more or less effective. One basic characteristic we would expect to find in a persuasive communication is a conclusion which follows from the facts in the case. This is elementary but can be overlooked. Moreover, the conclusion must follow from the facts *as far as the jurors are concerned.* When it is clear that some conclusion is based on facts which are made explicit, most jurors will try to decide whether or not they believe these facts. They will then decide if the conclusion follows from these facts.

Why do jurors ignore facts after an attorney has told them these facts are important and that his case rests upon their truth? The answer is quite simple. Jurors do not always choose to regard matters the way attorneys do. They may have attitudes and beliefs in place which render them unable to accept certain facts or to avoid these facts altogether and come at the case from an entirely different perspective, a perspective of which the attorney may not be aware.

Trial attorneys are generally excellent communicators. They usually do not make the error of presenting facts which fail to support the conclusion they wish to draw. When their messages have credibility problems, it is generally because the facts on which their arguments are based are rejected. They suffer a defeat in the case because they are arguing from premises which are simply not acceptable to the jury from an attitudinal standpoint.

Research has demonstrated that jurors frequently make end runs around technical arguments. They may even decide that the whole argument advanced by an attorney, the whole passel of facts and conclusions, is simply not a part of what should be considered. These jurors may be stubborn, but they are not imperceptive or unintelligent. At the end of the trial, they may not even remember the attorney's argument, at least not until their minds are jogged. This is because they have been off on a completely different line of reasoning on their own, with its own "facts" and conclusions.

Thus, from the lawyer's perspective, the question of making arguments logical is not an easy one to resolve. Most jurors will expect logic in a trial presentation; but the denial of emotional factors may compromise credibility in cases where there is an obvious emotional component. This is particularly true in cases where severe, if not tragic, personal consequences have formed the basis of plaintiff's claim.

The Strategic Use of Emotional Messages

Emotional appeals can be of two basic kinds. One kind of emotional appeal is one in which the message is accompanied by a positive emotional context. The communicator may attempt to convey good feelings or arouse positive feelings in the audience. On the other hand, many persuasive messages are delivered in a negative emotional context. Foremost among these are messages which in one way constitute fear appeals or attempts to frighten the receiver of the message into some kind of action or attitude change.

Messages which contain positive emotional context can often prove useful in court. Whenever an attorney can do something which will make jurors feel good, an advantage will probably be created. Of course, this must stop short of something that jurors recognize as frivolous, or an attempt to be ingratiating. Humor is the most obvious way to cloak a persuasive message with positive feelings. Interesting anecdotes or story elements can add interest to an attorney's presentation. Reassuring jurors that they are doing their work well and attentively, or that they will be able to cope with something coming up in the trial that will make special demands upon them, may also be useful. Serving on a jury in a long trial can be tedious. Providing small moments of pleasant relief for jurors will help win their allegiance. However, lawyers must be careful about the use of humor. If it is excessive or inappropriate to the context, it can seriously decrease the juror's perception of credibility by undermining his sense of how trustworthy the lawyer is.

The second type of emotional appeal is one which tries to persuade through the use of some kind of fear appeal or anxiety-provoking element in the message. There are many opportunities in the course of conducting jury trials for using a fear appeal of some kind to try to influence jurors. Fear appeals are the most common kind of emotional argument and are quite familiar. Politicians often threaten the electorate with some harrowing consequences if their policies are not supported. Advertisers threaten dire problems in health and hygiene if their products are not used. Fear appeals are commonplace from the pulpit. Messages from service organizations against drunk drivers depict a body covered with a sheet lying alongside a smashed car. An anti-smoking commercial depicts the ugly inside of a diseased lung.

Do people actually change their attitudes and behavior in response to this kind of appeal? How well advised is an attorney in a personal injury case, for example, to try to scare the jury into identifying with his client's suffering? Research into fear appeals or "anxiety-provoking stimuli," as they have been called, has produced mixed results. One of the major problems with fear appeals is that many messages intended to induce fear may not do so. It is not easy to manipulate the level of fear of a juror. Lawyers should not assume that their fear appeals will have an effect until they test it out first.

Fear appeals will be successful persuasive devices when they are quite strong, when the premises of the fear appeal are believed by the recipient, and when the recipients believe that the recommended procedures for avoiding the dangers illustrated in the appeal do in fact work.

This can be applied to a common situation found in litigation in which a fear appeal might be appropriate. Suppose the plaintiff is a quadriplegic and claims his condition is the result of a defective automobile. Very large monetary damages are being requested. To successfully employ a fear appeal strategy, experienced plaintiff counsel recognize that the fear appeal must be strong, unrelenting, and unambiguous. In addition to graphic details of plaintiff's past, present, and future suffering, the jury must be provided with unpleasant, frightening, or anxiety-provoking associations to make the fear appeal credible.

In a case alleging a design defect in automobile tires, jurors were shown various color photographs of the plaintiff lying in a hospital bed with surgical skull tongs implanted in his head. After seeing the pictures, the jurors were then presented with an actual skull tong as an exhibit. The tongs were passed from one juror to the next as they listened to a neurosurgeon describe the implantation procedure as equivalent to medieval torture. Later in the same trial, jurors were shown video tapes of tires literally disintegrating and flying apart at high speed. Post-trial interviews with jurors confirmed that plaintiff's counsel had indeed developed a sense of frightening association with the defendant's product.

Can fear appeals be taken "too far"? Generally, the more fear that is induced, the greater the effectiveness of the argument. However, if a message is too gruesome or unrelenting it may fail to arouse fear because jurors may engage in psychological self-protection and pay little attention to it. As an example, a brief appearance of a disfigured burn victim is far more powerful than having the individual present in the courtroom every day throughout the course of a long trial. Jurors become accustomed to the individual and over a relatively short period of time; the plaintiff's situation, while tragic, becomes less shocking or horrifying. The victim's condition takes on a state of altered normalcy. This is a trap plaintiff lawyers frequently fall into when showing "Day In The Life Of" videos. A short five to ten minute video of a person suffering the indignities of assistance with personal hygiene, or an individual racked with pain while attempting to complete some everyday human activity, can frequently overwhelm the jury's emotions. A 45 minute or hour presentation of the plaintiff's plight will allow the observer to construct defense mechanisms to alleviate many of the psychological reactions the video was designed to evoke.

When using fear appeals, it is very important that the jurors believe the remedy sought will ameliorate the conditions depicted in the fear appeal. If the jurors think, even subconsciously, that "all the money in the world is not going to help this poor plaintiff," they will be inclined to limit the monetary award. If, however, jurors accept the suggestion that by returning a large verdict, the message sent to the manufacturer might help reduce or eliminate the conditions that led to the production of a defective product (and the horrible consequences to the plaintiff in this particular case), they are very likely to award substantial punitive damages.

Rhetorical Questions

Studies have demonstrated that if people are not intensely involved in a topic of discussion, rhetorical questions will tend to make them pay closer attention to what they are hearing. This would suggest, however, that when jurors are paying close attention and are quite intensely involved with the subject matter, the use of rhetorical questions will do little to enhance communication effectiveness. At other times in the trial, when jurors are not attentive and are less involved, rhetorical questions can be an excellent device to arouse and recapture attention.

When arguments are not particularly strong or convincing, rhetorical questions can have the effect of calling attention to the weakness of the argument. This means, among other things, that if the attorney is not careful, the use of rhetorical questions in this situation can be counterproductive. At the same time, using rhetorical questions to call attention to weaknesses in an opposing argument can be an excellent communication strategy.

Of course, since rhetorical questions are likely to be viewed as argumentative, they will have to be used sparingly in the opening statement. When employed carefully and at certain key junctures, they can make a definite positive impact.

Repetition

Not only is it important to persuade jurors by changing their attitudes or beliefs, but it is also critical to sustain those attitude changes over time. It does no good to make a telling point in the opening statement of a six month case only to have it forgotten one week later. Attitude change will be more enduring when jurors are made to systematically analyze messages. Repetition of a theme or an argument is an extremely effective way of obtaining lasting attitude change.

Repetition causes jurors to create a greater number of mental connections with their thoughts and feelings. The attitudes jurors develop from listening to repeated arguments are more readily available and retrieved from memory. In addition, the more jurors are exposed to an argument the more they will feel comfortable with it. There is comfort in familiarity. If the jurors already agree with an argument then repeated exposure to it will make them more polarized toward it.

However, repetition can be overdone. Jurors may become satiated with the message. No longer will they come up with evaluative thoughts that are consistent with the message, but they might start to have more critical thoughts. Over-repetition may lead to a sense of tedium where jurors simply get sick of the message. Finally, there may be psychological reactance. Jurors may develop a sense that their freedom of choice is being restricted in some way and react by doing the opposite of what is being asked.

Research has shown that the more complex the message, the more important it is to repeat it. Jurors will then have more of an opportunity to learn and to respond to the message in an evaluatively consistent manner. One way to offset the risk of overexposure is to vary the message somewhat over time. In this way, the attempt to persuade does not appear to be overt. Finally, repetition should not be confused with continuous exposure to enormous amounts of information about a single subject. This may just simply overwhelm jurors with information they do not understand.

Strategy in Organizing the Content of a Communication

One of the most compelling questions in the organization of a persuasive communication is whether the argument should be one-sided or two-sided. The relative effectiveness of one-sided versus two-sided communications has been investigated by researchers in communication, and there is some reason to believe that an argument which presents only one side of an issue will be recognized as containing an obvious bias.

Richard Hibey* provides an example in a wrongful death action. The plaintiff outlined in opening statement a litany of horrors visited upon the decedent by the nursing home staff. In giving this side of the argument, to be proved by the testimony of decedent's relatives, counsel failed to disclose to the jury the circumstances which brought the decedent to the nursing home in the first place. This provided counsel with the opportunity to do three things in his opening statement:

1. Make ample reference to the myriad illnesses afflicting decedent;
2. Explain that while cancer was one of those illnesses, the nursing home was not claiming that it contributed to his death; and
3. Offer the nursing home's explanation of what happened, which credibility took into account *all* aspects of the decedent's condition and laid the groundwork for a defense on the issues of cause of death and adequacy of care.

Hence, the defense's opening argument gave context to the case where none was availing in the plaintiff's presentation and thus appealed to both cognitively-oriented and affectively-oriented jurors.

In almost all instances, two-sided communication is more effective. This becomes even more so when the jurors are familiar with the issues

---

* Richard A. Hibey, *Anderson Hibey Nauheim & Blair, Washington, DC.*

being tried. In general, one-sided communications seem to be more effective when the group hearing the communication is initially favorably disposed to the point of view being espoused. One-sided communications are also most effective in strengthening a pre-existing belief. Where there is no initial agreement between sender and receiver, however, a communication which presents both points of view can often be more effective in bringing about a change in conviction than one which contains only one point of view.

Use of one-sided versus two-sided arguments in jury trials can comprise a subtle strategic dilemma. Deciding between these two approaches will require knowledge of whom the jurors are and a sophisticated appreciation of the strength of one's position going into the trial. Credibility is the ultimate criterion.

First, consider the example of a case in which there are many good arguments which can be put forward on behalf of both sides. Suppose, further, that pre-trial juror research has revealed a good deal of support among jurors for both the plaintiff and the defendant and that many potential jurors face the dilemma of feeling there are identifiable strengths on both sides. Let us suppose further that the jurors who are actually chosen to serve in the trial are cognitively-oriented, that is, they are people who are going to be active information processors in the trial and make a decision on a largely factual basis. They are people who like to think with a certain amount of "logical" rigor and base their decision on the facts as the lawyers know them.

Given the above kind of situation, an attorney who completely ignores the position of the other side will risk losing credibility. There is good reason to suppose that in such a case the most credible approach will be one in which the arguments for the other side are presented and ultimately transcended or refuted by an appeal to a more reasonable, more just, and better-grounded set of counter-arguments. To pretend that the position of the other side does not exist, or have any validity whatsoever, risks being censured by jurors who themselves acknowledge that there is a certain amount of strength on both sides and who believe that the arguments for both sides are worth taking seriously.

Of course, your strategy will have to take into account whether or not you are coming at matters from the side of the defendant or the plaintiff. As we shall see in the next chapter, one of the most important occasions on which to decide whether or not to use a two-sided argument is the opening statement. When the defense is giving its opening statement, the jury will already have heard the plaintiff's arguments. If defense counsel proceeds to present the defense case with no reference to the plaintiff's position, he or she may experience a problem of credibility. From the plaintiff's point of view, it will sometimes be good strategy to present a two-sided argument which anticipates and refutes the defense opening statement. This technique, called inoculation, is based on the idea that opposing arguments will be heard by jurors, or occur to them, sooner or later and that there is advantage to be gained by having jurors hear these arguments in the context of their refutation. We will come back to the techniques of inoculation in the context of voir dire later in this book.

In situations where pre-trial research reveals that the case for one side is much more convincing to jurors than the case for the other, lawyers for the side which rates highly among potential jurors should not raise counter-arguments. When dealing from a position of great strength, an attorney will probably appear most credible by sticking to a basically one-sided presentation. Certainly raising and refuting arguments from the other side that jurors are not inclined to take seriously would compromise credibility.

When a careful analysis of the case has been undertaken and juror predispositions dictate that a two-sided argument will be useful, there is a proper method for formulating such an argument. This method is based on the use of primacy and recency effects, that is, the tendency to remember those parts of an argument which come first and those parts of an argument which come last. These effects dictate that it is best to begin with a strong presentation of the "pro" point of view. Given that a two-sided message strategy was selected, it is anticipated that there will be some resistance to this initial presentation. In order to enhance credibility and to support the initial arguments, the attorney next demonstrates a knowledge of the best arguments which will come from the other side and refutes these in the most effective way possible. Finally, the argument concludes with a forceful restatement of the initial pro position.

Conclusions

Communication strategy is an important aspect of any overall trial strategy. The attorneys are the basic senders of persuasive messages in a trial, and communications strategy centers on what attorneys can do to be effective in this role. If the sender perceives that the intended message has not produced the intended effect, the sender can modify the message and try again. Thus, feedback makes face-to-face interpersonal

communication highly efficient.   In the courtroom, however, effective
feedback is frequently difficult because the attorney and his intended
audience are physically separated. Hence, a smile, an affirmative nod, a
frown, or some other type of response may represent the extent of
available feedback. Jurors, as message receivers, are initially an unknown
in the equation. One of the basic objectives in small group research is to
develop knowledge about jurors and how they are going to exercise their
function as message receivers.

One of the most valuable contributions of communication psychology
to litigation has been to focus attention on the message as a distinct
element in a communication. By studying specific messages like opening
statements, witness testimony, and graphic exhibits, and the way they
influence jurors, we can solve the two basic problems of all communication. These are making certain that the message sent and the message
received are the same and that the persuasive intent of the message has
been fulfilled.

One of the principle strategic objectives of any trial is to carefully
insure the credibility of witnesses.   Aside from the obvious characteristics that we all like in other people, the witness must have recognized
expertise, there must be a perceived high degree of co-orientation
between the witness and the jurors, and the jurors must be convinced that
the witness is not committed to any specific outcome in the trial.

Obviously, the matter of persuasion and credibility is of paramount
importance from the earliest stages of trial preparation. It is another area
in which communication and social psychological theory can combine to
yield important strategic ideas.

CHAPTER 4

How Jurors Use Information

During a recent mock trial exercise, Fred Morris,[*] carefully observing his jury panel, became convinced that one of the women jurors was defense oriented. She seemed to smile and nod her head at times when he thought he was scoring points. She did the same thing during his summation when he hit upon what he thought were his strongest arguments and the plaintiff's weakest. When he retired to watch the deliberations on remote video, he was chagrined to discover that this juror strongly favored the plaintiff rather than the defense. From this and other experiences with jury research over time, Fred has concluded that a juror's demeanor in the courtroom may have nothing to do with his orientation toward the case, or the facts upon which he is likely to rely!

In this chapter, we will examine how jurors focus on and process the information they receive in the courtroom. We will show that they rely on a number of common sense rules for understanding and making judgements about complex information. Regrettably however, jurors frequently make systematic errors when applying these rules. These errors can be traced to our incapacity as human beings to perfectly process information and come to conclusions. And they have profound consequences for the ways in which jurors will treat evidence and arrive at verdicts.

---

[*] Frederick W. Morris, *Leonard Street & Deinard, Minneapolis.*

Jurors as Message Receivers

Jurors are message receivers and information processors. The messages they receive and the information they process become the basis for their decisions. Through conducting extensive pre-trial and post-trial research, it has been discovered that jurors can be classified into a dichotomy based on their decision-making style. By decision-making style, communication psychologists refer to the way in which jurors decode information, what information they are willing to decode, and how they will use this information in making decisions. The basic distinction into which jurors can be placed is the two-fold dichotomy of *affective* versus *cognitive* thinkers. It is important to emphasize that this distinction focuses on decision style and not intelligence. Bright and dull people are found in each category.

Affective Jurors. From a lawyer's perspective, an affective juror is one who makes decisions on an emotional rather than a rational basis. Affective jurors are generally impulsive decision-makers. They often base their decisions on highly selective perception and organization of what they see and hear, rather than reserving judgment until all the facts have been gathered. When information is presented to them, they are inclined to reformulate and shape it until it fits their previously held world view or set of conclusions based on how they feel about the matter. These jurors tend to be responsive to what the particular parties in the litigation symbolize—for example, "big business" and "the little man." Consequently, they are heavily swayed by the images an attorney may create of the parties involved. This is especially the case if the parties are portrayed in stereotypic terms that are consistent with the affective juror's preconceived notions. Affective thinkers are people who come to conclusions without making much of an effort to sift the evidence, review the facts, or critically analyze the subtleties of witness testimony.

Who are the people most likely to be affective jurors? Some generalizations from research on this subject reveal that affective jurors are more likely to be deeply devoted to religious principles or philosophies of life. They are often members of minority groups. Affective jurors are typically not college educated, but if they are, they have frequently majored in the arts or humanities rather than in one of the physical sciences. Affective jurors tend to dislike numerical concepts and abstractions. They tend to be creative and may be "artsy-craftsy." These people are the poets of the world; people who frequently conduct their lives on the basis of how they "feel," what they believe, and what "ought to be." In a debate or argument, an affective decision-maker might say, "Don't tell me that, I don't want to hear it!" Are all artists or all people who dislike mathematics affective thinkers? The answer is clearly "no!" These descriptions of affective jurors are clearly generalizations and must be viewed as such.

Cognitive Jurors. What are some of the descriptions of cognitive jurors? First and foremost, they are usually very orderly and logical decision-makers. They are information seekers because they are information processors. Cognitive thinkers balance their checkbooks, organize their lives (as well as the lives of others), and are generally intellectually fastidious and controlled. They are the kind of people who can always find the warranty to their five-year-old lawn mower because they inevitably have a file marked "lawn mower warranty." Jurors who are cognitive thinkers make "to do" lists and methodically do everything on the list. Affective thinkers, on the other hand make such lists with the best of intentions and inevitably lose the lists.

Cognitive thinkers have an intrinsic curiosity and, hence, will seek out facts and information. They are stereotypic inductive problem solvers. Cognitive jurors are often young MBA's or people who have majored in mathematics, drafting, bookkeeping, accounting, engineering, or one of the physical sciences in college. They may also be carpenters, electricians, or mechanics—people who rely upon detailed instruction and precision. Cognitive jurors tend to be intellectually rigorous, logical, and usually less empathetic than their affective counterparts.

It is important for lawyers to understand this affective/cognitive distinction. First of all, many lawyers are cognitive thinkers and generally anticipate that others will be so as well. As cognitive thinkers, lawyers not only view their case in "logical" cognitive terms but also construct their arguments and encode their messages from a cognitive perspective. When jurors fail to respond appropriately or render verdicts "inconsistent with the evidence," attorneys frequently assail jurors as stupid, inept, or incapable of dealing with complex or sophisticated issues. In many cases, the problem resides not so much with jurors but rather with lawyers who fail to make their communication consistent with the characteristics of the message receivers. In the vast majority of cases, jurors diligently attempt to do a good job. In too many cases, lawyers frustrate or inhibit the ability of jurors to do so.

Another reason why the affective/cognitive dichotomy is important relates to the design and structure of intended messages for the jury. If the lawyer is confronted with cognitive jurors, the information, testimony, and lawyer arguments should be consistent with this decision-making style. If, on the other hand, the jury is composed of affective jurors, communications should be constructed to reflect this orientation. What course of action should be pursued if the jury represents a mixture of both kinds of jurors? Fortunately, there is an easy answer to this dilemma. Affective jurors will require affective structures and affective arguments. Even though cognitive jurors will not particularly like an affective approach, they typically possess the rigor to place a cognitive structure on affective arguments. Hence, the rule is to attend to the affective jurors; cognitive jurors will be able to attend to themselves!

Having observed many trials over the years, it is interesting to note that successful plaintiff personal injury lawyers are frequently masters at structuring affective communications. At the same time, most defense lawyers adhere to a highly structured cognitive approach.

Heuristics

Jurors are continually asked to make judgements about uncertain or ambiguous events. They must decide which of two experts are more credible; whether a scientific study does, in fact, prove what it purports to; whether a criminal defendant is guilty or innocent; the probability that a certain chemical leached into the groundwater; how likely it was that a corporate defendant was aware of the risks associated with its product before it marketed it; and so on. All of these judgements involve an assessment of the likelihood that a particular conclusion is correct. Indeed, most of the judgements we all make in everyday life involve a certain degree of uncertainty.

Unlike scientists in the laboratory, we do not have sufficient time, inclination or training to examine all the available data in a methodologically sound way before we make our decisions. If we are deciding whether to take the train or plane from Washington, D.C. to New York and we are concerned about safety and promptness, it is very unlikely that we will examine all the available data on accidents per mile or all the studies of on-time arrival for trains versus air in order to decide our route of travel (let alone conduct our own study). What is more likely is that we will think of other times we have travelled on an airplane or a train and what that was like. Perhaps we might ask friends or acquaintances who have taken the train or flown between Washington, D.C. and New York to describe their experiences.

When we do this we are using a form of *heuristics*. Heuristics are simplifying strategies which we use to reduce complex decision making tasks to manageable proportions. While the use of these strategies may lead to satisfying results (we decide to fly to New York and arrive ten minutes early and without a scratch), they are clearly less accurate than reasoning strategies that incorporate all or most of the available information. Not only are they less accurate but they also lead to making systematic errors. Most importantly, the very same errors are equally likely to be made by both plaintiff and defense oriented jurors. They are part of being human—part of the built-in mechanism of humanness that entails imposing order, establishing patterns, and creating meaning.

In the mid-1970's, two social psychologists by the names of Amos Tversky and Daniel Kahnamann described some of the heuristics we use in everyday life and some of the common errors to which they lead. Since then their ideas have been tested and amplified. We continually see their ideas in practice as we watch jurors make decisions. One of the major heuristics jurors employ is the *representativeness* heuristic. This is a short hand method for deciding the probability that something caused something else.

Representativeness. How do we decide whether an object A belongs to class B? How does a juror decide whether a criminal defendant belongs to the class of guilty people? What is the probability that a corporation belongs to that class of corporations that infringe the patents belonging to others? How likely is it that a defendant polluted some ground water or engaged in insider trading? One way in which we make these decisions is to judge how similar or representative A is of B and then to use this assessment of similarity to make a judgment: We would expect that someone who is a rapist will resemble our conception of what a rapist is like, and so on for evil corporations, greedy defendants, and incredible witnesses. We find that when jurors see that two things possess some similarity (no matter how superficial that similarity may be) they think that these things must be connected in some way, e.g., "like attracts like," big effects must have big causes. In many instances, these kinds of judgements will be quite valid. But they quite often lead to serious errors. One of these errors is the base rate fallacy which we explore below.

Ignoring the Base Rate Frequency. In an experiment, respondents were told: "The following description is of a man selected at random from a group composed of 70 lawyers and 30 engineers. 'John' is a 39 year old man. He is married and has two children. He is active in local politics. The hobby that he most enjoys is rare book collecting. He is competitive, argumentative, and articulate." The respondents were asked to estimate the probability that John was a lawyer rather than an engineer. The median estimate was that there was a 95% chance he was a lawyer. Another group of respondents was read the same scenario, except they were told that John was selected from a group of 30 lawyers and 70 engineers. This group also estimated that the probability that John was a lawyer at 95%! The respondents looked at how similar John was to their preconceived notion of what a lawyer is like. They ignored the frequency with which lawyers appear in the population (the base rate frequency). We have seen jurors manifest exactly the same behavior in cases involving eyewitness identification, estimations of risk, the reliability of various forms of scientific tests, and many other scenarios. Is it any wonder that jurors tend to give so much more weight to anecdotal evidence (where similarities are much more obvious) than to the testimony of epidemiologists?

Research was conducted in a product liability case where the plaintiff alleged that a medical device was defectively designed, that the defect had caused the device to fail, and that this failure had caused her serious injury. Results revealed that most jurors consistently ignored testimony that the device had only a 1 in 10,000 chance of failing. They were much more concerned with how the features of the injury the plaintiff suffered were consistent with their preconceptions of what a medical device failure is like—catastrophic, instant, and inexplicable by any other cause. Social psychologists have also shown that people often ignore sample size when they judge how likely something is to have occurred. This may explain why jurors have such a hard time evaluating the reliability of scientific studies. Even though a study that shows that 90 out of 100 people exposed to a chemical did not get sick may have great reliability because of the sample size, jurors may be equally or more convinced by a study that shows that four out of five people exposed to the same chemical did get sick.

Jurors may conclude that evidence is proof of something even if there is little relationship between that evidence and what they believe it proves. For instance, we find that the greater the revenue of a corporation, the more likely jurors will be willing to believe that the corporation acted in an intentionally evil way although there is no demonstrated relationship between revenues and venality. Other research shows that an unattractive defendant in a criminal case is more likely to be judged as guilty although there is no relationship between a propensity to commit crimes and physical attractiveness.

Seeing Random Events as Ordered and Meaningful. People make frequent errors in judging whether or not something happened by chance. For instance, nurses in maternity wards will construct elaborate theories to explain streaks of boy or girl births. Most people believe that athletes go through streaks or have "hot hands." A fascinating study by Thomas Gilovich showed that basketball players on the Philadelphia 76's were no more likely to make a shot after they had made (or missed) one, two, or three shots in a row. Players on the Boston Celtics made 75% of the second free throws after making their first, and 75% after missing their first. The reason people believe that streaks or "hot hands" exist is that they have difficulty in figuring out what a chance sequence looks like. We expect the coin to come up heads after it came up tails (the so-called gambler's fallacy). Yet in a series of 20 tosses there is a 50-50 chance of getting four heads in a row, a 25 percent chance of five in a row, and a ten percent chance of getting six in a row. Since most basketball players make about 50 percent of their shots, it is not unreasonable to expect that purely by chance they would frequently make four, five, or six shots in a row. When random events cluster together it is difficult for us to see them as random. An example from a product liability case illustrates this problem:

> Plaintiff alleged that a defective tire was the cause of a serious injury and claimed that the tire manufacturer should have been aware of this defect and either corrected it or taken the product off the market. The jurors were very impressed by the defendant's evidence that it inspected all of its tires before they left the factory and that only one in ten thousand was found to have a problem. The positive effect of this evidence disappeared, however, when the plaintiff showed sequences of tire inspections where two or three tires in a row were rejected, or where a high percentage of tires in a batch were rejected even though statistically we would expect this to happen purely by chance.

This propensity to see clustering where it does not exist was found among residents of London in World War II who believed that the German bombing occurred in definite patterns, making some parts of London more dangerous than others. In fact, the bombing was random. Despite this, Londoners discerned a pattern in this randomness. We find this propensity on the part of jurors to see spatial clusters particularly apparent in toxic tort cases where the plaintiff alleges that the release of a chemical into the environment has caused an increase in disease. Whether or not an actual disease cluster exists, jurors will be very willing to believe that one does.

This willingness for jurors to see order in randomness clearly favors the party that is positing a relationship between the presence of one thing and another—a chemical and a disease; the presence of a defendant and the commission of a crime; a hiring pattern and discrimination. It penalizes the party that tries to convince the jury that these events occurred together because of chance.

More disturbing, social psychologists have found that once a person has concluded that a random pattern is a real phenomenon, he will provide an explanation for that phenomenon that can be incorporated into his pre-existing attitudes and beliefs. In a penalty to defense attorneys, jurors will hold onto these beliefs even when faced with disconfirming evidence.

Regression to the Mean. Elementary statistics show that when two variables are related, extreme values on one tend to be matched by less extreme values on the other. That is, extreme events tend to be followed by less extreme events. We know that the height of parents is related to the height of their offspring. Yet while very tall parents are likely to give birth to tall offspring, it is unlikely they will be as tall as their parents. A very poor performance on a test is likely to be followed by a somewhat improved performance. An extremely good year in business is likely to be followed by a worse one. In all these examples, all of the subsequent events were closer to the average (mean) than the preceding ones. This is called statistical regression.

However, people expect predicted performance to be the same or better than present performance—people believe the predicted should resemble the predictor as much as possible. When this fails to happen we invent various explanations (rather than realizing that it may be the result of statistical regression). When our children do very poorly on a test we may punish them for their poor performance. When our children do well we may reward them. The next time they take a test, statistics would predict that the poorly performing student will do better and the good student will do worse. Consequently, it appears to us that punishment works and reward does not. This is an accepted but spurious finding in much of everyday life. Perhaps that is one reason jurors are so willing to award high punitive damages when plaintiff counsel exhorts jurors to "send a message to corporate headquarters," to teach the defendant a lesson.

Many business disputes that end up in the courtroom rely on trend lines (company sales, profits, etc.) One party or the other may attempt to prove that changes in the trends were due to some action. Jurors will be very willing to accept these explanations even if the changes may only be the result of statistical regression. Once again we see the tendency of jurors to impute meaning to patterns that may simply be the result of chance events.

Availability. Another heuristic is that of availability. Here we find that people are likely to judge the probability that a relationship is true based on the ease with which they can recall examples of this relationship. We find jurors constantly using this heuristic. When we watch jurors deliberate, they are much more likely to recall anecdotal evidence, case studies or their own personal experiences than they will recall the testimony of expert witnesses. Post-trial juror interviews we have conducted indicate jurors spend more time talking about personal experiences than they do about the evidence.

In a highly publicized coverage case, a large petrochemical company was suing a number of insurance companies to recover the costs of cleaning up a hazardous waste site. One of the key issues was whether the insured either expected or intended pollution to occur. Post-trial juror interviews revealed that the key piece of evidence in the case was a description of ducks dying around one of the disposal ponds. This anecdote was vibrant and simple. Jurors remembered it—it was available—much more than the testimony of highly paid experts. Like the heuristic of representativeness, the use of the availability heuristic can lead to systematic cognitive errors.

The use of the availability heuristic is just part of jurors' willingness to base conclusions on incomplete or unrepresentative information. Because they do not recognize that they are using incomplete information as the basis of their belief, they are more likely to believe that their conclusions are a logical outcome of an objective assessment.

How Instances are Retrieved

Those instances which are more easily remembered will appear to be more numerous than those which are less easily remembered. People will believe in the validity of some fringe medical treatment because they can more easily remember instances where others reported a cure from the treatment than where people failed to do so. These instances are also more easily remembered than instances where people report a cure from more conventional medical treatment.

In a contract case the plaintiff was a small company that contended that the large corporate defendant had failed to honor a contract and purchase a product from the small company. This had led to the plaintiff's bankruptcy. In their research, defense counsel watched jurors deliberate and found that many were able to easily recall situations where either they or their friends or relatives had personal experiences where small companies had been forced into difficult situations because of the actions (albeit legal ones) of larger companies. This made it easier for the jurors to conclude that there was a relationship between the defendant's actions and the demise of the plaintiff. At the same time, however, there were some opportunities for the defense. First, the research demonstrated that jurors were able to recall many instances of small companies that had failed due to being overly ambitious and expanding too quickly. Second, the research suggested a two-fold strategy. The defense was to present the history of the defendant company emphasizing how it was dependent on successful relationships with other small companies (many of which became much bigger). In addition, the defense began to craft a mismanagement theme that emphasized the plaintiff's own self-inflicted problems.

The Saliency and Recency of What Is Recalled

The more salient and recent something is, the more retrievable it is. This will bias the conclusions that jurors make. If what happened to the plaintiff was similar to what happened to the juror last week, the juror's experience will play a much greater role in his decision making than if it happened to an acquaintance some time ago.

We see this phenomenon operating when lawyers engage in jury selection. An attorney is much more likely to excuse all accountants from a jury if he got killed by an accountant in his last trial as compared to a trial a year ago, or if he heard of a colleague that lost a case because of an accountant. This will be so even if there is absolutely no relationship between how the potential juror feels about the case and whether or not he is an accountant.

Elizabeth Loftus found that lawyers tend to be overconfident in their predictions of how successful they will be in any particular trial (a harmful error that may affect propensity to settle, expenditures on experts, etc.). This may be because lawyers are better able to remember past instances of their success than their failures in similar cases. When they do remember failures, they may attribute them to uncontrollable events (while successes are their due).

Over-Reliance on Information That Is Confirmatory

When making evaluations, jurors tend to overly rely on evidence that confirms the existence of a relationship. In trials where the plaintiff alleges that x caused y (a chemical caused a cancer, insider trading caused an increase in the price of a stock, etc.) a more effective strategy for the defense may not be that x did not cause y, but that z caused y. In the contracts case discussed previously, it was much more effective for the defense to argue that mismanagement caused the small business to fail than to argue that there was no violation of the contract and therefore this did not cause the business to fail.

One explanation for this phenomenon is that confirmatory evidence may be more easy to cognitively deal with. It is more difficult to conceptualize negative assertions. It is easier to argue that a chemical caused a disease than to argue that the absence of the chemical did not prevent the disease. It is also easier to argue that something other than the chemical caused the disease, than to argue that the chemical did not cause the disease.

False Consensus

Often, one of the greatest surprises jurors encounter during the course of a trial is when they first begin deliberations. They are shocked to learn that their opinion of what happened in the case is not shared by the other jurors. This is a telling example of a much wider phenomenon called the "false consensus effect." This is the often mistaken belief that the majority of others share our opinions. There are a number of reasons why this happens. The major one is that we tend to remember most things that confirm our opinions and those instances become more easily retrievable. It is not just jurors that have this problem. Lawyers often assume that their assessment of the strength of a case or what the major issues are will be shared by their colleagues. Judges often believe that all the parties to a dispute see the reasonableness of their rulings. Expert witnesses, in reporting what the consensus of opinion is in a particular field, may be simply stating their own opinion and assuming it is shared. Finally, people fall victim to the phenomenon of false consensus because our cultural norms prevent us from openly contradicting those with whom we disagree (especially if they occupy positions of authority, like a judge). Hence we tend to only hear opinions that agree with our own. This problem becomes compounded because we mix primarily with people who are like ourselves and who therefore will be more likely to share our opinions anyway.

Ambiguous and Unambiguous Information

The color black is almost universally associated with evil and death. In an experiment, social psychologists asked trained referees to view one of two videotapes. One tape showed a football scrimmage in which the aggressive team wore black and the other team wore white. The other tape showed the opposite. The referees who saw the black uniformed version were far more likely to award penalties than the referees who saw the other tape. This is a clear example of how our expectations will bias the way in which we perceive information when that information is ambiguous.

Unambiguous information is not easily distorted or ignored when it clearly contradicts what we believe or expect. What jurors often do when confronted with unambiguous information that runs counter to their pre-existing beliefs is subject that information to much closer scrutiny than information that confirms our beliefs. They will also be much more critical of that information. That criticism may or may not be appropriate, but the key point is that confirmatory information is not subject to the same level of scrutiny. By rejecting the non-confirmatory information, jurors become even more convinced of their original positions. That is why we find jurors so often becoming polarized to their initial verdicts during deliberations. In a toxic tort case, both sides presented studies that the chemical at issue either was or was not harmful. Those jurors who came to the trial believing that all chemicals were harmful spent their time in deliberations attacking the validity of the defense's study showing no harm. They ended up even more convinced that all chemicals are harmful.

Smoke and "PCBs"

We represented an architect/engineer who had designed the heating, ventilation and air conditioning ("HVAC") system for a high-rise building. There was a fire in the basement in the building creating smoke laden with trace amounts of polychlorinated biphenyls ("PCBs"). An action was filed to recover the costs of cleaning up the building, and it was alleged that the HVAC system acted as a conduit to spread the PCB-laden smoke throughout the building.

We retained world-renowned epidemiologists, who were prepared to testify that the amounts of PCBs in the building were harmless. Based on this testimony, we intended to argue that the level and consequent cost of the clean-up was grossly excessive in view of the harmless nature of the trace amounts of PCBs in the building. After several jury focus group studies, however, we learned that a jury would never accept the proposition that PCBs were harmless. More importantly, we learned that a defense based on the harmless nature of the PCB contaminants could backfire, because the jury would likely conclude that we would not present the defense unless we were conceding that the HVAC system was responsible for spreading the smoke throughout the building.

As a result of the jury focus group studies, we changed our strategy to emphasize that the HVAC system was well designed and, in fact, did a salutary job in preventing the spread of the smoke. We also emphasized how the insurance companies seeking recovery for the cost of the clean-up were attempting to blame others for the risk of loss that they assumed.

H. James Wulfsberg
Lempres and Wulfsberg, Oakland

Hindsight Bias

This bias becomes particularly manifest when jurors are asked to ignore or disregard certain evidence or information in reaching their decisions. As we all know, jurors often have difficulty following such instructions. A conventional explanation is that jurors resent being restricted. However, research has shown that it is the hindsight bias that is in operation.

Consider a product liability suit. In deciding whether to award damages to the plaintiff, jurors are asked to focus only on the behavior of the defendant prior to the occurrence of the plaintiff's injury. Thus, questions regarding adequate design, testing, and exercise of due care become relevant. Yet in making those judgements, it is difficult for jurors to ignore the fact that the plaintiff has been injured and to exclude that knowledge from their conclusions regarding the defendant's actions. This is precisely the problem a defendant faced in a case involving a group of plaintiffs alleging they had been injured by exposure to asbestos in the work place. In multiple pre-trial research exercises, surrogate jurors were unable to discount the claimed injuries of the workers when deciding whether the defendant, a manufacturer of an asbestos-containing product, had acted properly in continuing to market the product. The obvious strategy that emerged was to have the case bifurcated between liability and damages. When jurors are made aware of the outcome or conclusion of some event, they will utilize their hindsight knowledge to adjust or evaluate the facts of intermediate events leading to the conclusion.

Counter-Factual Thinking

We have been discussing how jurors estimate the probability that some event or outcome is true, real, or likely, and some of the errors that enter into this process. Equally important in jurors assessing the probability of an event is their assessment of the normality of an event. If jurors conclude that an event is normal, they will be much less likely to be emotionally affected than by events that are seen as abnormal or unusual.

Social psychologists have found that the more easily a person is able to imagine alternative outcomes (counter-factual thinking) to an event, the more likely that that event will be seen to be abnormal, and therefore the stronger the emotional reactions. They use as an example the way people react differently to the deaths of two passengers in a plane crash. One passenger had booked his ticket on the plane three months earlier. The other passenger ended up on the plane because the flight he was booked on had been canceled that day. Even though the probability of being killed in a plane crash was the same for each individual, people typically feel far more sympathy for the latter passenger.

Why is it that the more abnormal a victim's fate, the more sympathy it elicits? One factor is how easily we can imagine undoing the event. "If only the flight hadn't been canceled," or, "If only he had taken another airline," etc. The shorter the temporal or spatial distance between the outcome and the imagined alternative outcome, the more abnormal the event. A soldier killed 24 hours before the end of a war evokes far more sympathy than one killed six months before the end even though the probability of death and the severity of the outcome may have been the same in each instance. In addition, outcomes that follow unusual actions (the cancellation of a flight) are judged as more abnormal and will bring out more of an emotional response.

An example of this counter-factual thinking is frequently seen in accidental death cases. A horrible accident occurred at a construction site when a large steel beam fell from several stories up onto the street below. Those killed by the beam were a construction worker on the site, two people on their way to work, and a tourist. Research revealed that jurors would probably award higher damages to the estate of the tourist than to the estates of the two people going to work. They were significantly less generous to the construction worker's estate. This was so even though each victim had suffered the same injury and had no role in causing or contributing to the accident. The different rates of compensation were due to jurors' judgements of how unusual it was for each individual in this situation to become a victim. It was much easier to imagine alternative scenarios that would have placed the tourist elsewhere than it was to imagine similar scenarios for the construction worker.

Defense attorneys would be well advised to "normalize" the circumstances of the plaintiff as much as possible in this case. For instance, in the example above, the construction site was next to a popular entertainment attraction. It was important for the defense to emphasize that there were always a great number of tourists in the area. In addition, the construction site had a fence with view holes cut in it. Many people would stop and look through the view holes. Therefore, the death of the tourist in the accident appeared a little less unusual. The damages awarded the tourist's estate declined. By the same order, it would be a wise strategy for the plaintiff attorney to emphasize all the unusual circumstances that led to the plaintiff's situation.

As Jim Bruen[*] points out, "normalization" can begin during voir dire. In a toxic tort case where plaintiff alleges that his/her personal injuries resulted from exposure to a "chemical soup," defense counsel could ask whether prospective jurors have been periodically exposed to strong liquids made from a mixture of chemicals (e.g., drain cleaners, carpet stain removers, oven cleaners, etc.), whether they have developed any illness(es) at any time after one or more of these exposures, and whether they have blamed the liquids for the illness(es). The typical prospective juror will report exposure(s) and subsequent illness(es), but no blame. Thus, plaintiff's circumstances will appear "normal," but the ensuing legal claim will not.

Some Common Heuristics Used By Jurors

As we have seen, heuristics are "rules of thumb" that jurors use for making decisions about complex issues. Based on research conducted by cognitive psychologists, we have found that there are a number of "rules of thumb" that jurors commonly use:

1) "Statements by recognized experts can be trusted." We will examine this heuristic in more detail in Chapter 5 in our discussion of credibility. However, the most important consequence of this heuristic is that there are many circumstances where the perceived expertise of a witness will be far more important than what the witness is saying.

2) "Consensus implies correctness." This is a heuristic that lawyers implicitly know that jurors use. In any trial that involves a dispute over the safety of a substance or device, a major thrust of either side will typically be to show the jury what some government agency, academic group, or trade organization thought about the product. One of the strongest

---

[*] James A. Bruen, *Landels Ripley & Diamond, San Francisco.*

arguments that can be made to a jury is "how can all these experts be wrong and the plaintiff (defendant) be right?"

This idea that "if everyone is saying it, it must be true" comes into powerful play during deliberations and is often the major reason that minority viewpoints will capitulate to the majority. Perhaps the most subtle way in which this heuristic may come into play is during the trial itself. A great deal of research has shown that individuals are more persuaded by an argument when they believe that others in the audience are also persuaded. In a courtroom, jurors and spectators are enjoined from demonstrating their approval or disapproval of testimony or of counsel's comments. They cannot applaud or hiss. Yet, individual jurors are extremely attuned to the actions and responses of those around them. An effective technique that has been employed in more than one case is to have spectators in the courtroom who nod or shake their heads in unison at critical times during the trial.

3) "Length implies strength." In complex cases where comprehension is low, jurors may resort to the use of this heuristic. In essence they are saying, "with so much to say, the speaker must have a valid point, even though I have stopped listening." This is consistent with the idea that the sheer number of arguments made, regardless of their strength or validity, may be persuasive. Jurors do not always engage in heuristic processing. It is, however, important to understand the conditions under which they are likely to do so.

When Will Jurors Use Heuristic Processing

We have discussed a number of factors that influence how well we can persuade jurors. Some of the factors relate to features of the argument itself (order effects, one-sided versus two-sided arguments) and some refer to contextual variables (the credibility and likability of witnesses) that are independent of the argument. When is the persuasive impact of the argument itself greater than the impact of the context in which the argument is given? To answer this question, we must understand the difference between *systematic* and *heuristic* information processing.

When jurors engage in systematic information processing, they are actively attempting to understand and evaluate arguments as well as assessing their validity in relationship to the arguments' conclusions. They are likely to expend effort to pay attention to the content of arguments, analyze the arguments, and integrate their thoughts into what they already know. Jurors will give thoughtful consideration to issue-relevant information. Whether or not a juror is persuaded will depend to a great degree on the quality of the arguments made. When jurors engage in heuristic information processing, they are relying on cues that are outside the message itself (for instance, "he's an expert, he must know what he's talking about") or any of the other short cuts in reasoning in which they listen to only partial aspects of an argument as we discussed in Chapter 3.

Jurors are likely to engage in systematic processing and pay attention to issue-relevant information when they are motivated to do so. Two key motivations are the level of interest or involvement by the juror in the issue and an ability to comprehend what the issue is about. For instance, we generally find that there is much greater issue involvement in personal injury, toxic tort, libel, and product liability cases than there is in other types of civil litigation. The lower the involvement and the lower the comprehension of the juror, the less likely he is to engage in systematic information processing and to take all or most of the relevant information into account when coming to a decision. In these instances, jurors are more likely to use the kinds of heuristics we have described above.

Heuristic processing is much more likely to be seen in certain types of civil cases: contracts, intellectual property, and accounting fraud top the list. These tend to involve complex and arcane evidence and issues. The exceptions to this observation occur when the parties to the suit are well known and jurors have strong opinions about them, or when the topic of the lawsuit has received a lot of media attention or is perceived to be central to lives of ordinary people.

Common sense may tell us that in very complex and technical cases, the content of arguments is far more important than how the witness looks, how likable he is, or his degree of trustworthiness. However, psychological research indicates that just the opposite is true. These are cases in which jurors are not likely to be very involved and in which there will not be a great deal of comprehension. Hence, in these situations, we should expect to encounter jurors who will be paying far more attention to *how* messages are being delivered and by *whom* than *what* is being said.   Research also indicates that these type of trials almost always require more dynamic trial participants.

A Stipulation of Undisputed Facts

Several years ago, I had the pleasure of trying the case of Brown v. McDonnell Douglas *before Judge William Schwarzer in the U.S. District Court in San Francisco.   The case involved an airline disaster which occurred when two airliners had a mid-air collision at about 30,000 feet over a navigation facility in Zagreb, Yugoslavia.   The case was a cause celebre in Europe due not only to the large loss of life, but also due to the fact that the Yugoslavian authorities sentenced the air traffic controller to eight years in prison for criminal negligence.*

The claim against my client was that there was a pillar in the cockpit windscreen which was too wide, thus preventing the crew from seeing around it and detecting the other airplane and avoiding the collision.   The defense was that this was not the case, and even if it were, the two aircraft had a closure rate that was about the velocity of a Sten gun, and the accident was the fault of the air traffic controller and unavoidable by either crew.

As one can imagine, it was a hotly contested case with able counsel on both sides.   Since the case was estimated to take several weeks or months to try, Judge Schwarzer, who doesn't suffer long presentations gladly, advised us that he didn't intend to clog up his calendar with counsel taking weeks to try factual issues to which there could be no dispute.   He required us to enter into a stipulation regarding all undisputed facts. As one can imagine, the complicated facts involved a foreign   air traffic

(continued)

(continued)

situation and several airliners in a three dimensional environment. The primary source of information was an official investigation report on which the British and the Yugoslavians had collaborated. Trying to reduce this mass of technical data into a stipulation which could be understood and learned by a jury was a prodigious task. Our team put its mind to it, and after some time, had a draft of what we would propose to the plaintiff. I had spent many years trying aircraft cases and felt that the stipulation was a model of clarity.

As a part of our pre-trial preparation we had engaged jury consultants. A panoply of research was in progress, but one of the services we decided to use was a "trial simulation." This is where one tries a somewhat truncated case to subjects demographically similar to those who are expected to be jurors in the case. Unlike a focus group presentation, real witnesses are put on and the case is argued, though in an abbreviated form.

One of the things we wished to test, in addition to the effectiveness of our witnesses and presentation, was whether or not we had simplified the stipulation enough to have the jury understand it.

After presenting the case, we watched the subjects deliberate through a one-way mirror. We noticed that they were ignoring the stipulation entirely, even though it had been presented to them in writing. I mentioned this to the psychologist who was helping us (and also happens to be the author of this book). He went into the jury room and pointed out to the foreman that it should be remembered that they had the written stipulation to rely on if they had any questions about the facts of this complicated situation.

As he left the room, we observed the foreman place his hand on the stipulation which lay on the table before him. He slid the stipulation aside and the jury returned to their deliberations relying heavily on the information given in the opening statement and the demonstrative evidence, which was ample.

(continued)

(continued)

In reviewing this exercise, we developed the strategy that the jury would probably not be too interested in the stipulation, no matter how clear and concise it was. Accordingly, the behavioral psychologists suggested that rather than clarify it, it should be made so complex as to be virtually incomprehensible. It was their suggestion that we rely on the demonstrative evidence which consisted of computer animations of the crash scenario and computer simulations of the radar presentation seen by the controller, as well as full scale mock-ups of the cockpit windscreen and a host of other toys and top flight experts.

The court's penchant for brevity led to a granting of a non-suit at the close of the plaintiffs' case. When we interviewed the discharged jury, we were interested in how they would have held and also their reaction to the plaintiffs' evidence. We were also curious as to their feelings about the stipulation which had been given them and which now was as incomprehensible as our trial team could make it. (It made the Internal Revenue Code look like a kindergarten reader.) They said they would have found for the defense if given the case and, oh yes, they paid no attention to the stipulation!

Edwin W. Green
Bronson Bronson & McKinnon, Los Angeles

When jurors engage in heuristic processing, not only are they less likely to pay attention to the quality of the arguments made but they will also pay more attention to peripherals. These peripherals include jurors' perceptions of the expertise of the lawyer or witness, how likable they are, their physical attractiveness, or how long they speak. These peripheral cues can become a critical element of persuasion.

The contrast between systematic and heuristic processing also has an interesting bearing on a question frequently of concern to trial lawyers. This is, how will jurors react to the fact that an expert witness has been paid a great deal of money for his testimony. This information will be more harmful when jurors are not paying attention to the content of the witness' testimony, but rather to peripheral cues. This is when credibility is important. As we have seen, an important component of credibility is trustworthiness. If jurors are concerned about witness credibility, fees to testify will have a direct effect on jurors' perceptions of impartiality which in turn will affect their perceptions of the witness' trustworthiness.

We should not assume that systematic processing is necessarily more accurate or better than heuristic processing just because it requires more cognitive effort and is more demanding. Systematic processing too is subject to bias and will be affected by jurors' prior knowledge, vested interests, and the degree to which they are committed to previously existing attitudinal positions.

The Rationality of Irrational Behavior

Recently, economists have begun to understand that in the same way that baseball players are able to catch a fly ball without any conscious understanding of parabolic curves or differential equations, so people realize in many situations that the best way to achieve their goals is by irrational, not rational, behavior. If we define rational behavior as the conscious pursuit of a goal by the most efficient means possible according to consistently applied rules, we may see many examples where rational behavior will not work and something else must be substituted. Take for instance, attempts to fall asleep at night. The more one consciously tries to do so, the less successful one is likely to be (the same applies to trying to get someone to fall in love with you, trying to act as a member of the upper class, and so on). We see the same dilemma appear continually in research on juror behavior. It manifests itself when jurors are faced with seemingly intractable problems. Most frequently, this occurs when jurors are deadlocked or when they must decide damage amounts. When the solution to problems is more obvious, it is easier to act rationally. But with difficult problems, jurors employ techniques that clearly violate "rationale" rules or are not goal directed. These include: flipping a coin, averaging, changing the subject, majority rules, and so on. Just as any economic theory based solely on a model of rational man is dangerously outmoded, the same is true of any theory of jury behavior similarly based.

Conclusion

In this chapter, we have examined some of the cognitive mechanisms jurors use to process information. These should be contrasted with some of the motivational processes we will describe elsewhere in this book. These cognitive mechanisms are not related to the satisfaction of psychological needs, or the possession of particular attitudes or beliefs. They are mechanisms all of us use that could well be evolutionary adaptations. Most importantly, this chapter has shown that when jurors use these mechanisms, they can lead to serious errors. Even though a juror may be quite convinced by a conclusion at which he has arrived, the method he has used may have caused him to be quite wrong.

These errors are not the company of laymen alone. Study after study has shown that experts engage in precisely the same form of faulty reasoning while at the same time believing they are being logical and scientific. Psychologists, sociologists, and other experts in human behavior have been known to utilize heuristics in forming judgements and making decisions. And as we have show, lawyers are not immune from committing these errors when estimating the strength of their case, selecting jurors, and defining key case issues.

## CHAPTER 5

Learning and the Attribution of Innocence or Blame

In many cases, jurors are required to learn new information, concepts, or ideas which are foreign to their education, background, training, or previous experience. Hence, the learning process and the concepts of memory and retention are a critical aspect of the development of effective trial strategy. How do people learn? What is the learning process? And how does learning relate to juror behavior? There are many forms of learning which reflect the various processes through which people seek to improve their adjustment to and control over their environment. Here, we are interested in how these learning processes relate to juror decision-making. Learning is one of the fundamental processes of human behavior and is certainly a basic part of the behavior that occurs in a courtroom. No other field of psychology has generated the volume or quality of empirical research as the study of learning. While we cannot do justice to this topic in this chapter, we will touch on some basic principles and concepts that are relevant to the process of presenting a case to a jury or judge.

Two Types of Learning: Voluntary and Involuntary

The process of learning is broken down into two general categories: involuntary and voluntary learning. Involuntary learning is traditionally referred to as Classical Conditioning and involves the association of a certain response with a particular stimulus. Pavlov, the Russian physiologist studying the digestion process at the turn of the century, conditioned dogs to salivate at the sound of a bell in the absence of food. He achieved this by repeatedly pairing the introduction of food with the bell. Eventually, the bell became associated with the food and conditioned salivation occurred. The name "involuntary" is used to describe this type of learning because the learner does not have to want to learn in order for learning to occur. All of us have many conditioned responses. We may feel hungry when we see a fast food commercial. We may feel pride when we listen to the national anthem and view the flag because of the way these symbols have been paired with significant ideas and events over our lives and throughout history. We have been conditioned to experience fear in dark places. In fact, many of our emotional responses are the result of involuntary conditioning.

In the courtroom, conditioned emotional responses may be built by the careful repetition of the plaintiff or defendant's name with some specific behavior. For example, the plaintiff in a personal injury case might continually refer to the defendant and "corporate greed." With this method, the plaintiff will attempt to build negative associations with the defendant. Using the same strategy, the defendant might continually refer to the plaintiff's "personal irresponsibility" in the presentation of his case. In both examples, the attorney attempts to establish a conditioned response to a particular stimulus. This type of conditioned association is quite powerful because it occurs automatically without much, if any, cognitive activity on the part of the juror.

Consider the impact of a series of long and dull depositions. Once jurors are conditioned to associate depositions with feelings of boredom, frustration and even anger, this association is likely to be reproduced throughout the rest of the trial when jurors are confronted with deposition testimony.

In cases involving banks, it is common for jurors to have been conditioned to respond with negative feelings when they hear or read about banks. They may associate feelings of anger about how they have been treated by their own bank. Yet in an employment discrimination case, a trial attorney may unwittingly attempt to present the bank as a caring and sympathetic employer in the courtroom. Similar examples occur with attorneys representing utility companies. Very frequently, there is the desire to present an image of the company during the trial as responsive and dependable. Yet the very jurors who are the recipients of this intended message have been conditioned to react to the contrary. *The lawyer's message is not only inconsistent with what the jurors think, it is inconsistent with what they feel.*

Voluntary Learning: Some Reinforcement Techniques

Voluntary learning refers to the behaviors people choose to emit because they expect a certain positive consequence, usually a reward or reinforcement, to follow. This type of learning is often referred to as Operant Conditioning. We are most familiar with this type of learning because it has been the focus of discussions ranging from how to educate our youth to how to deter crime.

Behavioral psychologists consider reinforcement to be central to the learning process. Reinforcement can be primary—for example, food, which satisfies a physiological need—or secondary, such as praise or affection, which satisfies an emotional or social need. It has been demonstrated that learning occurs fastest when a reinforcement immediately follows a desired behavior every time the behavior occurs. If we want Johnny to make his own bed every morning, we should reward Johnny appropriately (e.g., praise, money, candy) every time Johnny in fact makes his bed. However, it has also been demonstrated that the strongest learning occurs when reinforcement follows an intermittent schedule. In this scenario, Johnny is rewarded on average, every third or fourth time he makes his bed. Intermittent reinforcement has been used to explain the occurrence of habits, superstitions, and even gambling. It is relatively easy to stop behavior that gets rewarded every time. Just stop the reinforcement and the behavior will stop. Under an intermittent schedule however, it is more difficult for the learner to determine if the reinforcement has stopped or not. In fact, the learned behavior often increases in the absence of reinforcement with the expectation that increased responding eventually will result in reinforcement. "I know my luck is just about to change!"

In the courtroom, lawyers can use the principles of voluntary learning and reinforcement to promote desirable responses from jurors. For the most part, lawyers have little opportunity to provide the jurors with primary reinforcers (throwing pieces of chocolate to the jury during one's opening statement is probably objectionable in most courts). However, lawyers can make strategic use of secondary reinforcers to teach the jurors various information and behavior. Lawyers can reward jurors for attending to their evidence by presenting them with interesting information. Most people experience a sense of personal pride with the acquisition of new knowledge. This is particularly the case when the knowledge or information is considered socially relevant and not possessed by many other people. In these situations, jurors can develop an inner sense of self-satisfaction by having learned things that their colleagues, friends, or family members would like to know but do not. When the lawyer or his witnesses provide jurors with this experience, the juror can be said to have been rewarded. Another form of rewarding jurors stems from the lawyer's ability to satisfy curiosity. Human beings are innately curious. Establishing a problem or an unanswered scenario and later helping jurors arrive at a solution can be a rewarding experience. Jurors can also receive a psychological reward by arriving or being provided with answers to important questions. Unresolved issues and unanswered questions tend to produce psychological tension and frustration. The elimination of these conditions can function as reinforcement or reward. Finally, trial lawyers can reward jurors by the lawyer's performance in the courtroom. As an example, if the trial lawyer is direct, concise, and very precise in the conduct of this direct or cross-examination, jurors can be rewarded by this behavior in contrast to long, protracted, and unfocused examinations by the other side. As an aside, judges have often noted that nothing draws out the jurors' ire faster than an attorney's broken promise to be brief.

Participation in the Learning Process

A fundamental and thoroughly verified principle of learning is that active participation in the learning process increases the speed and amount of learning. The more a juror enters into the learning process in some way, the better he learns. For this reason, the lawyer may attempt to inject the juror more directly into the learning process by techniques such as providing jurors with exhibit books which they can review during recesses or at the end of the day. This can also be accomplished with physical sight inspections, representational models, or the ability to touch, feel, or physically contact important pieces of evidence. Demonstrative exhibits are particularly effecting in injecting jurors into a more dynamic learning environment.

Most jurors intrinsically enjoy learning and report in post-trial interviews that the most rewarding aspect in their jury service related to the fact that they learned so many new and interesting things.

Memory

After learning has been accomplished, there remains the important matter of *remembering* the information that has been learned. Some theorists believe that nothing is ever really forgotten but that the material in question is simply inaccessible to the conscious mind under normal conditions. Results from hypnosis and psychoanalysis tend to support this view. In the courtroom, we are primarily interested in knowing what information has been learned. Further and more importantly, the lawyer is concerned not only about what information has been learned, but also, the extent to which it can be recalled accurately over time.

Retention and Forgetting

The stability of learned material over time is defined as retention and the converse is forgetting. Forgetting is the tendency for learned associations to weaken over time. Weakening occurs primarily through lack of use, interference, or severe physical or emotional trauma. In the case of involuntary learning, a stimulus like Pavlov's bell is presented to the dog so many times without food, it begins to lose its conditioned qualities (incidentally, most phobias are treated this way—by repeatedly exposing the patient to the feared event in the absence of any real harm or trauma). With voluntary learning, it becomes clear that if reinforcement no longer reliably follows a given behavior, the behavior extinguishes.

Hence, at the most basic level, for jurors to remember significant events that occur in the courtroom, it is incumbent upon the lawyer to remind jurors frequently through repetition whenever possible. Most psychologists regard repetition as a key to successful learning. Without repetition, there is a significant decay in learned responses over time. Yet repetition must be done carefully so as not to patronize and/or bore the jurors. Effective repetition takes more planning and skill than most believe. One of the keys to effective repetition is to make the repetition meaningful. Each exhibit, witness, and argument presented to the jury should have a legitimate reason to contain the important message. The message should be presented in different and creative ways. As stated previously, memory is significantly enhanced with the use of visual imagery. Demonstrative exhibits are an excellent way to enhance understanding and memory of a message. Using these techniques, jurors are continuously exposed to the message without being bored or made to feel unintelligent.

The Power of Repetition

As a young lawyer, I was privileged to carry the brief case for Lawrason Driscoll, during the trial of Tool v. Richardson Merrill Co., *a case which made some law in California regarding punitive damages. The claim asserted by a most able and experienced trial lawyer, John Wynne Herron, was that the drug MER-29 (used to lower blood cholesterol), had serious side effects which had damaged the plaintiff. The facts included that the defendant had fabricated data during animal testing on monkeys which had previously died, and had suppressed reports of side effects during the clinical trials and after the drug was licensed for sale. The defendant had even been fined by the U.S. Food and Drug Administration due to the alleged misrepresentations, an unprecedented event.*

The case was heavily laden with expert testimony in fields like microbiology, pharmacology, chemistry, medicine, and more. Mr. Herron, who was a striking figure, concluded his cross-examination of each expert presented by the defense with a hypothetical question which was along the following lines: "Doctor, I'd like you to assume the following facts: Assume that during the animal testing of the drug MER-29 by the company scientists, one of the monkeys died and the scientists continued to record data for the monkey two months after his death. Assume further that test results of the animal testing were misrepresented to the FDA. As-

(continued)

(continued)

sume also that when clinical testing was being done there were many reports of ichthyosis, depressed libido, alopecia, areata, and lenticular cataracts. Assume further that upon licensing, over 200 of the users of the drug complained of these symptoms and that the company consciously suppressed this information, leading to the FDA fining the manufacturer for the first time in U.S. history. Sir, would those facts change your opinion?"

While I don't have a transcript of that question, it was very close to my description. It was, of course, his opening statement and his final argument, but it was said in the presence of the jury at least two times per day for several weeks of the defense case. As one might expect, the jury was seen to mouth the hypothetical question along with Mr. Herron. The verdict set a record for punitive damages. It was a powerful lesson for a young lawyer.

Edwin W. Green
Bronson Bronson & McKinnon, Los Angeles

Keep in mind that your opponent will attempt to interfere with the acquisition and retention of your messages by bombarding the jurors with contradictory messages and information. You are in a constant battle with your opponent for the jurors' attention, learning, and retention energy. The lawyer who wins this battle for the bulk of the trial usually wins the case as well.

In general, learning new information or a new task over time has been found to be superior to the concentration of learning in a limited amount of time. This conclusion suggests that:

- The case narrative and themes should be repeated and reintroduced as frequently as possible throughout the trial by the lawyer;

- The case narrative and themes should be repeated and represented to the jury whenever possible through witness testimony and demonstrative exhibits;

- The conclusions or most important aspect of an individual witness' testimony should be reinforced throughout that witness' direct testimony as frequently as possible.

- Witnesses should reinforce and review the testimony of those who precede them and, if possible, help set the stage for the important topics of those witnesses who are to follow;

- Demonstrative exhibits should be designed to repeat and represent the major issues in the case; and

- Careful attention should be devoted to demonstrative exhibits to ensure that repetition and redundancy are built in to exhibits in an attractive and appealing manner.

Causal Schema and Common Sense Explanation

People want to know the causes of their own and others' behavior. They want to be able to explain the behavior of individuals, corporations, and governments. Was the neighbor that failed to return the borrowed lawn mower being malicious or just forgetful? Did the defendant, a major corporation, manufacture the defective product because of greed, or did problems occur because of uncontrolled circumstances beyond its control? Was the assault perpetrated on an innocent victim or someone "who asked for it." Every day, we make countless causal attributions to explain what happens to us and others. Establishing causal explanations for our own and others' behavior allows us to better understand the world and to see the world as a more predictable place.

Many people believe that human beings engage in complex, quasi-scientific analyses of cause and effect before making attributions. Lawyers often incorrectly assume that jurors are motivated to find *accurate* causal explanations. In fact, in most situations, causal analysis is an efficient, if not automatic, process grounded in common sense, not "rational" scientific analysis. As noted earlier, when it comes to explaining the world, people are more than willing to trade *efficiency* for accuracy. The concept of efficient causal analysis is important because it explains why many people develop erroneous causal explanations for events in their life and at trial.

In the courtroom, jurors embark on a search for explanations for the events surrounding the case unfolding before them. They are determined to understand the motivation of the litigants and the causal explanations for what they view as the primary issues in the dispute. In short, jurors want to decide who is to blame for any damage or loss incurred by either party.

The way in which jurors go about establishing cause and assigning blame provides clues as to the types of strategies that would be most effective in influencing this process.

Throughout our lives, we develop a lasting inventory of causal principles for explaining human behavior. These principles are simple cause and effect statements such as "business success is the result of good ideas and hard work." These statements tend to be based more on common sense ideas than on rational analysis. Organized sets of cause and effect statements are called schemas which determine the types of explanations that we construct. Schematic processing involves fitting or matching incoming information to pre-existing schematic representations. If the information "fits," no further processing is necessary. If we observe a parent hitting a child, we may access a schematic representation of an abusive parent. If what we observe adequately matches up with this representation, we may conclude that the physical punishment is caused by the parent's underlying pathology.

It is important to note that schema are highly internalized and their influence on a person's thinking is often automatic. In other words, schema are activated with little or no in-depth analysis on the part of the person seeking an explanation. Common sense explanation requires very little information. When we encounter new behavior, we attempt to explain that behavior within the context of our pre-existing framework of causal principles. It is not uncommon for a person to construct an explanation that is not supported by the facts.

The basic dilemma that we face whenever we observe our own or someone else's behavior is deciding whether it is a result of personal or situational forces. When we learn that a colleague has made partner, we can attribute his success to his ability (personal force) or to some external factor like luck or office politics (situational forces). Personal forces can be expected to endure while situational forces are highly variable. When we make a personal attribution, we are making a judgement about someone's immutable characteristics. When we make situational attributions, we are concluding that the requirements of the situation produced the behavior that we observed.

Plaintiff lawyers often want jurors to attribute any undesirable behavior to personal characteristics of the defendant (the company is fundamentally evil). They want jurors to believe that not only did the company commit some transgression, but that the conduct was only one manifestation of a corrupt and greedy system. Persuading jurors to make this type of dispositional attribution increases the likelihood of significant damages. On the other hand, a defense attorney might attempt to persuade jurors that if in fact an undesirable event occurred, it was caused by situational forces outside the defendant's control.

Attribution I'll Never Forget

The first time I ever used a "shadow jury" was in a case pending in Federal Court in Orlando, Florida, before a visiting judge named Kellum, in a case styled Butler v. Gulfstream Aerospace. *A "shadow jury" (a concept originally developed by Dr. Vinson) is a group of people chosen by a behavioral psychologist to, as closely as possible, replicate the actual jury. The shadow jury sits in the back of the courtroom during all times that the actual jury is in the courtroom, and each evening they are debriefed by a person on the psychologist's staff. They do not know for whom they are performing this service. This technique allows the trial lawyer to get daily feedback on many aspects of his presentation. It can be very bruising to the ego, as I am about to relate.*

(continued)

(continued)

At the end of the plaintiff's case, which the shadow jury reported had not gone well for the plaintiff, a university professor of economics was presented for the purpose of describing the economic loss to the plaintiff for the jury. Since I had been getting encouraging reports of my dazzling (I felt) cross-examination of their witnesses, including experts in the fields of aerodynamics and mechanical engineering, I felt that the economist would be duck soup, especially in view of the coup de grace that I had prepared. After a rather long side bar conference with Judge Kellum, he allowed me to interrogate the economist on the fact that he had been convicted of a felony, to wit, smuggling illegal substances into his homosexual lover's jail cell. Furthermore, the record of the conviction had been sealed, because a large amount of the professor's income was derived by testifying on behalf of plaintiff's lawyers.

Any fool can cross-examine when he has the goods on the witness, and I had the goods. I felt that in this Southern jury's mind, I had not only damaged the witness' theories and opinions, I had undermined his credibility to such an extent that it would bleed over onto the entire case. The witness was on the ropes, I thought, and so was the plaintiff's case. It had been done with the savior faire of Darrow, Rodgers, and Erlich (all my trial lawyer heros).

I went back to my hotel room, a conquering hero, and awaited the telephone call from the psychologist, which I knew would be to rest at the close of the plaintiff's case and put on no proof for the defense.

The call came and the report floored me. I had not gained yardage, but in fact had lost it. It would now be necessary to put on economic evidence which we had not expected to need. The

(continued)

(continued)

information I received was one of the first realizations I had that juries don't see things as lawyers do. The psychologist advised me that it was the shadow jury's belief that for someone to have "gone through what the professor had and to have emerged and continued as a full professor at a major university in spite of that, he must have great strength of character."

After the verdict in favor of my client, the judge allowed me to speak with the actual jury. To my lasting chagrin, the jury felt exactly as had the "shadow jury." I unknowingly learned a little bit about negative attribution.

Edwin W. Green
Bronson Bronson & McKinnon, Los Angeles

Attributional Biases

Attribution is usually not a highly rational process. Not only are our causal explanations based on common sense analysis, they are often designed to enhance our own self-esteem. Self-serving attributions can lead us to make serious errors about the causes of others' behavior. Common biases that affect how jurors decide who is at fault are discussed in this section.

Fundamental Attribution Error. Suppose a juror observes a witness stammering during vigorous cross examination. What do you think the juror concludes? As you probably guessed, the typical person would conclude that the witness is lying. This example illustrates a phenomenon known as the fundamental attribution error: a person's tendency to explain others' actions in terms of personal rather than situational causes. We are prone to discount and ignore potential situational explanations when it comes to evaluating others' behavior. In the example above, the juror downplays or never considers the possibility that the witness is uncomfortable speaking in public, or is inexperienced in courtroom testimony, when making the causal attribution for the speaking difficulty.

Naive observers tend to focus on personal explanations even when the other person is not in control of his or her behavior. For example, if a defendant in an employee discrimination case argues that he was merely following company policy when he committed the discriminatory act, jurors will still tend to attribute prejudice to the employee. People either focus on other people's behavior and ignore the context in which that behavior occurs, or they fail to assign sufficient weight to potential situational causes.

Actor-Observer Effect. While people tend to make dispositional attributions about others, they typically attribute their own behavior to situational causes, particularly when the behavior in question is undesirable in some way. This bias is known as the Actor-Observer effect and has been well-documented. If you watch a stranger trip on the sidewalk, you tend to conclude that he is clumsy. However, if you trip, the crack in the concrete, the slick surface, or the slippery shoes are to blame.

Typically, the best way to counter this bias is to encourage people to empathize with another person by "standing in his shoes." Carefully and clearly describing other causes often allows people to better appreciate more favorable explanations for the observed behavior.

Of course, when the behavior is desirable, the equation changes. As a general rule, we take credit for good things that happen, and blame others for the bad things. When others do well, we talk about luck and easy tasks. The workplace only makes political decisions when we are passed over for promotion. The umpiring is only bad when we lose the game. When we win a lawsuit, we tend to credit our intelligence and good planning, and when we lose, we tend to place the blame on the judge, the client, the witnesses, or something else. Our attributions have a tendency to be highly self-serving. This self-serving nature turns out to have important implications for trying cases.

Confronting Positive Attributions

I recently tried a plaintiff's medical malpractice case in which my client, a 30 year old woman, claimed that the internist whom she had seen over the years had failed to properly treat her condition of primary ovarian failure and, as a result, she had premature osteoporosis. Primary ovarian failure is characterized by the lack of production of estrogen, and the lack of estrogen places women at an increased risk of developing osteoporosis.

Before trial I suspected that the jury panel would be predominantly made up of women, as it was. So I asked my wife and women at work about male doctors and female patients. I learned that many women go to female rather than male physicians because they feel women doctors listen better to women than men doctors. Armed with that knowledge, I asked each prospective juror what he or she expected when they went to his or her doctor. The women almost without exception said that they wanted their doctor to listen to them. That, of course, was one of our themes.

I also wanted to focus jurors away from what I believed, and still believe, to be a strong deference to doctors. Everyone's personal physician is fine and I anticipate that, on one important level, a juror might not be able to distinguish his or her own doctor from the defendant. I asked each in his or her own turn to assume that the driver of an automobile had been inattentive and drove through a stop sign without slowing and struck and injured a pedestrian who was properly crossing the street. Would the juror have any difficulty holding the driver responsible for the injuries? With the exception of one person, all said with varying degrees of conviction that they would definitely hold the driver responsible. The one exception was a woman who insisted she would have to hear all of the evidence before making a decision.

(continued)

> *(continued)*
>
> *I struck her from the jury. In closing, I compared the physician to the driver who was inattentive. I also reminded the jurors of our theme throughout the trial that the physician did not listen to the plaintiff and related that to what they said they expected. The jury returned a verdict for the plaintiff.*
>
> *Frederick W. Morris*
> *Leonard Street & Deinard, Minneapolis*

Defensive Attribution. In product liability cases, jurors are often asked to evaluate the claims of someone who has been badly injured in an accident. Attorneys in these cases are often surprised to learn how common it is for jurors to "blame the victim." In fact, the jurors most likely to do this are those who share the most in common with the plaintiff.

In studying defensive attribution, researchers have sought to identify relationships between the victim and the observers. In the case of jurors, we might ask how the difference in age between the juror and the victim will affect the attribution process. Will attribution vary with the intensity of the accident? Does blaming the victim depend upon a feeling of identification with the victim on the part of the juror? Research has shown that if a juror perceives the victim to be like himself on some significant dimension, he may blame the victim. Why does this happen? In the jurors' minds, blaming the victim reduces the chances that they too will suffer a similar fate. Jurors confronted with the details of a terrible injury *want* to conclude that "this wouldn't happen to me." Jurors make defensive attributions as a way to cope with the anxiety created by the severity of the injuries and the apparent similarities between themselves and the plaintiff.

When a juror becomes familiar with the facts of an accident, there is a psychological tendency to worry about being involved in a similar situation. This concern can be increased dramatically to the extent that the juror identifies with the victim. They may have similar backgrounds, engage in similar activities or have friends or loved ones that they associate with this victim. They may be the same sex and age.

Psychologically, jurors will need to find reasons why what happened to the victim could not happen to them or to someone else of significance in their life. Most people possess a world view that insulates them from the reality that, as human beings, we are vulnerable to the horrors of disfiguring accidents, terrible illness, or premature death. When jurors are confronted with the facts and consequences of a serious accident or injury and they can identify with the victim in some way, they frequently evoke psychological coping mechanisms to deal with the situation.

One way to cope defensively with an anxiety-provoking event which has happened to someone else is to neutralize the possible impact of blind fate, or uncontrollable outside forces, and blame the victim. It happened to him because he is such and such a person who did such and such a thing, but it would not happen to me because I would not do that. So the reasoning goes.

The Intensity Factor. Researchers have measured the effect of varying the intensity of the accident on defensive attribution. It has been found that people will assign increasing responsibility to the victim as the intensity of the accident increases. When the accident is less severe, people tend to release the victim from responsibility.

What about the identification factor? If an observer identifies strongly with the victim in the case of a very severe accident, the likelihood of blaming the victim is increased even further. The implication that the observer may also suffer a grave accident is more threatening. By blaming the victim and stressing that he is a different kind of person, the observer can psychologically insulate himself from the threat of being involved in a similar disaster.

When did the Tire Fail?

In a case involving serious injuries to a young man alleging that a defective tire caused him to lose control of his new, high-performance car, the defense was concerned about the willingness of jurors to hold the plaintiff responsible for the cause of the accident. The young man was an "all American boy"—good looking, athletic, and hard working. Further, the defense was confronted with troubling documents and a series of similar claims and law suits alleging a design defect for this particular series of tires.

Notwithstanding the defense's difficulties, the behavior of the plaintiff on the night of the accident was suspect. The crash occurred at 3:20 A.M. The police estimated that the car had been traveling at more than 100 miles per hour when it left the highway, and empty beer cans were found in the vehicle.

Plaintiff's experts were prepared to testify that the defective design resulted in the tires' disintegration, and the driver then lost control of the car. The product had been marketed and sold as a high-performance, high-speed tire and was included as original equipment on a very fast sports car.

The defense experts, on the other hand, were convinced that the car was traveling at speeds vastly in excess of 100 miles per hour, and that the driver lost control of the vehicle. Various physical forces affecting the tire after the car left the highway resulted in the tire's disintegration.

As one element of our pre-trial research, our consultants undertook a telephone survey with over 1,000 participants in a similarly matched venue in the northeastern United States. Study subjects were read a scenario describing: (1) the accident; (2) the driver who was referred to as "Jim"; and (3) the nature and consequences of his injuries.

(continued)

(continued)

Included among the many questions that were asked were: (1) "How responsible was Jim for the accident," and (2) "How likely is it that this accident could have happened to you?" We also collected a large amount of demographic, attitudinal, and consumer information about the people who participated in the study.

Jim's age was varied in the accident scenario described to the subjects in the study. We found no connection, however, between the answers to the questions listed above and the extent to which Jim's age did or did not correspond to the age of the respondent. However, answers involving an identification with Jim provided highly significant correlations. The responses to the questions were given on a three point scale: very much, some, and not at all (with grammatical modifications for the different questions). We separated the group of respondents who answered "very likely" when asked: "How likely is it that this accident could have happened to you?" We then examined how many of these people thought Jim was responsible for the accident. Jurors who thought the accident could have happened to them were the same ones who found Jim responsible. This group also thought that Jim had been careless and did not think the accident had been the result of chance factors. For those people who thought "it can happen to me," the victim of the accident was blamed and held responsible.

After the trial in this case, a defense verdict, we interviewed members of the jury. It was clear from our discussions that the results of our pre-trial research were consistent with the dynamics of the jury's verdict.

William H. King, Jr.
McGuire Woods Battle & Boothe, Richmond

Strategies for Voir Dire Based on Defensive Attribution

What are the implications of defensive attribution theories from a defense strategy perspective? Suppose the defendant is the government agency responsible for maintaining the road. Plaintiff alleges that the shoulder was poorly maintained, that the outside stripe marking the edge of the pavement was too indistinct, and that the road grade itself was improperly designed and unsafe. To begin with, we want jurors who think a similar accident might happen to them. Voir dire questions, then, might be designed to find out whether or not a juror engages in behavior similar to the plaintiff's. Is there anything we can learn about jurors which would indicate that they might find themselves in a similar situation? Do they travel the same road as the plaintiff? Do they travel at the same time of the night? Are their driving habits similar? Do they, or would they, drive at the same speed? Would they operate their automobile the same way under similar circumstances? Can we find jurors who regularly travel in the early morning at speeds in excess of 60 miles per hour? Can we find jurors who drive similar cars?

While jurors who believe that they could have a similar accident will make good defense jurors, we must be wary of jurors who have already had a similar accident. The latter will sympathize with the victim because of the reluctance to blame themselves for their accident.

Consistent with defensive attribution theory, a juror who thinks he or she could personally have such an accident will possess a deep need to rationalize the situation. This rationalization must lead to the ultimate conclusion that such an accident would not occur with the juror as driver. In order for this conviction to stick, the juror must explain what happened. If the juror drives a similar car over a similar route at a similar time of day, he must find a unique fault with the plaintiff indicative of human error.

In a venue where extensive voir dire is permitted, the defense will want to explain the situation, then ask prospective jurors if they have ever been involved in a similar accident. The prospective jurors can then be asked whether or not they think the accident could have happened to them. Through the use of such questions, attorneys for the defense should be able to identify jurors who are likely to be positively or negatively disposed toward the defendant. Plaintiffs, of course, will want to know the same information. Plaintiffs will obviously want jurors who are unlikely to blame the victim.

From a defensive attribution perspective, defense lawyers should also make reference to items or events identified in voir dire which are of significance in the jurors' lives. For example, if defense counsels learn from voir dire that the vehicle involved in the accident is similar to a juror's, the attorney should go to some length to describe the car in detail. This sort of thing should be particularly aimed at defense-oriented jurors.

Complex Causal Analysis: Location, Controllability, Stability

Although causal analysis is usually automatic and one-dimensional, some situations result in more complex analysis by the decision-maker. Whatever the reason, we know that there are times when a person consciously attends to incoming information and engages in additional searches for causal explanations. For example, if a juror believes that chemical companies harm the environment, but learns that defendant company has spent a lot of time and money protecting the environment, the juror must try to explain this inconsistency.

Complex causal attribution involves the analysis of three different dimensions: whether the observed behavior was due to personal (internal) or situational (external) causes, whether the cause was controllable or uncontrollable, and whether the cause is constant (stable) or variable (unstable). Of these three dimensions, perceptions of controllability seem to have the most impact on how people assign responsibility and blame.

For example, after a highly publicized hotel fire, the partners who owned the hotel along with other defendants who manufactured some of the products used in the building were sued by the families of those who were killed. A particularly tragic aspect of this fire was that it had been intentionally started by disgruntled employees during a labor dispute. The hotel had an inadequate fire safety system which had not been improved despite warnings from the fire department and despite the occurrence of several small fires in the past. The partners had no direct management responsibilities and were never on-site. They planned to make a corporate veil defense.

Pre-trial research showed that jurors believed that the terrible loss of life was caused by ineffective and unresponsive local management which created an attitude of indifference to fire safety. Jurors believed this orientation was due to unconcerned and uninvolved owners who didn't care about anything except making money (an internal cause). Jurors uniformly believed that the fire was preventable had the owners chosen safety over profit (a controllable cause). They also believed that the previous fires revealed a pattern of neglect and greed (a stable cause). Jurors who drew these conclusions were extremely enraged. They were in no mood to consider the complexities of a defense based on limited liability.

While the owners wisely settled, other non-owner defendants involved in related litigation used this information to build strategies that reinforced jurors' attributions by stressing how much control the owners had and how little control suppliers could have exerted in areas of fire safety. Traditional product defenses were downplayed. This strategy allowed defendants to build an emotional bridge with the jurors and gave them a rationale to find against the plaintiffs in a very difficult case.

"Compliance With Standards" Defense: An Application of Attribution Theory

Another way in which trial strategy can be based on attribution theory can be illustrated by the compliance-with-standards defense in product liability trials. In product liability actions, the defense may be inclined to base its case at least in part upon the fact that the defendant has been in compliance with some private organization or public agency that has established standards for quality and safety as they apply to the product in question. Such a defense raises problems which can only be addressed by attitude and attribution theory. This chapter will conclude with a discussion as to why this strategy is one of the more problematic approaches the defense can pursue in product liability cases.

The attribution aspect of a compliance-with-standards defense is twofold. First, the jury will evaluate the defendant on the basis of whether or not the act of being in compliance with certain standards is enough to make the defendant a "good," "responsible," or "honest" manufacturer of the product. In other words, what kind of reflection is it upon the defendant to have been in compliance with standards? What kind of attributions will be made as a result of compliance? Further, what kind of negative attributions will be made with regard to defendants found not to be in compliance with standards?

The second way in which attribution becomes germane in these cases concerns perceptions of the organizations which establish standards. What kind of attributions will jurors make about a government agency, an industry association, a private research foundation, or a research and

standards institute associated with a large university? Are jurors
impressed by any or all of these organizations? What sort of attributions
do jurors begin to make when the name of a particular organization is
invoked?

The attributions jurors make in the case of compliance versus non-
compliance with standards are also linked to juror attitudes. We might
suppose, for example, that jurors with initial negative attitudes towards
industry and business will be more impressed with compliance than jurors
who do not harbor such negative attitudes. We might discover other
kinds of attitudes which are relevant, such as attitudes and beliefs about
the standard-setting organizations themselves. We would not normally
expect a juror with a strong anti-government bias to be impressed with
a firm which has been in compliance with standards set by a government
agency.

Attributions with regard to compliance with standards may also be
correlated with demographic factors. Do the sex and age of jurors make
a difference? Do income or education matter? All of these questions
must be answered before a strategy involving a compliance defense can
be evaluated.

A Case Study. In order to develop some general orientation toward
this strategy, an investigation was carried out using a number of fictitious
scenarios which involved typical products cases in the automobile and
pharmaceutical industries. In each of these areas, there have often been
large compensatory and punitive awards, and defendants have frequently
relied heavily on the compliance defense. In each of these test scenarios,
defendants had either met or failed to meet government or industry-set
product standards.

The initial hypothesis in the study was to test whether or not a
defendant's compliance would be an important factor in jurors' minds.
From an attribution theory perspective, it was felt that if a defendant had
been in compliance, jurors would be less willing to attribute the harm
which plaintiff suffered entirely to the defendant's actions. In contrast,
when the defendant had not been in compliance, it was supposed that
jurors would see the cause of injury associated with the defendant's
behavior. Just about all of these assumptions were soundly refuted by the
data.

Research Findings on Compliance Attributions. On a scale
measuring approval, with "1" being low and "8" being high, the highest
score that a defendant received who had been in compliance with specific
manufacturing standards was about 4.5. This related to government

agency standards. At best, it was discovered that jurors were not impressed with claims of compliance with government standards. Compliance with these standards did not lead jurors to make positive attributions where defendants were being evaluated. Where industry standards were at issue, compliance was even less of a factor in favorably impressing jurors. Here, there was strong evidence that a defense based on compliance would elicit no more than a neutral reaction among jurors. These neutral reactions would not be sufficient to induce the desired external attribution, that is, the attribution that the harm to plaintiff occurred as a result of factors outside the defendant's control.

When considering compliance in this context, jurors are influenced by what is known as the discounting principle. Discounting refers to the tendency to downplay the importance of any potential cause of another person's behavior to the extent that other possible causes exist. In this example, jurors are likely to believe that defendant's compliance was the result of low standards rather than defendant's motivation to behave properly. The compliance effort is not regarded as having a great deal of significance.

Based on these findings, one might suppose that when a defendant has not complied with standards, it will not matter much to jurors. Not so. When the defendant is a non-complier, evidence suggests that jurors will be quick to form a negative opinion. In fact, non-compliance has potentially disastrous consequences for the defendant. On the same approval rating scale of 1 to 8, defendants in a non-compliance scenario score very low and were regarded unfavorably by jurors. There is reason to believe that if the plaintiff pursues a strategy of demonstrating that the defendant is in non-compliance with established standards, defense counsel will have a difficult time bringing jurors up to a position of mere neutrality toward their client on this issue. Jurors will readily make damaging internal attributions associating injury or damage with the defendant's non-complying behavior.

Do these attributions, which vary from negative to neutral, merely reflect pre-existing negative attitudes? In order to assess this factor, jurors were asked a series of questions about corporations in general. Based on the answers to these questions, jurors were classified as either pro-business or anti-business. Jurors who were classified as anti-business exhibited extremely negative attitudes toward product liability defendants who were not in compliance with industry and government standards. This is not particularly surprising. However, pro-business jurors displayed an equally negative attitude toward non-complying defendants.

In fact, when pro-business jurors were asked to evaluate a pharmaceutical defendant who was not in compliance with government standards, they made an extremely negative evaluation, even more negative than that made by the group of anti-industry jurors. Apparently, the pro-business group made such a negative attribution precisely because they held a pro-business predisposition and were incensed by what they regarded as the defendant's "breach of faith."

Thus, there seems to be little difference between pro-business and anti-business jurors when it comes to making negative attributions toward product liability defendants when the issue of compliance with standards is raised. What differences there are seem to indicate that jurors with pro-business attitudes in place are harder on the non-complying defendant than anti-business jurors. Overall, it was discovered that initial juror predispositions or biases and the nature of the industry, either automobile or pharmaceutical, make little difference in the way attributions are made where compliance with standards is an issue.

The Two Strategies of Enhancement and Denial

Given the way in which jurors make attributions when the matter of compliance with standards comes up in a trial, there are two basic strategies which can be followed: enhancement and denial. When a defendant wishes to employ compliance with standards as part of an overall trial strategy, it will be necessary to "enhance" the importance of meeting standards in the minds of the jurors. This is so because, as we have seen, jurors generally are not overly impressed with the fact that a product liability defendant has been in compliance with standards set by some testing agency. On the other hand, when plaintiffs make the argument that non-compliance with standards is significant, the defendant must deny the importance of these standards. The same strategies, enhancement and denial, can be pursued by the plaintiff. When the plaintiff attacks the defendant for non-compliance, the importance of the standard which has not been met should be emphasized. When the defendant is using compliance as a line of defense, the plaintiff can pursue a strategy of denying that the standard has any real significance.

Using denial and enhancement strategies effectively will involve knowing how jurors make attributions regarding organizations which set standards. These perceptions are important. Research has shown that jurors make very different kinds of attributions relating to these various groups, agencies, or organizations.

Knowing what we do about how jurors evaluate organizations which establish standards can also tell us when not to attack them. Jurors invariably rank consumer protection groups and university research centers as very effective in setting standards and measuring compliance. This rating is so strong that an attorney who attacks these groups may very well compromise his own credibility. Standards set by major corporations and industry trade groups are regarded as quite ineffective by jurors. Attacking such standards, or denying that they have any real importance, is much more likely to win favor. Thus, the success or failure of a compliance defense will depend in part upon the agency involved. Compliance with organizations like consumer protection groups, university research centers, and independent testing laboratories will be more effective in persuading jurors, and this kind of compliance should be emphasized. If compliance with government and industry agencies figures highly in the defendant's behavior, then an effort must be made to show that these standards mean something. In general, when it is necessary to emphasize a client's adherence to standards, the proper procedure is to point to the professionalism, scientific thoroughness, and prestige of the specific agency involved. It can never be taken for granted that the public in general, and jurors in particular, will have a positive image of any standards-setting organization. Of course, when the importance of standards is going to be denied, the image, reputation, or effectiveness of the agency in question can be challenged using these same criteria: professionalism, scientific thoroughness, and prestige.

Generally, since we know that jurors make different kinds of attributions, both with regard to the effectiveness of those setting standards, and the culpability of defendants who are and are not in compliance with standards, any strategy using compliance or non-compliance should be tested prior to trial.

Research has also shown that there are some sex and age differences in the way jurors perceive the significance of compliance. It has been found that women and people over the age of thirty are notably more harsh in their attributions toward corporate defendants than are men and those under thirty. All other things being equal, defense counsel will want to seek out young men as jurors, while the plaintiff would prefer to have older women. People under thirty, in general, are less impressed by either compliance or non-compliance.

By applying attribution theory to the question of the "compliance with standards defense," we have another example of research tending to run counter to the common sense conclusion. Defendants who meet standards for product safety appear to gain far less approval in the minds of jurors than defense lawyers often suppose. When compliance with standards is going to be part of the defense strategy, it is very important that these standards be enhanced and that jurors are persuaded of their legitimacy and reliability.

We have also found that general attitudes toward corporations are not good predictors of how the compliance with standards question will be evaluated. Instead of basing strategy on such general attitudes, it is important to learn about specific attitudes toward specific issues that are going to be raised in the trial.

Conclusions

One of the most striking things that emerges from social science research is that jurors are willing to make attributions of blame and cause on the basis of very slight and fragmentary evidence. Many jurors resort quickly to simple, if not naive, "causal schema" to explain the events they see around them. In making attributions, they can be wrong in what they remember and in what they predict. Self-serving biases are common, and there is a tendency to disregard fundamental information which should influence attributions.

The importance of previously held attitudes and beliefs has been demonstrated in our investigation into the compliance issue in product liability cases. Here, the use of attribution theory has enabled us to see that commonly held suppositions about this kind of defense are not nearly so well founded as many have believed. Being able to make use of knowledge about how these attributions will be made is critical when compliance is an issue in a case.

In accident cases, the phenomenon we call defensive attribution may be applicable. Whether or not jurors can be induced to blame the victim will often determine the success of the defense. Ensuring that jurors do not blame the victim is a critical task of the plaintiff. Defensive attribution theory can also assist attorneys in identifying jurors who may be oriented toward a verdict for one side or the other.

It is important to recognize, however, that strategies based upon defensive attribution theory must be carefully researched prior to their utilization in a trial. While there have been instances where this concept has been extremely useful, there have been other cases in which strategies based on defensive attribution would have been counter-productive. Where the theory works, it works well. Only well-designed studies can identify the applicability of the approach for a specific case.

An attorney's ability to make use of what we know about attribution is an invaluable strategic asset in the courtroom. Insights based on attribution theory and research can be used in voir dire and in case presentation. Once research has uncovered the fact that jurors are going to make critical attributions in the trial, it is often possible to base major trial strategy on this finding.

CHAPTER 6

Persuasion in Voir Dire

A consideration of psychological strategies in voir dire must begin with the recognition that the rules governing the conduct of voir dire vary from place to place and from court to court. Typically, judges in federal court control voir dire and may or may not allow attorney participation. In some state courts, such as those in New York and Texas, voir dire is an open-ended process in which attorneys are permitted wide latitude in questioning prospective jurors. This does not, however, imply that in federal courts the strategic implications of voir dire are completely negated. Many federal judges will entertain the use of suggested voir dire questions.

There are two essential reasons for asking questions in voir dire. Questions can be asked because it is important to know the answers. Questions can also be asked because it is important to communicate something to the jurors through the questions. Voir dire, then, is actually the process of assessing the responses of prospective jurors, as well as providing them with persuasive information.

Juror Assessment

Judgements made about jurors involve estimates as to how they are likely to behave with interest focused on the verdict they are likely to render. Secondarily, it will be important to evaluate the role jurors will play in the deliberation process. To many non-lawyers, the term "jury selection" implies selecting the jurors that you want. In actuality, of course, jury selection really means juror elimination; that is, exercising a limited number of challenges in order to remove jurors from the panel. Voir dire is largely a process of identifying jurors who, for a variety of reasons, will be wrong for the case. It is essentially an exercise of looking for the "wrong people." A particular juror may be an inappropriate candidate for a wide variety of reasons. The individual may possess intractable bias or prejudice against one of the litigants. Intensely held values, attitudes, and beliefs may exist which will have the tendency to interfere with a fair and impartial evaluation of testimony and other evidence. Finally, the trial lawyer may simply dislike the juror for idiosyncratic reasons of his own.

While trial lawyers are generally comfortable structuring their own voir dire questions and assessing the verbal component (what is said) of the prospective juror's answer, most are less experienced at analyzing paralinguistic cues (how it is said—such as pauses, stuttering, tone, pitch, and breathing patterns), and kinetic cues (body language—such as posture, gestures, facial expressions, and eye contact). Herein lies a wealth of information not attainable from the verbal component of communication. Whereas verbal behavior is used to communicate events external to the speaker, paralinguistic and nonverbal cues are used to express emotions and anxiety. Furthermore, true feelings are more easily assessed through nonverbal communication when deception is taking place. Throughout voir dire and also in the delivery of the opening statement, attorneys have an opportunity to gain instantaneous feedback from jurors in the form of nonverbal cues. Attorneys can be attentive to signs of discomfort. Some of the most obvious of these include nodding, fidgeting, doodling, and other indications that something is going awry in the communication process. Jurors may also display positive nonverbal feedback. Attentive looks, as well as note taking, may be positive indications that the jury is paying attention. These positive cues, however, are less reliable than negative ones. Jurors frequently use positive cues to conceal a negative or neutral inner reaction. While we can often deceive with the words we choose, it is much more difficult to prevent our inner feelings from "leaking" through our nonverbal behavior. In recognition of this, some attorneys have begun to use trained observers to assess these subtle clues to a potential juror's biases and beliefs.

Jurors Who Smile So Sweetly

When pressed to exercise a peremptory challenge, I am inclined to revert to and act upon the belief that, as expressed by Mark R. McGarry, Jr., "you will do best with a juror whom you feel comfortable with—whom you could strike up a friendship with—or whom you admire." Mark R. McGarry, Jr., Do-It-Yourself Voir Dire, Litigation, Winter 1983. at 38. *I can rationalize that inclination by positing that the friendly juror also is likely to be one who subscribes to the same core of beliefs that I do and who is likely to share my arguments. However, I recall the representative story of one trial lawyer who tells of the lovely juror with whom he fell in love, who smiled at him so sweetly and in whom he had complete confidence—and who voted against his client's cause with alacrity and firm conviction.*

The one irresistible lesson is that selection of the most receptive jurors, and the best arguments for those jurors who are selected, requires as much information as can be obtained in voir dire concerning each individual prospective juror's attitudes, unvarnished by the tendency to provide socially correct responses to voir dire questioning. There is a great art to designing evocative questions to penetrate natural defenses and reveal true attitudes. But that art will be unavailing in any event unless the questioner has determined in advance what attitude set is likely to be favorable, and what attitude set is likely to be unfavorable, to his or her case. That may well require, as indicated in this book, carefully designed pre-trial research study.

It perhaps also deserves mention that the best voir dire questioner will stop when he or she has enough information, keeping in mind that all information elicited also informs the other side, and any questioning always carries the risk of offending the person being questioned or other members of the jury panel.

(continued)

(continued)

*One subject hinted at in Chapter 2 also deserves empha-
sis—the subject of jury dynamics—what happens in the jury room.
The identification of potential leaders in jury deliberations—an
important feature of that subject—is in itself a fine art about
which at least this trial lawyer, guided by the trial lawyer's
"instincts," knows a good deal less than I think I do. Perhaps Dr.
Vinson's greatest contribution in jury research will prove to be the
techniques he has developed for identifying the strength and depth
of jurors' convictions. Not every committed juror will be a leader,
but every committed juror at least represents the beginning of the
formation of a majority. Surely every litigant and every trial
lawyer would sleep better during the course of a trial if he or she
felt confident that there was at least one juror who could be
counted upon to stick with his or her cause throughout the jury
deliberations.*

*Jack E. Brown
Brown & Bain, Phoenix*

Bias: The Behavioral Science Definition

As we have noted elsewhere, no one comes to the courtroom with his
or her mind as a blank slate. All jurors possess pre-existing attitudes,
beliefs, experiences, and knowledge. This must inevitably affect, to some
degree, however small, the ways in which jurors will judge a case.
Similarly, all jurors employ ways of processing information that
inevitably lead to approximations and errors. From a behavioral science
standpoint, all jurors are biased. Fortunately, the concept of bias forms
a continuum. If bias were an either/or proposition it would be impossible
to impanel a jury. It does mean, however, that no juror can be completely impartial. If jurors were all completely impartial (unaffected by the
history of who they are), there would be no hung juries. What we must
be concerned about is where on the bias continuum a particular juror lies.
Specifically, we must find out how salient, intense, and intractable the

juror's pre-existing attitudes and beliefs are. This can be accomplished with various psychometric scales and research techniques, which will be discussed in Chapter 11. When a juror has a belief that is germane to the issues in the case, when the juror's belief is important to the juror, and when the juror is unwilling or resistant to listening to arguments that run counter to his beliefs, the juror is likely to be at the extreme end of the bias continuum.

Verdict Predisposition as a Form of Bias

The legal definitions of bias rest on some demonstrated connection between a juror and a party or issue in the case or the juror's *own* assessment of his subjective state of mind. This may be related to a verdict predisposition on the part of the juror. But, in a sense, all jurors enter the courtroom with *some* degree of verdict predisposition. Verdict predisposition is no more than a mild form of bias. It alone should not be grounds for excluding a juror as it would imply excluding all jurors. The fact that seven out of ten prospective jurors have a verdict predisposition in favor of one party does not mean the other party cannot get a fair trial and that a change of venue should be granted. Even with a verdict predisposition, a juror may be quite open to listening to arguments or evidence that run counter to his predisposition.

If a party in a lawsuit faces an unfair burden in having a juror consider its case presentation with intensely held and intractable negative attitudes or beliefs, then the juror has a degree of bias that should warrant exclusion for cause.

Voir Dire and Impression Management

Voir dire in its traditional form is not a reliable way to identify psychological bias. This is because most people actively manage the impressions they create for the benefit of others. We all have a tremendous psychological investment in creating and maintaining our "public self." Most people feel uncomfortable disclosing their intimate beliefs and experiences in front of a group of strangers, particularly when these disclosures would undermine their public self image. Further, most people desire to portray themselves as fair individuals and do not desire to be classified as partial or biased. They know that society places a high value on fairness in the courtroom and want to present themselves in a manner consistent with that value.

Trial attorneys often forget that it is common for prospective jurors to be nervous and embarrassed during voir dire. Jurors are typically apprehensive about being scrutinized and evaluated, and about having to speak in public. Sometimes, their nervousness interferes with jurors' ability to listen and respond to voir dire questions. In a product case a juror who had personally experienced a significant problem with the product was not struck because she did not volunteer this information during voir dire, even though she had been asked specifically. After the trial she reported that she didn't remember being asked to disclose this information. She may have not been listening, felt uncomfortable about sharing this information with the group, and/or had some unusual motivation to sit on this particular jury and therefore tailored her answers accordingly. It is also interesting to note that jurors who have been called to serve for a period of time and who get recycled back into the jury waiting room if they are not seated on a case, eventually grow frustrated with the process. They learn what types of answers increase the probability of having a strike exercised against them and they avoid these types of responses. In general, the longer jurors have been waiting to get seated, the harder it is to get them to reveal relevant biases. People who have served on previous juries also frequently possess the experience to manage or manipulate the voir dire process.

Juror Questionnaires

Questionnaires given to prospective jurors in advance of voir dire are very useful in identifying juror bias. People are more likely to disclose revealing information when responding to a questionnaire than in public. Further, sensitive questions can be asked without the juror associating the question with one of the lawyers, thereby reducing the "tainting by association" effect that lawyers fear when faced with the prospects of asking personal questions. People are also less likely to feel pressure to conform when they are responding to questions in writing. Finally, jurors tend to take written questions more seriously than oral questions, feel compelled to answer all the questions, and are less likely to lie or grossly distort reality when committing their answers to paper. Juror question-naires are being used in an increasing number of courts around the country. Unfortunately, many times these questionnaires contain the same tired and essentially useless questions that are fixtures in traditional voir dire. The juror questionnaire is an opportunity to collect valuable information about key juror attitudes, values, and experiences, and should not be mainly comprised of demographic information about the prospective juror and his or her spouse and children.

Jury Questionnaires

In a case involving sensitive personal issues pertaining to female anatomy and a prescription drug used during pregnancy, counsel convinced a federal district trial judge to utilize a specially prepared juror questionnaire and if there were "red flag" answers, to interrogate those jurors in chambers. The purpose was to obtain knowledge of the preconceived perceptions of the jurors on these sensitive issues, but the answers to the questions submitted, if given in the presence of the entire jury panel, could well have prejudiced counsel's client. The questionnaires were given to the jurors as soon as they reported to the courtroom. The completed questionnaires were then copied and given to counsel before the general voir dire questioning began. After the general voir dire questioning was complete, the court allowed counsel to interrogate on the record in the court's chamber separately each juror who had submitted affirmative answers to these sensitive questions. Counsel for both sides were allowed to ask questions of the prospective juror. The juror did not know which counsel had requested the private interrogation. The court struck for cause several jurors based upon the answers given on the questionnaire and the follow-up answers given in the discussion with counsel on the record in chambers. This result would not have occurred but for the use of the juror questionnaire and the subsequent interrogation outside the presence of the rest of the panel. It is an approach to the problem of handling sensitive subject matters on voir dire which will keep the entire panel

(continued)

(continued)

from being tainted with a juror's potentially prejudiced statements and which will allow the court to have a much better basis for exercising a strike for cause than if handled in the usual manner in the presence of the entire panel.

Lane D. Bauer
Shook Hardy & Bacon, Kansas City

In summary, the principle objective of voir dire questions is to encourage jurors to reveal relevant information about themselves. Jurors tend to present certain images of themselves in voir dire which are self-flattering, or even self-aggrandizing. This is particularly true when questions are psychologically or socially threatening. Responses to questions may also reflect a bias toward either wanting or not wanting to serve on the jury. Jurors who want to serve will try to avoid offending attorneys for either side. Where the rules governing voir dire are liberal, a number of different questioning techniques are available to help the lawyer assess potential jurors.

Questioning Techniques

Asking open-ended questions that reveal relevant attitudes and values will provide useful information for sizing up prospective jurors. For example, a defense lawyer in an antitrust case strongly believed that small business owners were automatically pro-plaintiff. Research convinced him to probe beneath the surface by asking small business owners whether they saw themselves as successful or not, and whether their success or failure was due to internal or external factors. Pre-trial research had indicated that small business owners who attributed success or failure to factors within their control were excellent defense jurors.

In cases where voir dire is expected to go on at length, projective questions can provide very useful insights into what jurors believe and how they are likely to react. Projective questions are those in which jurors are asked to talk in general terms about some person, experience, or event which serves as a stimulus. In reacting to this stimulus, jurors may provide subconscious or unguarded responses reflecting their attitudes, values and beliefs, patterns of motivation, and personality. These responses can then be evaluated against pre-trial juror research findings.

When voir dire is more limited and it is necessary to use a small number of focused questions in the most efficient manner, areas of inquiry should be tied directly to behavioral variables found to be positively correlated with salient case issues. The development and testing of these questions can be undertaken with a variety of research techniques prior to trial.

When the opportunity to ask questions in voir dire is severely limited, or non-existent as it is in many federal courts, the ability of lawyers to obtain information about jurors is obviously restricted. In these situations, attorneys have to rely upon whatever knowledge they can obtain about the panel from whatever source. This is frequently limited to nonverbal behavior. Clinical psychologists have developed a number of techniques of passive observation. Social scientists trained in participant observation research and unobtrusive measures can detect many details of human behavior of a nonverbal character that normally escape the attention of other people. Such an observer stationed in the courtroom during voir dire can contribute helpful insights to the attorneys conducting the examination of jurors. The observer might note, for example, that several prospective jurors have indicated a strong desire for social acceptance through nonverbal actions like excessive smiling and head nodding. Other potential behaviors such as passivity, aggression, depression, feeling of inferiority, and alienation can be frequently detected. While observations of nonverbal behavior are important tools at the lawyer's disposal, they must be used with caution. The kinds of data available from courtroom observation provide global and generalized impressions of jurors at best. Whether or not observed characteristics are in any way related to a juror's evaluation of evidence, perception of testimony, or the ultimate verdict is unknown without having undertaken prior research.

There is a true story of a lawyer who became enamored with a woman juror who nodded and smiled a lot at him during voir dire and the trial. The lawyer began to rely on her as his barometer for how the case was going. When she nodded and smiled, he concluded that things must be going well. When there was less nodding and smiling, he became concerned about his position. After the trial, this woman disclosed that she had been high on cocaine and had been oblivious to much of what had transpired in the courtroom. Fred Morris[*] gives another example. Several years ago he tried a case in which a male juror always initiated greetings and made friendly comments in the common areas. In every respect, he showed friendliness. That was interpreted as favorable to the defense. While the verdict was a plaintiff's verdict but, in reality, a defense outcome (nominal damages), Morris learned that this "friendly" juror was, in fact, the strongest proponent of liability and wanted to award large damages. The obvious lesson from these antidotes is beware of ambiguous nonverbal communication!

Looking for Inconsistencies in Juror Behavior

Jurors, like other people on public display, will endeavor to present a positive or attractive image of themselves. It is useful to analyze and interpret this image in terms of inconsistencies and contradictions which signal things the juror wishes not to reveal. These inconsistencies can include words and how they are used, or discerned by reading between the lines of what a juror does or says. Inconsistencies can also be detected in a juror's attire or physical appearance. People who wish to avoid being labeled as blue collar workers may "dress up" for court. Careful observation of style and coordination of the individual's clothing may suggest that in his everyday life, this person is not the person he appears to be in the courtroom. In a recent trial, a juror described himself as a food handling technician, thereby making himself acceptable to attorneys who felt that people with technical backgrounds would be favorable to their side. A post-trial interview revealed that the juror was, in fact, a busboy in a hotel. In this instance, as in many others, there is a natural tendency among jurors to inflate their positions in life. They are not telling lies, but they can indeed deceive. One of the ways to avoid being beguiled by what jurors say is to carefully observe inconsistencies between what they say and the signs or signals of behavior.

---

[*] Frederick W. Morris, *Leonard Street & Deinard, Minneapolis.*

Techniques of Persuasion in Voir Dire

Voir dire functions traditionally and primarily as a means of selecting and rejecting jurors. However, it also represents the only opportunity for jurors to directly interact with counsel or the judges who communicate counsel's queries. As such, it provides a unique opportunity for the presentation of one's case. The experienced attorney recognizes that the trial does not begin in earnest with the opening statement. Indeed, juror perceptions are amenable to influence from the moment the jurors enter the courtroom.

Various techniques of persuasion can be employed in voir dire. These include juror self-persuasion, forced compliance, sensitization, inoculation, and techniques which warn of the opponent's persuasive intent.

Inducing Juror Self-Persuasion. Social psychologists know that there are various circumstances under which people become self-persuaders. Among jurors, self-persuasion can take place when jurors make up their minds, or reach conclusions, without being directly persuaded to do so by an external message or communication specifically directed at leading them to this conclusion. What seems to occur in cases of self-persuasion is that jurors suddenly become aware of something "they knew all along." Jurors may emerge from a state of doubt into a state of certainty regarding some issue. They will spontaneously realize that they have reached a conclusion about something they had previously not considered.

One of the most striking kinds of self-persuasion occurs when a set of attitudes or beliefs appears to be firmly in place and information counter to these attitudes is suddenly presented in an unexpected way. Initially, there will be strong resistance to this information, but somehow a nagging doubt will have been planted, and after a time lag, the attitudes which resist the information suddenly crumble and disappear. This is particularly likely to occur in the wake of the kind of strong frontal attack which can be presented in the form of a voir dire question or set of questions. There will be strong initial resistance, but inroads will have been made. A given juror may continue to be disturbed by the attack but ultimately integrate the new information into his belief system.

Frontal attacks using counter-attitudinal information, or information which contradicts existing attitudes and beliefs, are particularly appropriate to voir dire. They have the best chance of success when they are based on some incontrovertible fact which cannot be ignored. Attitude change comes after a delay and occurs because new information has forced a rearranging of beliefs within a juror's mind. The key to why this works and the reason why it is appropriate to voir dire is that jurors must not be aware that an attempt is being made to persuade them. The attitude change occurs because jurors are unaware of the working of any outside influence or stimulus. They are convinced that they have changed their minds by themselves.

Since self-persuasion is a delayed process which takes place within a juror's mind, it can often be set in motion by a rapid "hit and run" attack, a rhetorical thrust, or the almost surreptitious planting of a key piece of information. Knowledge of self-persuasion techniques, combined with the knowledge that the proper attitude context may exist, makes voir dire a good opportunity for using self-persuasion strategies.

Social psychologists have established that people often come to know their own attitudes, beliefs, and feelings about something through the observation of their own behavior. Thus, through their own self-perceptions, jurors can sometimes be led to express an attitude or belief they did not know they had. Having heard themselves express the thought, they will later be willing to defend it. The theory of attitude change or reinforcement through self-persuasion can often be used in voir dire. Jurors can be led to make admissions which are consistent with the position of one of the litigants. When they do so, they will have psychologically positioned themselves to cognitively defend an attitude that might have been previously neutral, flexible, or ambiguous.

The most effective way to modify attitudes through self-persuasion theory is to induce jurors to play a role. When people play a role, they are often doing something with which they are initially uncomfortable. They may, for example, be forcing themselves to say something they do not really believe. It is often possible in voir dire to induce jurors to play roles and, in doing so, force them to comply with a position they would otherwise avoid. Roles which are at variance with what people think they believe are called attitude discrepant. When jurors assume a role which is attitude discrepant, they may change the underlying attitude so that what they believe is now in conformity with what they are doing. Their attitude changes because people are more likely to believe something when they hear themselves saying it than when they hear someone else saying it.

There are many commonplace examples of the "try it, you'll like it" syndrome. Self-persuasion techniques involving role playing are often used, for example, with children who shy away from the unfamiliar, whether it be a food or some new experience. "Think how much you're going to like this," the mother will say as she tries to persuade her child to do something he doesn't want to do.

Two points can be made about the matter of attitude change through role playing. First, people are often persuaded to change attitudes toward something by observing their own behavior when playing a role. Second, people are more likely to learn, or change attitudes, when they adopt the role voluntarily than when they feel they are being pressured to do so. Studies have shown that even thinking about playing a role can bring about a modification in attitude. If a juror can be made to see himself doing something, for example, it will increase the possibility of his doing it. When someone goes from making the statement, "I could never do that," to the statement, "I could see myself doing that," there has already been an attitude change.

Forced Compliance Through Induced Role Playing

Voir dire offers numerous opportunities to induce juror role playing in a way that will force compliance with a particular attitude or belief. A defense attorney might ask the following question in voir dire:

> Put yourself in the place of people who work for Company X who have tried their best to manufacture products with the highest standards of quality and then find themselves accused of making something defective and harmful to people. Do you think that because someone is injured using a product, there must be something wrong with the product?

In a contract dispute, a plaintiff attorney might ask:

> Put yourself in the place of Mr. Johnson. He thought he had a deal; he shook hands on it. Is there anyone in this courtroom who doesn't believe that major corporations have the duty to behave according to the standard of honesty and integrity that people like you and I do?

Self-perception theory offers another voir dire strategy for altering more central and ambiguous beliefs. The application of this theory is straightforward. For example, the defense could question a particular juror along the following lines: "Mrs. Smith, do you believe that consumer advocates are sometimes overzealous or just plain wrong in their attacks on some products?" Jurors responding positively to this kind of question may well leave the voir dire with some new skepticism about consumer advocates. Thus, by observing their own responses to the attorney's carefully worded questions, they will conclude that they do not strongly believe everything said by consumer advocates.

When Forced Compliance Didn't Work

In a products case that was tried in the midwest, I was confronted with a jury pool from a very rural town, and its environs, of 1500 or so people. It also was the plaintiffs' "home" town. An important issue in that litigation was whether or not the product's advertising was "false" and whether anyone really relied upon it anyway. I described a scenario for the jury panel: they were to pretend they needed to purchase an automobile; they had a week within which to make their decision; they had unlimited resources available to them; they could buy new or used and any model or make, and they had to return to the courtroom and tell all what they bought and why they bought it. The purpose of this role playing exercise was to have each person articulate that advertising plays no significant role in the decision to buy an automobile. Other factors such as prior experience, the experience of others, consumer reports, opinions of friends, family, and neighbors, etc., are very important in driving the ultimate decision about what to buy while advertising is simply an "attention getter."

The exercise seemed to work just fine. Each prospective juror seemed relaxed, spoke with animation, and freely and comfortably described what they bought and why they bought it. In one way or another, each stated that advertising was not important beyond generally describing the car. Not one relied upon the advertising in his or her decision to buy. One woman even used the magic phrase without any prompting—"advertising is just an attention getter."

The jury returned a verdict for the plaintiff. And regrettably, the woman who had described advertising as just an "attention getter" was one of the strongest jurors against my client!

Frederick W. Morris
Leonard Street & Deinard, Minneapolis

Group Sensitization

It is often possible to use self-persuasion techniques on the part of the entire jury panel to modify an attitude or belief, or to plant a new idea. Sometimes, through a series of questions, the panel can be sensitized to an argument. This occurred in a recent case involving a sudden and unexpected automobile accident in which a driver lost control of his car. Plaintiff alleged that the blowout of a tire had occurred because it had been defectively manufactured. Counsel for the defense wished to make the point that there are numerous alternative explanations for what happened. Defense counsel also wanted the jurors to make an internal causal attribution, that is, to blame the driver for what happened. To induce this kind of attribution, the attorneys suggested that what happened in this case is not what would happen to most people in this situation. Jurors were immediately sensitized to this line of defense in voir dire through a series of questions. The attorney asked:

How many of you drive? (All raised their hands.)
How many of you ever had a flat tire? (All raised their hands.)
How many of you have had a blowout? (All raised their hands.)
How many of you have lost control of your car in this situation? (None raised their hands.)

With this simple series of questions, the case for the defense was presented in microcosm.

The "Stalking Horse"

It is my belief based upon nothing other than observation and intuition that appropriate questioning of some jurors may be used to build a consensus or drive opinion in other jurors. Questioning all jurors alike is not feasible and certainly unwise for a variety of reasons. A juror or two may be chosen to pursue a certain line of questions for the purpose of building a consensus among all jurors or driving opinions or thoughts. All jurors

(continued)

(continued)

cannot be asked those same questions but one presumes that all jurors will give some thought to the questions when asked of others and to the responses that are given. I sometimes will use a juror as a "stalking horse" for a particular issue when I know there are good reasons not to pursue the same issue individually with all jurors. There are, of course, certain issues in every trial that I feel must be covered individually with each juror. When I do that, I try to make the exercise interesting for the jurors, believing that there is a greater chance of getting what I want if I attract jurors to the topic than if I herd them to it.

Frederick W. Morris
Leonard Street & Deinard, Minneapolis

Warning Jurors of the Opponent's Persuasive Intent

There are many instances in our lives in which we observe someone trying to change someone else's opinion with a persuasive message. When this is particularly overt, people normally become very sensitive to these efforts. Evidence shows that we are less likely to be persuaded by a speech, taped message, or written appeal if we think it is designed to influence our opinions than when we do not possess such knowledge.

Jurors resist persuasive messages when they have prior knowledge of the intent to persuade. This is particularly true for attitudes they consider important. Prior warning sets in motion the formulation of counter-arguments. These counter-arguments are then in place when the persuasive message arrives.

Voir dire is an appropriate time to warn jurors that they are going to be subject to various arguments from the other side during the course of the trial. We may know, for example, that certain juror attitudes are likely to be aligned in opposition to the case for the other side. Often, the results of pre-trial research into juror attitudes can be usefully employed in this connection.

Suppose, for example, the case involves a contract dispute. Our client, the defendant, has been accused of failing to perform alleged contractual obligations. It will be argued that these obligations were not the intent of the contract. A voir dire question might ask:

The plaintiff is going to claim that this contract obligated my client to provide for the maintenance of the flood control system after the installations were in place. Do you feel that you'll be able to evaluate this contract objectively and find out what it really says?

With this, and related kinds of questions, jurors will have been forewarned about the plaintiff's principal arguments. They will have an opportunity to begin formulating counterarguments in their minds at the same time they state they can be "objective."

Inoculation

Inoculation against the opponent's opening argument is another effective, though underused, voir dire strategy. In this regard, research on attitude change has shown that persuasive attacks on unquestioned beliefs (those beliefs for which the juror has no alternative viewpoint) can be astonishingly effective when the belief has gone unchallenged for some time. Self-generated counterarguments (arguments raised by the listener to counter the position of the speaker) will be weak during this kind of attack, and the listener will be highly susceptible to persuasion. This is of particular concern when trial strategy depends heavily upon attitudes jurors are expected to bring with them into the courtroom. The possibility exists that a direct assault upon favorable attitudes by the opposition may succeed in creating confusion, doubt, and the possible abandonment of the juror's original position. This threat can be reduced by inoculating against arguments which may come later in the trial.

Inoculation is most effective when a mild attack on a belief is supplemented with counterarguments that a juror may not easily generate on his own. For example, suppose a company is being sued for allegedly manufacturing a defective airplane involved in a fatal accident. One argument for the defense could be that, "The FAA has approved and certified this airplane for production and use." Although most people have a generally high regard for the FAA, they know little about it and have had little need to defend their opinions about it. This kind of unquestioned belief is highly vulnerable to effective counterarguments that derogate the competence of the FAA. The defense could inoculate against these attacks by asking:

Some people think that all federal agencies are inefficient and
bureaucratic; but is there anyone here who does not believe that
the FAA rigorously reviewed this airplane before it was put on
the market? Is there anyone here who does not believe the FAA
is concerned about and dedicated to the safety of the traveling
public?

Several queries along these lines would provide the necessary
inoculation against attacks on unquestioned beliefs. Thus, a mild dose of
the plaintiff's "virus," supplemented by the defense's "antibiotics," will
help develop stronger defenses that can deal with a more potent attack at
a later time.

Another example of inoculation can be seen in a feminine hygiene
products case in which the defendant-manufacturer was a very old,
reliable, and highly regarded company. Pre-trial research had established
that the jury panel as a whole would be positively disposed toward the
defendant. Many jurors remembered the company's other products from
their own childhood. The research further revealed that jurors would
possess the belief that the company had upheld a particular kind of trust
which is fundamental to its responsibility as a producer of household
baby products. The defense counsel felt that plaintiff would wage a
strong attack on this attitude-belief constellation in the opening statement.

Since the defense suspected that positive attitudes among jurors
would be based more on a "halo" effect of positive childhood memories
than on any factual substance and that these beliefs had gone unexamined
for many years, there was concern that plaintiff's attack might succeed.
In order to guard against this possibility, the defense elected to launch a
mild attack on the beliefs in question, supplemented with counter-
arguments that jurors would not be able to readily generate on their own.

The defendant had carefully constructed an image in the public mind
of compassion and reliability, mainly through the sale of its baby
products. There was a long-standing, ongoing advertising campaign
based on these values. Plaintiff was going to allege that the company had
been deliberately negligent in marketing a line of products without
knowing whether or not they would be dangerous to the user. The
defense knew that the plaintiff would put forward the argument that the
company had acted precipitously, without adequate testing, in order to
maintain its market share. By implication, the company management was
governed by pure profit motive and a disregard for the welfare of its
customers. In this case, the defense used voir dire questions like the following:

There's a lot of cynicism about big business today, and there are no doubt a fair number of people who think there's a wide gap between the advertising image of a company and its actual business practices. Do you think you can lay aside some of these current ideas and judge this case on its merits?

The plaintiff is going to ask you to believe that a company like Bakes and Hubbard, which has enjoyed the public trust for over fifty years, would suddenly throw out its standards of quality. Are you willing to look at the record without prejudice in this matter and see that the record speaks for itself?

It's hard to believe that anyone would think that a company which has been dedicated for generations to making products like Bates and Hubbard baby powder, Bates and Hubbard baby oil, and numerous other products would suddenly take leave of its senses and enter the market with an untested, dangerous product. Are you willing to consider the possibility that what happened to the plaintiff had no connection with Bates and Hubbard products at all? Are you willing to look at this matter with no prejudice toward the defendant?

For effective inoculation, a number of queries along these lines should provide the necessary protection against attacks on the jurors' unquestioned positive attitude-belief regarding the defendant and its products.

In sum, inoculation, like the other persuasive techniques discussed here, is part of an effort in voir dire to get jurors to psychologically position themselves to cognitively defend attitudes favorable to your side.

Voir Dire: The Elimination Decision

It was stated earlier that voir dire is an exercise in finding the "wrong" jurors. This means evaluating what each juror as an individual brings with him into the courtroom. It also means assessing how each person will fit into the group in which he will be placed.

At times, a juror must be eliminated strictly on the basis of individual characteristics, but more often than not, the decision will also incorporate an assessment of how much these characteristics are likely to matter in the context of a group. This is because individual traits are subject to group influence, and through this influence individual traits can be muted or exaggerated. Just how this will occur will depend upon the personality and motivational characteristics of all the jurors and how they interact.

Suppose a juror has beliefs in place which are unfavorable to your side. Whether this juror should be eliminated depends upon how much these beliefs will matter in the context of the group. Suppose the individual is a passive, follower type, with low self-esteem. Such a person will probably be led to a verdict by other jurors. Hence, it may not be necessary to eliminate this juror.

A feeling of affiliation or liking may lead a juror to subordinate certain cognitions and make decisions on the basis of these affiliations. On the other hand, a juror with weak favorable beliefs may have to be eliminated because it is clear that this individual will have strong feelings of aversion toward the attorney for your side, or toward the litigant. Racial or class prejudice is an example of this kind of aversion.

In choosing jurors by a process of elimination, it is necessary to decide how much a particular juror can hurt. This will be a decision based on individual juror characteristics and the role a juror is likely to play in the dynamic of the juror group decision-making process.

Voir Dire: The Elimination Decision

I tried a plaintiffs' products liability case last year which involved a claim that the defendant manufacturer's furnace was defective as a result of negligent design and manufacture and that the defects resulted in the release over several years of subacute levels of carbon monoxide (CO) into the living atmosphere of the plaintiffs' residence. The youngest daughter in the family was about six at the time of the alleged release of CO and she slept next to a hot air register. She was the only member of the family with any significant symptoms, e.g., headaches, nausea, flu-like symptoms, and the only one in the family for whom medical attention for these symptoms was sought. These symptoms persisted on and off for several years. It was claimed that the symptoms ceased, at least in their unusual frequency, once the defect in the furnace was discovered and repaired.

(continued)

(continued)

I became involved in the case somewhat late in the game. After some exposure to the family and private meetings with the parents and each of the three children, it was clear to me that the family was significantly dysfunctional for reasons unrelated to the furnace. The youngest daughter, 17 at the time of trial, had suffered from bulimia for several years and only shortly before the trial had apparently brought it under control. The defense had a psychologist who would and did testify, based upon his testing and examination of the young girl, that her emotional problems arose from causes having nothing to do with the furnace.

Among the jurors selected was a young woman who worked at the University of Minnesota, who had a degree in psychology, and who had worked at the bulimia clinic at the university. She was working on her Masters degree at the time of the trial. She was alone among the jurors in her educational background and her special experience with bulimia patients. We left her on the jury with some misgivings about her experience because there were others whom we thought were better to strike. While we did get a plaintiffs' verdict, it was a 5-1 decision with the university employee as the lone but staunch holdout. In interviewing the jury afterwards, it was clear that she saw the family as dysfunctional and the youngest child's bulimia as a symptom of that dysfunction. At no time did the defense call the family dysfunctional but it would have been clear to any close observer of the trial that there were problems with the family, particularly between the children and their parents.

(continued)

(continued)

In retrospect, we should have used a peremptory strike to dismiss the university employee because of her specialized background. The gamble did not hurt us this time because the other jurors, none of whom were as well educated, were not moved by her opinions. In another situation, someone with her experience and background might be a leader of opinions on the jury.

Frederick W. Morris
Leonard Street & Deinard, Minneapolis

Jury Myths and Voir Dire

Most of this book has focused on the many ways that jurors' belief systems and perceptual errors influence their decision making. However, lawyers, being human, are also subject to similar influences. Nowhere are these influences more apparent than during voir dire, where it is common to see lawyers rely upon certain "rules of thumb" or correlating classifications about human behavior to make key decisions about jury composition. Of course when utilized, they are viewed as irrefutable laws that define the outcome of jury verdicts and are typically held with great conviction by the lawyers who use them.

Jury selection myths, not unlike other folklore, are strongly held, yet largely unfounded, beliefs about what motivates jurors to decide for one side or the other in a lawsuit. Myths tend to be very resistant to change and often take on a superstitious or magical quality that allows them to persist even in the face of contradictory information. Although typically interesting and often humorous, myths can lead to dangerous jury selection errors; the following are common characteristics of jury selection myths:

1. They are expressed as a simple, absolute relationship between one observable characteristic and a behavior. "Women always respond favorably to an attractive male witness."

2. They are based on very few observations, and frequently on no observations whatsoever.

3. Most are described in the form of a war story.

4. They are handed down from one generation of attorneys to another with no clear origin.

5. They typically originate from a negative experience and have a fairly strong emotional component.

6. The essential factor(s) is easily observed in the courtroom (race, clothing, weight, sex, age, etc.).

7. They take the form of a stereotype.

8. Contradictory information is discounted, distorted, or ignored.

9. They are very resistant to change.

Selection myths proliferate because evaluating a jury is a very complex task. The lawyer is asked to predict how total strangers will behave, not now, but sometime in the future, based on extremely limited information provided under abnormal conditions and severe time constraints. Effectively revealing jurors' attitudes and values is quite difficult using traditional voir dire techniques. Under the circumstances, it is easy to understand how myths survive. Myths offer simple decision rules that can be used quickly and efficiently. These rules can be universally applied without detailed observation and analysis.

Unfortunately, myths also lead to many errors in judgement. A myth is a general categorization rule based on surface level information. On the other hand, as we have seen, juror behavior is determined by underlying cognitive structures which are often unrelated to surface characteristics. Altogether too frequently, myths are very unreliable and inefficient predictors of juror decision making.

As a typical example, one well known lawyer automatically strikes postal workers because he believes a letter carrier was responsible for an adverse verdict in a case he tried years before. The problem is that by selecting jurors according to his "Postal Worker Rule," he will never able to find out if his theory is correct. If he wins, he attributes his success, in part, to his ability to keep postal workers off his jury. Nothing makes a myth grow stronger than a clear-cut victory. If he loses, he attributes his loss to other factors, but the myth is unaffected. Interestingly, if for some reason a postal worker is seated on the jury, and *the case is won*, the myth is preserved through rationalization ("That was an unusually intelligent postal worker!").

The reader may enjoy the following encountered jury selection myths that have been proposed by real lawyers in real cases over the last 15 years:

- Anyone whose occupation begins with a "p" should be struck (postman, plumber, painter).
- Women with thin lips will help a plaintiff.
- Low income groups award high (or low) damages.
- Good looking women will always find for a physically attractive male lawyer.
- People who wear business suits are pro-business.
- Men with "crew cut" hair cuts are defense jurors.
- Highly educated jurors are better in complex cases.
- Widows award high punitive damages.
- Railroad workers are automatic plaintiff jurors.
- Anyone with a beard is a punitive juror.
- Fat women hate plaintiff lawyers.
- Blacks are bad for corporate defendants.
- Young women sympathize with criminal defendants.

Fred Morris[*] suggests that among the jury myths that might be added to the list is "public employees are plaintiff oriented."

He tried a case during the summer of 1987. The theories going to the jury were negligence, strict liability, warranty, and fraud. The venue was Lansing, Michigan, and he faced a jury pool full of public employees—employees of the state, county, and Michigan State University. Of the 12 people on the jury, at least 75% were employed by one or another government agency. While the verdict was for the plaintiffs, the jury returned a verdict on the negligent misrepresentation and warranty counts only and found the plaintiff 49% at fault for damages that were nominal given the amount requested. The total damages were around $160,000

---

[*] Frederick W. Morris, *Leonard Street & Deinard, Minneapolis.*

but the request had been more than $1 million.

Conclusions

The basic purpose of voir dire is juror selection, bur voir dire must also be viewed as an initial opportunity to present the case in microcosm and to begin the process of persuading jurors. Psychological techniques of persuasion, like those proposed here, can be employed in a variety of ways. Once the general thrust of the case has been determined, and pre-trial research is complete, it is possible to map out voir dire strategy that will effectively achieve the dual purpose of choosing a favorable jury and presenting the main outlines of the case to follow.

Psychological research offers a number of helpful suggestions that taken together improve typical voir dire strategies. More efficient use of paralinguistic and kinetic cues will aid in detecting true juror feelings. With carefully selected questions in voir dire, the lawyer can inoculate jurors who may be susceptible to attacks on previously unchallenged beliefs. Further, jurors led to make an admission that is consistent with the position of one of the litigants will "psychologically position" themselves to cognitively defend an attitude that was previously neutral, flexible, or ambiguous.

Finally, trial lawyers must constantly strive to avoid becoming victims of their own mythologies. The best way to keep myths from misleading them is to become aware of what their particular myths are and how they influence the lawyer's behavior during voir dire.

CHAPTER 7

Juror Selection Strategy

Jury selection is one of the most challenging and complex applications of the social sciences to litigation. Depending upon the particular jurisdiction, background information on prospective jurors may be quite limited, and lawyers may also be required to exercise their strikes in a short period of time. Where lawyers have wider discretion with voir dire, there are still, nevertheless, severe limitations on the ability to learn very much about the people seated in the jury box. The judge and/or lawyer can ask questions, but jurors clearly control what they want you to know.

Juror Selection: The Primary Approach

Lawyer experience with jurors in the venue is the basic starting point of any juror selection strategy. Most trial attorneys possess "feelings," "hunches," "gut feelings," or "instincts" about the type of people they want or wish to avoid for a particular case. For the most part, these views are based on stereotypes about human behavior. While these may be unscientific and impressionistic, they represent an inventory of beliefs about people based on a lifetime of experience with other people in a variety of social contexts. These ideas are important because the trial lawyer must be comfortable and self-confident with his audience. But as we discussed in Chapter 6, these feelings may or may not accurately reflect the ultimate behavior of a given juror in a particular case. When properly employed, behavioral science research and courtroom observation techniques can assist the lawyer to confirm or reject instincts and perceptions about prospective jurors.

If, for example, an attorney feels that middle-aged housewives will be positively predisposed to his client, this can be tested in a research setting. If he feels that blue collar workers will be antagonistic toward him or his clients, this can be tested as well. Thus, the primary approach to juror selection is one in which behavioral science research and lawyer intuitions are juxtaposed. However, juror selection strategy should not be limited solely to testing lawyer impressions about jurors. These impressions are a starting point. Many other hypotheses based on concepts and theories about human behavior with which lawyers may be unfamiliar can be subjected to empirical verification. Pre-trial research aimed at developing juror selection strategies will generally pursue a program of investigation into both the psychological and sociological characteristics of jurors. Pat Lynch of Los Angeles relates an ironic example of jury selection strategy in *Memorex v. IBM*, an antitrust case.

Predicting Jurors—What the Experts Know

This was a six-month antitrust trial charging IBM with multiple acts of monopolization. By stipulation, the parties had a jury of 12 members, and a unanimous verdict was required. The jury deliberated for 30 days. Each day the IBM team watched the jurors come and go, and had convinced themselves (a) that the majority of the jurors were on their side and (b) that they could identify one juror who was definitely voting against them. On the 30th day, the jury advised Judge Conti that they were hopelessly deadlocked. Judge Conti called the lawyers into chambers and suggested that they stipulate that each side could strike two of the jurors to see if that would result in a verdict.

(continued)

(continued)

Since Lynch and his team believed that they were ahead, they were intrigued with this idea. They consulted their jury advisory, and the Memorex lawyers did likewise. Ultimately, no stipulation was reached and a mistrial was declared.

Comparing notes many months later, IBM's lawyers ascertained that if they had excused the two jurors recommended by their advisors, they would have excluded one of the two jurors who had been consistently voting for them. Ironically, if Memorex had excused the jurors selected by its advisors, Memorex would have removed the juror who had been most consistently in favor of Memorex.

Patrick Lynch
O'Melveny & Myers, Los Angeles

Juror selection decisions really represent the lawyer's predictions as to how members of the panel will arrive at their ultimate verdict. This, of course, implies an evaluation of individual people as well as an assessment about how these people will operate as a part of a decision-making group. Hence, jury selection must include considerations of potential jurors at two levels: the psychological and the sociological. Psychological characteristics are the traits jurors display as individuals. Sociological characteristics consist of the traits jurors display as members of a group. Verdicts represent a unique norm of human decision making. Clearly, the decision of a group is not the mere amalgamation of individual decisions. Thus, juror selection strategies must also involve a consideration of social class memberships, cultural and sub-cultural identifications, and concepts about how individuals function in a decision-making environment. It will be useful to look at these factors in greater detail.

Psychological Characteristics

In addition to the cognitions that jurors bring with them into the courtroom, it is important to think about prospective jurors in terms of a number of psychological variables like motivation, personality characteristics, and the feelings jurors have about themselves. Each of these concepts has been investigated in great detail in university research settings. Much of what has been learned can be helpful in assessing how jurors will do the things they do in the courtroom and during deliberations.

Motivation

Human behavior is not random or accidental. It proceeds with certain motivations and goals in mind. Motivation propels action and stimulates the individual to engage in some behavior. Jurors, as human beings, possess general motivational patterns. Their behavior will be consistent with these patterns. Motivation involves self-protection, the gratification of needs, the reduction of tension, and the enhancement of the individual and his concept of self. Jurors are actuated by all of these motives when they come into court.

An important element in jury selection is the discovery of the extent to which juror behavior is linked to certain general patterns of motivation. Although there is not complete agreement among psychologists as to the nature of motivation, most accept the idea that certain needs are fundamental and that they probably exist in some sort of hierarchy. Motivation grows out of this hierarchy of needs in individuals and even in entire societies. Basic physiological needs, like the need for food, water, and safety, must be gratified before other "higher" needs emerge. These higher needs will include the need for love and affection and a need to feel a part of some group or society. When these needs have been fulfilled, still higher needs make their presence felt. Needs for self-respect, prestige, recognition, and achievement emerge. Finally, there is the need for self-actualization, or the belief on the part of a person that his or her potential is being fulfilled.

Jurors may be motivated to serve on a jury to achieve social recognition or prestige. Jury service may also provide the opportunity to fulfill needs associated with a social or political cause or some other set of intensely held beliefs. Once empaneled, jurors may, for example, pay attention to a particular witness or area of testimony because of motivational needs associated with learning new concepts or information.

Differences in motivational patterns among jurors can frequently be seen in the courtroom. Needs and the ways in which they are manifested among ghetto blacks are very different from the way they are disposed among upper class whites. These people will have entirely different approaches to life and may differ in the extreme when judging the motivations of litigation and of issues relating to equity and justice. At the same time, professional, college educated jurors will be motivated by different needs from blue collar, working class jurors. These differences will emerge in their expectations of the courtroom participants as well as in their expectations of other jurors. When various theories of motivation are considered, a number of important notions about jurors can be inferred and later incorporated into the jury selection process.

John Nyhan[*] gives an example of jurors motivated to sit on a jury. In a highly publicized trial of a products liability case with television cameras in the courtroom, several potential jurors seemed impressed with the flamboyance of plaintiff's lawyer, Melvin Belli. A University of California professor of philosophy wanted so badly to sit on the jury that he refused to describe what the concept of freedom of choice meant to him. After remaining silent for five minutes, he stated that he could not answer the question.

In the same trial, another juror was so strongly motivated to serve that she failed to answer voir dire questions truthfully with respect to her tolerance of cigarette smoking by others in her presence. A co-worker who shared an office with the juror was moved out of the office at the insistence of the juror who complained to supervisors about the co-worker's smoking. The co-worker saw a televised excerpt of the trial and observed the juror sitting in the jury box during opening statements. The co-worker later advised defense counsel that this juror was obviously biased but had not been disqualified. Based on the co-worker's testimony, the juror was disqualified for cause before the trial resumed.

---

[*] R. John Nyhan, *Pillsbury Madison & Sutro, Los Angeles.*

Freud's Psychoanalytic Theory of Motivation

One of the most important theories of human motivation is the psychoanalytic theory of Sigmund Freud. Freud's thinking has had a major impact on modern thought in general and is of particular importance for determining why people behave as they do. Freud emphasized the role of basic biological drives in motivation and argued that the way in which the personality becomes organized is a direct result of the need to gratify these basic drives or instincts. According to Freud, the personality which governs motivation is organized into three basic systems or processes. These are the *id*, the *superego*, and the *ego*. The id is comprised of biological drives generally defined as aggressive, destructive, pleasure-seeking impulses. The superego is made up of a system of moralistic inhibitions imposed on the id by parents and society. The ego is a mediating system which arbitrates the impulsive urges of the id and the suppressive nature of the superego. The conflicts which ensue among these three processes can lead to frustration and anxiety. The ego, or reality principle, seeks to cope with this frustration and anxiety through the use of a variety of mechanisms. These defense mechanisms, as they are called, often deny or distort reality in order to help the individual control or overrule internal motivations which are socially unacceptable. Defense mechanisms can also be used to resolve internal conflicts between the superego and the id. These conflict resolutions occur beneath a level of conscious recognition by the individual. One of the most important insights propounded by Freud is that a great deal of human behavior is determined by subconscious motivations.

The usefulness of Freudian insights for the study of juror behavior relates to understanding the existence of subconscious motivation and the use of defense mechanisms. A complete discussion of Freudian theory is beyond the scope of this book, but some of the defense mechanisms relevant to jury selection applications are identification, projection, displacement, and rationalization.

Identification is a very common and very powerful mechanism people use to copy and imitate others. If the individual is placed in a situation where his ego structure is rendered inadequate, the person may compensate by imitating someone else. For example, a juror with a low level of education and limited social or interpersonal experience may attempt to emulate jurors he considers to be more knowledgeable and sophisticated. The imitation of "opinion leaders" is common among jurors. It is important to identify the possible existence of jurors who could provide an opinion leadership role model and those who could become their followers. John Nyhan notes that another form of identification can occur when a juror identifies with plaintiff as victim. In one simulated trial, a juror who claimed to have been rendered sterile by a defective IUD described her own condition as identical to that of the plaintiff, whose immune system allegedly had been activated. This juror argued in favor of exorbitant compensation for the plaintiff's alleged injuries based on her own experience in having been denied compensation for her injuries.

In addition to the identification phenomenon occurring among members of the jury panel, attorneys should consider the possibility of extended influence; that is, identification occurring between a particular juror and a member of the trial team, witness, or a party. This factor has been a significant influence in a number of cases involving jury selection decisions. Chuck Preuss[*] notes that if the plaintiff is a celebrity, such as an athlete, entertainer or other well-known figure, this identification phenomenon can often produce a result which might not otherwise occur. For example, in three separate cases involving an athlete, a television celebrity, and a night club singer, all as plaintiffs, each prevailed and was awarded higher damages than was anticipated in light of the liability picture and nature of the injury involved.

A second defense mechanism is the phenomenon of projection. Projection is the opposite of identification. Projection consists of attributing to others motives and forms of behavior which the individual subconsciously recognizes as undesirable or unwanted within himself. This can be very dangerous when a juror views a litigant in this manner. Projection can often be the motivation behind certain kinds of causal attributions. In a wrongful termination case for example, a juror who is personally rigid or dogmatic may attribute these characteristics to a supervisor or executive as an explanation for an employee's alleged unfair treatment. In rape cases where the defendant is a physically attractive male, female jurors have been known to vote for acquittal notwithstanding very strong evidence to the contrary. This may even be the case where the man admits to having had sex with the woman. In post-trial interviews, these jurors reveal that they found the defendant so handsome or physically attractive that the purported victim must have also found him sexually appealing. Projecting their own subconscious sexual desires

---

[*] Charles F. Preuss, *Bronson Bronson & McKinnon, San Francisco.*

to the accusing woman, they conclude that she either "asked for it" or surely consented to the sexual encounter.

Displacement is a defense mechanism which transfers energy from one object to another. People who are underemployed in terms of their education and intelligence may be inclined to channel their frustration by blaming others for their plight. They may even blame a particular class of individuals. Some psychologists argue that one of the elements of racism is a displacement phenomenon: people find themselves dissatisfied with their own lives and find solace in blaming some racial group for their misfortunes. Displacement can also work in more subtle ways. A fight with one's spouse might be followed by a spending spree or some other form of impulsive behavior. Instead of directing energy against the other person, the energy is rechanneled into another form of unrelated behavior. Jurors may use displacement mechanisms as part of their motivation in rendering punitive verdicts. As an example, a juror who has lost a job or whose spouse has been fired may direct his anger and hostility toward a corporate defendant in a completely unrelated matter.

Finally, one of the most widespread of all defense mechanisms is the one called rationalization. Rationalization consists of providing ourselves with acceptable reasons for actions which are troubling, unacceptable, or in some way inexplicable. Pre-trial research frequently reveals that jurors will have to engage in rationalizing behavior in order to render verdicts in certain cases. In traumatic personal injury cases, jurors may have to develop rationalization for awarding or refusing to award large damages to the plaintiff in order to protect the jurors' own sense of self-worth. Knowing in advance which kinds of people are likely to engage in which kinds of rationalization can be a critical element of jury selection strategy.

Neo-Psychoanalytic Approaches

Various disciples and critics of Freud have promulgated ideas about motivation which remain within the basic psychoanalytic framework of unconscious drives and the development of mechanisms for their gratification. Adler felt that all human motivation grows out of a fundamental need to establish superiority and to overcome childhood feelings of inferiority. Fromm argued that all of our behavior is motivated by a need to overcome a certain existential loneliness, while Sullivan put forth the idea that all of our motivation should be understood in terms of the drive to form relationships with others.

Although none of these theories of motivation offers a complete explanation for all juror behavior, they are often suggestive of how certain jurors will behave in certain situations. Loneliness is a good example. While everyone suffers the pangs of loneliness and estrangement on occasion, the problem is particularly acute for people who have suffered the death of a loved one, for single people living in strange cities, or for divorced jurors forced to live alone for the first time.

In one of the IBM antitrust cases, an elderly, divorced juror felt intense anxiety and depression over the ending of the trial. This individual had come to view a number of the pro-IBM jurors as "close friends" who provided "affection and support." Interestingly enough, post-trial interviews revealed that those other jurors viewed the lonely divorcee as a social isolate who had little interaction with the rest of the jury and was "never really a member of the group but would vote the right way."

Jurors who exhibit certain traits, like loneliness, often play a key role in the jury both because of their motivation to deal with other jurors in particular ways and through the processes by which they are motivated to perceive issues in the trial.

Motivations Found Among Jurors

Jurors are likely to possess many different motives which, individually or in various combinations, may be aroused during the course of the trial. When pre-trial research indicates that certain motives are associated with significant aspects of the case, a careful scrutiny of potential jurors along these dimensions becomes a critical element of selection strategy. Some of the more frequently encountered motives observed in work for clients over the years include the desire for social approval and status, the need for security, the pursuit of personal interest or curiosity, the drive for self-realization, and the need to give and receive affection.

Social Approval. Jurors are often motivated by the need for social approval and status. For example, jurors who possess a great need for social approval will frequently dress and behave in ways conforming to their perceptions of social standards. This may include displays of excessive formality or politeness, or exacting attention to personal grooming and attire. In a series of product liability cases, one important element comprising the overall profile of desirable juror types for the client included certain characteristics of middle-aged women. In addition to other criteria, one important research finding suggested identifying women jurors in this age bracket who displayed fastidious attention to the coordination of their clothing, makeup, and adorning jewelry. While attire itself was not a predictor variable, it was a good surrogate reflecting a basic need (social approval) that was indeed correlated with verdict predisposition.

Status is related to social approval, but status is a form of social approval in which one's superiority over others is acknowledged. This may involve being able to wield power over others, command wealth and possessions, or receive deference from others. Identifying jurors who are motivated by high status needs may be important because of an association with courtroom perceptions and/or verdict predisposition. At the same time, such needs can be a good predictor of potential relationships among members of the jury panel.

The Need for Security. The need for security is commonly found as a basis for motivation in juror behavior. People with a prominent need for security feel that they must protect themselves and their loved ones both physically and/or psychologically. If testing issues or compliance with standards are expected to play a predominant role in the trial, it may be critical to identify jurors who possess this characteristic. This can also be true in matters involving allegations of financial, medical, or legal negligence or malpractice.

Curiosity. The pursuit of personal interests and curiosity seeking are motivations displayed by jurors at one time or another. Quite often a juror will have a personal interest in some salient aspect of the trial. An engineer might have an interest in design procedures and find this interest stimulated in a patent case. The engineer might be motivated to assert his interest and thereby become an "expert witness" during deliberation and possibly dominate other jurors. In a childbirth defect case, a nurse might have a personal interest in some arcane aspect of genetics. And, even though she may lack an accurate understanding of the topic, her professed mastery of the testimony presented in the trial combined with her formal credentials may allow her to exert a distorted influence on other jurors. In cases where the defense intends to present sophisticated or highly technical evidence, these people may be good candidates for peremptory challenges. Contrary to the conventional wisdom of wanting jurors who can understand the facts of the case, the old adage, "a little knowledge is a dangerous thing," may well apply. Clearly, if the voir dire process will permit, lawyers should attempt to ascertain the depth of knowledge the juror possesses in order to make this determination.

People with intense personal interests in a trial often turn out to be particularly dangerous to one side or another.

Self-Realization. A few jurors may wish to serve on a jury as an exercise in self-realization. They want to achieve some personal goal by serving on the jury. They may be anxious to convict or anxious to award damages. They may wish to achieve intellectual satisfactions of some kind through service as a juror. Through use of certain questions, juror research can identify potential jurors highly motivated by the need to achieve self-realization and predict how this kind of motivation may be linked to verdict predisposition in a particular trial.

Need for Affection. Jurors who are motivated by a strong need to give and receive affection may also play a special role in a given case. These people may react to courtroom events through the feelings they have for one of the attorneys or one of the litigants. They can also play a unique role in the group dynamics of the deliberations by spending their time seeking approval and affection from the other jurors.

While motives may be difficult to assess by untrained observers, they are an important element in the overall evaluation of potential jurors.

Rationalizing Evidence Against the Plaintiff

A case which illustrates the interplay of several of these motivations involved a child who was seriously brain-damaged after aspirating on a baby aspirin administered by her mother when the child was two years of age. As part of the jury selection process, a request was made to have the child present during the jury selection, so that the prospective jurors could be observed and questioned to determine whether their natural sympathies for the child's plight would influence their decision regardless of the evidence. This approach was successful in excusing a potential juror who admitted her strong feelings for the child's misfortune would cause her to favor a verdict on the child's behalf.

After the jury selection process was concluded, the evidence showed that the child aspirated on a larger pill of a different color

(continued)

(continued)

from the one alleged to have been administered by the mother. In addition, the bottle produced as the one from which the pill in question came was shown to have been manufactured after the date of the incident. Although this evidence was persuasive to seven of the twelve jurors, which included the more educated among the group, three jurors, who were among the less advantaged on the jury, were adamant that the child should receive an award to assure its future care regardless of the evidence.

Although it was anticipated that these three jurors would defer to their more educated colleagues, two factors led to the jury hanging eight to four in favor of the defendant manufacturer. First, the majority group was too forceful and demeaning in attempting to impose its will, which led to intransigence on the part of the smaller subgroup. Second, the three jurors found a protector in a soft-spoken chemist who had moved to the small town in which the trial took place from a faster paced life in a nearby large metropolitan area. This chemist stated in a post-trial interview that he always considered it his responsibility to stand up for those less fortunate than himself. This dominant motivation led to rationalizing the evidence against the plaintiff, to cast the pivotal vote to hang the jury and to instill the will within the subgroup to stand up to the pressure of the majority group.

Charles F. Preuss
Bronson Bronson & McKinnon, San Francisco

Personality

A second major psychological construct that must be included in any evaluation of potential jurors is the concept of personality. While there is a wide variety of conflicting and oftentimes competing theories of personality, most behavioral scientists agree that the personality of an individual is a useful predictor of behavior. Fortunately, unlike many of the other psychological concepts discussed in this book, behavioral factors defining an individual's personality are often observable. These include recurring patterns of specific behaviors which are related to personality traits. Personality traits are the set of relatively permanent and broad behavioral tendencies that serve as the building blocks of an individual's personality and are frequently correlated with deeply held values, attitudes, and beliefs. For example, when we describe someone as having a trusting personality, we are tracing the root of some behavior back to an underlying source which is believed to be an enduring personal characteristic.

Psychologists have identified many different behavioral expressions of personality traits. They range from the jobs we choose, the friends we make, the way we rear our children, the way we deal with crises and many, many others. Personal appearance characteristics are perhaps the most obvious ways that we express our underlying personality traits. Dress and grooming style can reveal much about an individual's personality. The use of certain products can also be related to personality traits. The kind of automobile, the consumption of certain foods, and the use of various consumer goods can all reflect the personality of an individual.

Psychologists have suggested many different theories of personality. Some theories are more amenable to empirical validation than others. All provide unique insight into human behavior and careful study is recommended to the trial attorney who is looking for creative ways to understand juror behavior. One theory that is particularly well known and is often credited with stimulating the subsequent development of many new theories of personality is Freud's theory of psychosexual development. Freud developed a personality typology based on his beliefs about infant sexuality and the manner in which this sexuality develops in the behavior of mature adulthood. Freud argued that people pass through clearly marked phases in their sexual development and that fixation at any given stage will determine an entire set of personality characteristics which are manifested later in life. An individual who traverses a normal path of sexual development will arrive at what Freud described as the genital state. Such a person will be interested in other people and the world outside himself. Much of his energy will be geared toward the attraction of people of the opposite sex, becoming socialized, joining groups, planning a career, getting married, and raising a family— all components of the so-called normal personality. Freud also felt that people who did not succeed in reaching the genital stage were neurotic in various ways. These people may be compulsive, narcissistic, overly aggressive, and competitive. They may also display tendencies to be sloppy and disorganized or compulsively neat.

There have been many attempts to derive other explanations of personality from Freud's basic ideas. One well-known typology posits that the predominant personality of an individual can be associated with one of three general categories. These personality traits are described as aggressive, compliant, or detached. Aggressive people are motivated to move against other people and to dominate and control their environment. Compliant people move toward or with others; they tend to acquiesce to social influence. Detached people move away from others and engage in avoidance behavior. Since Freud's time, many other psychologists have developed complementary and competing theories of personality, all of which share the basic concept that personality is a relatively enduring set of behavioral tendencies which are reflected in how a person responds to the environment.

While a comprehensive review of personality theory and research is well beyond the scope of this book, it should be understood that underlying the somewhat superficial characteristics of personal appearance and the use of certain products, one can often discern less obvious and perhaps more abstract characteristics of a juror's personality. For this reason, it is often valuable to inquire into a broad range of behaviors that may range beyond the immediate scope of the case when constructing juror personality profiles.

Personality, then, is a key factor in the assessment of jurors. By carefully observing the overt behavior of a person, personality traits can be inferred. These inferred characteristics may be compared to personality inventories contained in juror profiles or previously found through pre-trial research to be associated with significant issues in the case. In his experience, John Nyhan has found that inferred characteristics based on observation of a person's overt behavior can identify certain types of jurors. For example, in one trial involving alleged risk of injury due to exposure to asbestos contained in fire-proofing material, one member of the jury used asbestos gloves in her work as a laboratory technician and was aware of risks as well as benefits of the substance. She thought little of the exaggerated claims asserted by plaintiff. This juror became the foreperson and persuaded the other jurors during deliberations to ask a question they knew to be spurious: Could they award damages for breach of warranty, a theory neither pled nor argued. When asked about this question after deliberations, the foreperson stated the jurors had no interest in awarding plaintiff anything and simply wanted to tweak all of the lawyers and make them wonder what was taking the jury so long to come to a decision.

In addition to being useful as predictors of behavior, are personality variables associated with persuasion? There are no consistent findings in psychology that show that certain types of personality traits are more persuadable than others. One explanation may be that personality traits can both enhance and inhibit persuasion at the same time. For instance, an intelligent juror may be more likely to comprehend the evidence (and thus be more persuadable) but at the same time, be more likely to question it (hence, inhibiting persuasion). A juror with low self esteem may have little confidence in his own judgements and hence be more easily persuaded; at the same time, this person may also have little interest in what is going on around him and therefore pay little attention to the evidence.

The Jury as a Social Group

In addition to the characteristics that jurors display as individuals, trial lawyers must evaluate the individual's potential interaction with other members of the jury panel. Thus, a person may possess attributes which would ordinarily disqualify him as a desirable candidate but nevertheless be acceptable because of potential social group influences; and, of course, the opposite may be the case.

Group processes represent more than an aggregation or collection of individual behaviors acting together. Individual traits, when combined with those of others, may become exaggerated or modified. Hence, groups frequently become more or less than the sum of their parts. Group behavior is unique.

First-time jurors are literally "strangers in a strange land." The pressures of a new environment where the rules governing behavior are unique, formal, and associated with an unfamiliar vernacular frequently place jurors in an atmosphere of stress and uncertainty. In such an environment, group identity and mutual support can become very important to the individual. Group identity is strengthened by juror interaction during the course of the trial. These interactions facilitate the formation of group norms as well as the development of negative and positive affiliations toward other members of the panel.

An important part of the decision-making process is that jurors learn early in the proceedings where their colleagues stand. Without discussion, they learn the position of other jurors through patterns of social influence, verbal and nonverbal cuing, and the formation of subgroups. John Nyhan provides a humorous example of how jurors often find ways to communicate nonverbally. After a lengthy trial, jurors disclosed they were so tired of hearing the same theme repeated by one side's witnesses that whenever the words "risk of harm" were uttered, one juror sitting in the front row whose hands were hidden below the front wall of the jury box, waved her hands like a conductor whenever the same old tune appeared. This is an example of a message carried so far as to be boring. The social interaction that leads to group formation, in fact, is one of the most important aspects of any jury. The formation of subgroups is also a preparation for the action of convincing others. Those who hold a particular position seek to build a network and set of defenses early in the trial. This is useful in anticipated confrontations over the verdict. Subgroups will thus consist of people who think alike and who have the same understanding about how they will carry out their roles as jurors.

Jurors are in an artificial, closely controlled environment, which precludes them from interacting in the very areas that, to them, are of social significance. They are jurors, but the very business of being jurors is just what they are not allowed to discuss.

Perhaps this can be more clearly understood through an analogy. Suppose that a group of employees were told that they could discuss anything among themselves except their job, their work environment, what they were doing, how they were doing it, and how their thoughts, observations, or opinions impacted upon them or the organization for which they worked. It is obvious that such a social environment would produce a great deal of stress.

The need to form subgroups seems to stem from two sources: a desire for interpersonal communality and the anticipation of who will be who vis-à-vis the verdict. Post-trial interviews with jurors who served on the *Calcomp v. IBM* trial demonstrated the tremendous importance of subgroup formation. While IBM received a directed verdict after plaintiff's case-in-chief, post-trial interviews revealed that before the defense began its case, three distinct groups had formed: the pro-IBM group, the pro-CalComp group, and the group of the unannounced. Each group formed around a strong opinion leader.

The IBM group was led by a woman who was a doctrinaire believer in free enterprise. She and her husband regularly read the Wall Street

Journal and together maintained a small portfolio of stocks they carefully tended. They followed an ultra-conservative lifestyle, and she, in particular, was a dogmatic and opinionated person who served as a kind of Pied Piper for this group. They clustered around her and through her found support and protection for their point of view. This group was educationally oriented and interested in current events, economics, and political issues. Thinking of themselves as philosophers, they were condescending toward the pro-CalComp group, whom they considered to be their intellectual inferiors and generally ill-informed.

The pro-CalComp group tended to form in reaction to the pro-IBM group and was much less pro-active. Its focal person was a woman who worked in a factory. She had a high school education, was very religious, and tended to be opinionated. She also disliked IBM and its lawyers intensely.

The third group, the unannounced, was made up of those who, although they were probably committed to one side or the other, did not announce their predispositions through any sort of signaling as to how they would have voted. In many ways, this group provided a major source of cohesion; a conduit through which cooperation and negotiation would have to flow. The unannounced group would have played an important role in shaping group identity and in arriving at a verdict had the case gone to the jury.

Interviews also indicated that the jury foreman would have come from the unannounced subgroup. This individual was a 40-year-old construction foreman employed by the state of California who was particularly well-qualified for the role of foreman in this case. He was a mature individual, strong without being aggressive, and a person who could take charge. He was a facilitator, pleasant, thoughtful, and trustworthy.

Subgroups among jurors can be seen in seating arrangements around a jury table, in car pooling, and in who goes to lunch with whom. They also are marked by the use of "safe talk." Since jurors cannot talk about the reason for their collective existence as jurors (the trial and their role in it), they invent safe topics which become the central thrust of their interaction in small subgroups. These frequently include common interests, work, sports, politics, hobbies, families, neighborhoods, and other mutual concerns. This use of safe talk is a frequent occurrence in juries. Safe talk enables jurors to find significant others, that is, people like themselves, and allows posturing and the formation of alliances.

The most typical safe topic used in the IBM case, as well as in many others, was food. Women brought in cakes, pies, cookies, and rolls. Inevitably, this became competitive. In other cases, when there are no men on the jury, women frequently bring food to the judge and the bailiff.

Among the people in the pro-CalComp group, food was the most frequent topic of safe conversation. The members of the pro-IBM group regarded the Cal-Comp group as silly and intellectually deficient. They, in turn, considered the woman who led the pro-IBM group as "phony" and having unjustified intellectual pretensions.

Talk among members of the pro-IBM group was mainly about politics and current events. Members of this group spent much of their time sitting at their end of the jury table in their appointed places discussing these safe topics.

The moderates, or the group of the unannounced, centered on sports as their principal topic of safe talk. They saw the woman who led the IBM group as dogmatic and opinionated, but they did not necessarily dislike her. From the point of view of the IBM group, the group of the unannounced, with its talk of sports, was clearly inferior and plebeian.

Juror Roles

All groups undergo a process of socialization. From the time a group forms until it disbands, it functions like a society in miniature. The major social process which takes place within a group is the formation of roles. The roles jurors play are related to the function of the jury as a group: to reach a verdict. Initially, jurors play the role of observers and investigators. Shortly after deliberation begins, they shift into the role of persuader and decision maker. At this point, their roles may become adversarial.

The most important role that a juror can play is that of the opinion leader. One of the objectives of juror research is to identify people who are likely to become leaders and to determine the kind of influence they will exert on the rest of the group. The cluster of traits which seem to determine opinion leadership among jurors includes: a strong drive for responsibility and task completion; persistence and vigor in pursuit of goals; venturesomeness and creativity in problem solving; self-confidence; and a drive to exercise initiative in social situations. Leaders are willing to drive decisions forward, to absorb stress, and to accept the consequences of the decisions they make and actions they carry out.

The juror foreman may or may not be the group opinion leader. While the foreman is the titular leader of the group, he may merely carry out certain formal tasks. Indeed, the jury foreman may exert very little influence on the ultimate verdict. Oftentimes trial lawyers express a great deal of interest in predictions about which person will become the foreman of the jury. In reality, this may be misplaced attention. The real focus of attention in juror selection from a sociological perspective should be the identification of potential opinion leaders. Recognizing the opinion leader is a matter of carefully analyzing the past experience and background of jurors and attempting to discover which jurors have played the role of opinion leaders in other walks of life. It also includes an evaluation of those who display the capacity to lead vis-à-vis the composition of other people on the panel.

The Juror who "Has Been There"

An opinion leader may not always be easy to identify. One covert opinion leader that turns up all too often is the juror who "has been there." Even the most unassuming, uneducated, or retiring juror may assume a leadership role if he or she is perceived to have inside knowledge about the subject matter of the trial.

When I first started trying personal injury cases as a young plaintiff's lawyer, in one matter we were allowed a relatively thorough state court voir dire with the exception that the judge was adamant that we not state facts to pre-sell our point of view. The jury was impaneled and the judge said: "This case involves a motorist who took his car to a service station, had a tire changed, drove on to the freeway where the wheel came off and an accident resulted." One juror timidly raised his hand. "What is it?" the judge demanded. "Well," the juror said, "last week

(continued)

(continued)

I put my car in a service station to change a tire, drove on to the freeway, the wheel came off and I was in a terrible accident. Should I be sitting here?" Although that was rather dramatic, I wonder how often it happens in an oblique way and isn't caught.

In another case, I was involved in a jury simulation supervised by a leading trial research firm. We were trying the actual case in Indianapolis, and Columbus, Ohio, was chosen as the surrogate city for the mock trial. The issue was alleged fraud in the sale of hundreds of residential lots in Colorado. After screening many dozens of potential mock jurors and impaneling 24, one of them turned out to have actually purchased one of the Colorado lots in issue.

Thomas J. McDermott, Jr.
Rogers & Wells, Los Angeles

Juries work because not everyone wants to be a leader. Many people feel more comfortable playing the role of followers and facilitators. People normally defer to others who have greater ego-strength, greater skills, or higher intelligence. Jurors may also defer to other people they like. Liking can produce deference, as can fear. What kind of people are likely to defer to others and become followers instead of leaders? Followers can be identified in jury research by looking for certain traits and motivations such as the ones discussed earlier in this chapter. Jurors who conform easily, move toward people, and who have a strong need to give and receive affection are likely to be followers.

Personal Influence: How Leadership Works

People will defer to others they consider significant in their lives. These can be athletes, teachers, religious leaders, media stars, or anyone else who seems to embody some ideal or provide information which can be used as a basis for decisions and actions.

People also can defer to others because of the perception that some individual is in a unique position "to know" through special training, education, or experience. The opinion leader may, in fact, possess none of these special attributes, but the perception that he does in comparison to other people in the group may propel him into a leadership position.

The "Expert" in the Jury Room

In many cases, the subject matter is such that a member of the jury panel may well have particular expertise in the subject matter of the suit. The possibility of this expertise should be anticipated before jury selection begins. Questions for ferreting out this expertise should be prepared in advance and thought given as to whether such a juror should be retained. An incorrect decision can be devastating. For example, in a case in which a tampon manufacturer was alleged to have provided an inadequate warning of toxic shock syndrome (TSS), the plaintiff contended that the company could have performed certain tests which would have led it to ascertain that TSS was being experienced by consumers who had reported certain ill-effects from using the company's tampon, even though TSS had not yet been associated with tampons by the Center for Disease Control, or in any scientific article. The pivotal juror was an engineer, who informed the jury (which was hung seven to five for four days in favor of plaintiff) that based on his experience, the inadequacy of the company's testing program was demonstrated by the paucity of the testing documents produced by the company. This viewpoint, coupled with his repeated reiteration to his fellow jurors that, so strongly did he believe in the correctness of this viewpoint, he was willing to spend the December holiday season deliberating until a plaintiff's verdict was obtained. This pressure led two female jurors to change their votes in order to accomplish already delayed family preparations for the holidays, even though the two capitulating jurors regarded the damage award as excessive. Beware of December trials.

Charles F. Preuss
Bronson Bronson & McKinnon, San Francisco

We create opinion leaders because we need them. Leaders on juries owe their leadership position to their ability to help other jurors accomplish the task at hand. Leaders initiate structure. They state the issues, organize what is taking place, and move the group toward its goal of rendering a verdict. This leadership may be exercised with moral suasion, fear, affection, or logical argument, but the ultimate task of the leader is to drive the group to accomplish its stated formal role.

Personal Influence and Communication on the Jury

Patterns of communication among jurors can be described as a series of networks. Significant issues or salient pieces of information during deliberations will be filtered in some way through other members of the panel. Communication psychologists refer to this as a two-step flow of communication. When the jurors leave the courtroom to begin deliberations, they have not yet talked to each other about the case. When they do begin to discuss the trial, different jurors will remember different things and place differing interpretations on what they remember. The interpretations of some jurors will become a source of information for others. Strong-willed, dominant people with the best recall will generally contribute the most to this information recall process. People who become the most frequent source of information on the jury will have the most personal influence. They will tend to become leaders and to steer the group process. This will also tend to become circular and self-fulfilling. Those who have the most information will gain personal influence and, as they gain personal influence, they will become more and more important as sources of information for other jurors.

If the trial lawyer can determine which jurors are likely to perform this role, special attention can and should be devoted to them during the course of the trial. This can include various forms of nonverbal communication as well as efforts to insure that charts, graphs, and demonstrative exhibits are clearly visible to these jurors.

Conclusions

This chapter has discussed a number of behavioral considerations which go into juror selection strategy which can be employed to complement lawyer instincts and intuitions. Well-designed juror selection strategies begin with lawyer instincts which are then juxtaposed to the insights and findings of pre-trial juror research.

Juror selection strategies can be assisted by a number of concepts and principles from the behavioral sciences. These include a broad range of individual juror characteristics as well as the probable group process that will occur once the jury has been chosen.

Individual or psychological characteristics include patterns of motivation among jurors which will provide insights as to how jurors will regard the issues and participants in the trial. Although behavioral scientists are not in complete agreement about theories of motivation, all concur that people possess certain basic needs and are driven to gratify these needs. The way in which needs are disposed and gratified constitutes an individual's motivational pattern. Juror research strategy seeks, in part, to learn how motivational patterns will influence a juror's behavior in a given case.

Personality characteristics also influence juror behavior. Psychologists have established the existence of a wide variety of personality traits which are found to be repeatedly associated with specific behaviors. Pretrial research can be employed to demonstrate connections between juror behavior and these personality traits in a given case.

The second major area in which the behavioral sciences can contribute to juror selection strategy is in understanding the jury as a social group. Group identity and the way in which subgroups form within a jury is evident in many trials. This can be seen through the emergence of opinion leaders and through the observation of patterns of association, avoidance, agreement, disagreement, deference, and even conflict among members of the panel. Evaluation of how these patterns will occur and who will be likely to emerge as opinion leaders is an important aspect of selection strategy.

A final and important point about juror selection strategy is that pretrial research must be case-specific. Every case is unique, and research must be oriented toward this uniqueness. The jurors, the courtroom events, the trial participants, the venue, and the issues which will be raised during the proceeding will constitute a one-time-only occurrence. It is most hazardous to suppose that the results of jury selection research conducted for one trial can be applied in an unqualified way to another. The carry-over which can be reasonably expected from one trial to another consists of testing propositions about jurors which may have worked once to see if they will work again. To assume that they will work again without testing them in the new setting is improper from a scientific standpoint and potentially dangerous to the client.

CHAPTER 8

The Psychology of the Opening Statement

Over the years, there has been a considerable amount of discussion among trial lawyers and jury behavior experts on the importance and impact of opening statements. The analysis of hundreds of post-trial jury interviews and thousands of simulated trials provide consistent findings: The vast majority of jurors arrive at a verdict predisposition during or immediately after opening statements. Further, these initial decisions are remarkably consistent with the final verdicts that jurors render at the conclusion of the trial. This is particularly true in shorter cases. Does this mean that once the opening statements have been presented the remaining elements of the trial are superfluous? That these initial evaluations are immutable and impossible to change? The answer is certainly no! Nevertheless, the opening statement does indeed set the stage for winning or losing a lawsuit. It dramatically shapes and influences how and what jurors perceive during the case. For this reason, it is the most critical address the lawyer will deliver during the trial. Why are opening statements so important?

The beginning of the trial is the occasion when jurors are most attentive to the judge, lawyers, and courtroom events. They have not become conditioned to their new role, and the experience of being jurors is still novel and stimulating. As we have seen in previous chapters of this book, the opening is also the time when jurors possess the tendency to focus on and remember a great deal more of what is presented to them

161

than at any other time during the trial. All of this, then, points to the great strategic importance of the lawyer's initial presentation of his case to the jury.

Primacy-Recency

There have been numerous studies over the past sixty years investigating the order effects of new information on memory and retention. One relevant conclusion from this research suggests that people have a tendency to remember information that is presented first or last in a series of information. Absent factors to refocus attention, there is a U-shaped curve for memory and retention of material that comes in the middle. When student subjects participating in learning experiments are presented with a long list of names, they can later typically remember the names that appeared at the beginning of the list and names that were contained at the end of the list. Rarely can they recall names emanating from the middle portion of the list unless there is some unique or distinctive quality about a specific name. Replicating these studies with numerical data, subjects are presented with long lists of numbers. Experimental findings reveal that, if subjects can remember any of the numbers at all, they tend to remember once again the numbers that appeared at the beginning of the list and those at the end. For this reason, names appearing on election ballots in many states are randomly ordered. There is a statistical probability of prevailing in an election merely because a candidate's name appears at the beginning or end of a list of people seeking a particular office.

The implications of these primacy-recency effects have important strategic considerations to trial lawyers. As with subjects in psychological experiments, jurors have a tendency to remember what comes early in the trial—the opening statement—and that which comes at the end. The middle may tend to fade or blur.

Because of primacy-recency effects, opening statements address a critically important requirement at the beginning of the trial. If properly designed and delivered, the opening statement will provide an informational super-structure for the jury. We know that jurors will not attend to all of the *information* presented to them during the trial—indeed they cannot. Hopefully, the lawyer's themes will be learned, remembered, and employed to tie together otherwise potentially disparate documents, evidence, and witness testimony.

We should also point out that the concept of primacy-recency applies not only to the trial as a whole, but to its component parts. Within the opening statement itself, that which is said at the beginning and the end will be retained better. The same point can be made for the examination and cross-examination of witnesses, closing arguments, and the reading of instructions. This has important implications for the ordering of evidence throughout the trial.

Opening Statement Strategy

The problems involved in composing an opening statement really focus on identifying which specific issues, among all of the possible alternatives, jurors must hear at the beginning of the case.

As we have seen, attorneys and jurors may not approach a trial from the same perspective. Jurors may focus on issues or concepts without the most legal relevance, or even without any legal relevance at all. These salient points may represent factual issues in the case or some highly perceptible emotional issue which will have a particularly persuasive impact.

In a product liability case, a child had suffered brain damage *in utero*. The plaintiff alleged that a drug manufactured by a large pharmaceutical company to induce labor in pregnancy was the cause of the defect. It was further alleged that the company had received indications of adverse reactions from physicians treating other patients. Clearly, these were serious allegations for the company.

In this instance, the case was settled before the jurors had completed their deliberations. Pre-trial research, however, had revealed an issue that would have been invaluable to the defense had the case gone to judgement. Utilizing excerpts of the mother's videotaped depositions, surrogate jurors were provided with key portions of the plaintiff's testimony. After observing the tape, the jurors were all deeply disturbed by their perception of the mother's apparent lack of love for the child. This fact, a negative attitude toward the plaintiff based on natural instincts toward children, did not refute any of the plaintiff's evidence. It was hardly a legal point and was not even in dispute. Nevertheless, this attitude, disapproval of the mother's apparent lack of love for her child, could have proved critical had the case gone to a jury verdict. It was completely inconsistent with the common sense belief that mothers should love their children under all circumstances. In this case, the relationship between the mother and the child would have been an issue of paramount importance. It would have allowed jurors to bring common sense to bear on the case, and using common sense is what most jurors are inclined to do. As such, this extra-legal issue, the mother/child relationship, was selected to be one of the central themes of the defendant's opening statement. These central themes or key issues or key concepts can be referred to as Thematic Anchors.

Choosing a Theme and Sticking To It

Jurors, after all, are people, whose perceptions about the parties will bear heavily on the outcome of your case. Another example of this—and the need to focus themes accordingly—is seen in a major antitrust case tried in San Francisco. Not long after I first worked with Don Vinson in 1979 and had begun to focus more on the importance of stressing themes in opening statements, I was recruited to take on the re-trial of an antitrust suit against the Hearst Corporation, its San Francisco Examiner, *and the* San Francisco Chronicle, *brought by smaller regional newspapers and advertisers. The first trial of the case had resulted in a 1-5 hung jury in favor of the plaintiffs. The defendants, feeling fortunate to have barely escaped a verdict that would have wreaked havoc upon newspaper mergers across the United States, decided to bring in new counsel to defend the second trial.*

It was obvious that something different had to be tried. It was not so obvious what to do. After reading a three foot stack of transcripts, however, it was at least apparent to me that the most serious obstacle the joint defendants had failed to surmount in the first trial was in proving that the afternoon paper—the Examiner—*was in such danger of failure as would justify the defendants' recourse to an antitrust exemption under the Newspaper Preservation Act of 1970. The problem was that the* Examiner's *venerable publisher, Charles Gould, had repeatedly asserted in letters and memoranda to New York headquarters—right up to the time of the merger—that the* Examiner *was in excellent health and about to turn the corner into profitability.*

(continued)

(continued)

My first theme seemed clear: "Daily newspapers with different editorial voices are good for America, but they are dying out and so too will the Examiner unless allowed the protection of the Act's antitrust exemption." I knew that my second theme had to confront and somehow deal with Mr. Gould's inconsistent writings, but had no idea how it could be accomplished until I laid eyes on him. A tall and distinguished man in his early seventies, Gould radiated integrity. He had been among the deans of newspaper publishing for more than four decades, but had met his match in San Francisco, Hearst's flagship city. He had run a traditional newspaper with ancient equipment and boasted a wall of national awards for journalism, but he could not compete with the spicy, flamboyant Chronicle. It was also clear to me that Charles Gould could not face the possibility of failure in the winter of a brilliant career and that I should simply own up to the jury that he had either been lying to the home office or had been fooling himself. Whatever I did, I knew I had to take risks if I were to turn a 1-5 hung jury into a 6-0 verdict in favor of the defense. I began to hope that my major problem could be turned into an opportunity by a simple theme: "To destroy the Examiner would be to not only destroy competing daily editorial voices and attitudes, but a good human being as well."

With Mr. Gould's consent and encouragement, I then used the opening statement to hammer on these themes and never stopped during the next two and one-half months of trial—which resulted in a defense verdict.

John S. Martel
Farella Braun and Martel, San Francisco

Thematic Anchors

Work in the area of jury psychology has consistently shown that jurors normally base their verdict on a small number of critical points. These Thematic Anchors represent the two, three, but no more than four central themes or issues which support the overall story of the case. Lawyers may call these "case issues," "case concepts," "theories of the case," or "case touchstones." Whatever the terminology, they are the deductive framework jurors formulate early in the trial and use to organize subsequent details. These Anchors provide answers to nagging questions and are used to tie together loose ends and resolve lingering doubts.

If the jury remembers nothing else during the trial, hopefully they will remember the lawyer's Thematic Anchors.

Going into a trial, lawyers should be aware of what these Anchors will be since they will, in all likelihood, form the foundation of the jury's ultimate verdict. In most trials there are a variety of issues which can be presented. In one antitrust action, there were more than 400 individual issues which could be used to develop a theory of the case. In such instances, it is necessary to identify the three or four most important points on which the action will rest or fall. All of the evidence, testimony, lawyer argument, and significant demonstrative exhibits should relate to and reinforce these Thematic Anchors. If properly selected and employed, they tie together lawyer arguments, testimony, and demonstrative evidence.

Thematic Anchors exist in two forms. First, they can be descriptive and represent matters of fact: things about which documents are written, witnesses testify, and exhibits represent or explain. Factual anchors are the ones with which there is no dispute—the bridge collapsed, the plaintiff was injured, the bond default occurred. Reasonable people may argue over the cause or the consequences of an event, but descriptive anchors are rarely open to dispute.

It is interesting to note that descriptive anchors are the ones with which many lawyers feel most comfortable. Oftentimes, however, they are the least important to jury verdicts.

The second form of Thematic Anchors relates to matters of evaluation. These anchors are based upon the cognitions jurors carry with them into the courtroom. In a contraception product liability case, for example, issues relating to God, children, femininity, sexuality, motherhood, family, abortion, and death may be infinitely more important in verdict determination than testimony involving epidemiology, biochemistry, or arcane aspects of medical science. The legal, technical, or scientific facts of the case will evoke evaluative beliefs. If the trial lawyer fails to provide the jury with appropriate evaluative anchors, the jurors will employ their own. Without contributing strategic guidance in this "issue identification/issue selection" process, jurors may well focus on aspects of the case quite distinct and apart from the lawyer's intent.

What Anchors Do for Jurors—Overcoming Cognitive Dissonance

Thematic Anchors do several things for jurors. As we have noted, they enable jurors to organize the case consistent with their attitudes and beliefs. They also tend to provide jurors with a feeling of completion and security. They give jurors the rationalizations they need to settle the case in their own minds without lingering inner conflicts. When jurors render verdicts, they have to make judgements and evaluations. Psychologists know that when people are asked to make judgements, they seek reference points around which to anchor these judgements. Evaluations and judgements are not made in a void. They are made with reference to an initially consistent and comfortable framework. This framework is the familiar one of cognitive structure or attitude set. When jurors are confronted with information which is hard to reconcile with fundamental beliefs and attitudes, they frequently experience a condition referred to as cognitive dissonance.

Cognitive dissonance consists of feelings of discomfort and even anxiety. The cognitive dissonance jurors sometimes experience when confronted with hard to digest information, not consistent with what they believe to be true, can be very uncomfortable. It can even produce states of acute tension and psychological disequilibrium. To avoid this psychological tension or dissonance, jurors, like people in other decision-making situations, will engage in a variety of coping mechanisms. These include: (1) rejecting the dissonance inducing information; (2) distorting the information to make it consistent with previously held beliefs; (3) minimizing the importance of the new information; or (4) changing their original beliefs or cognitive structure. From the lawyer's perspective, the last condition is probably the most logical. However, as we have seen, it is incredibly difficult to change most centrally held beliefs by merely presenting people with new information. As an example, the beliefs that most jurors hold relating to sexuality, religion, interpersonal relations, concepts of right or wrong or fair play, political orientation, or economic risk are relatively immutable. These belief structures are typically very resistant to change. Lawyer arguments, witness testimony, or judges' instructions which assault these cognitions or are inconsistent with them are likely to produce cognitive dissonance.

The kind of general stress under which jurors labor is only compounded by cognitive dissonance. Jurors are in unfamiliar surroundings. They are strangers in a world in which the attorneys and the judge are at home. Yet they are being asked to shoulder responsibility for allocating blame and possibly awarding large sums of money. Under these circumstances, jurors work to reduce cognitive dissonance by screening out dissonant information.

The Anchor Never Stated

The importance of a Thematic Anchor can be seen in the following example: In a recent case, suit was brought by a 14-year-old boy for injuries received as a passenger in an automobile collision. The injuries were very serious—extensive orthopedic injuries and pronounced brain damage. By the time of trial, medical expenses had exceeded $230,000 and the upward exposure to a judgement against the defendants was in excess of $1 million. The plaintiff, Pablo Rivas, and the boy who was driving, Anthony Ruiz, and a third boy were joy-riding in a car belonging to the uncle of Anthony Ruiz. Both Anthony Ruiz and the third person in the car were killed in the collision, and Pablo Rivas was severely injured. Suit was brought against the father and the uncle of Anthony Ruiz on a theory of negligent entrustment and negligent supervision. Briefly, both Pablo Rivas and Anthony Ruiz were young Latinos living in the same Denver neighborhood. Anthony Ruiz was 14 years old and was below the age at which he could legally drive a car. There was evidence that Anthony was having a number of behavior and academic problems at school, and that on one or more occasions he was seen driving a family vehicle around school buildings during and after school hours.

(continued)

(continued)

On the evening of the accident, Anthony Ruiz's parents left
him and his brother at home under the supervision of the uncle
while they attended a concert. Without the uncle's knowledge,
Anthony left the house with the keys to the uncle's car. He drove
the car away and picked up Pablo Rivas and the third boy for an
evening of joy-riding and the fateful accident.

The problem facing defense counsel was (1) a fair amount of
evidence that the parents knew of Anthony Ruiz's truancy and
proclivities to drive a car unlawfully, and (2) the fact of Pablo
Rivas' extensive injuries and the need for a lifetime of medical
care. Additionally, the State of Colorado had entered the case as
a party plaintiff to seek recovery of the extensive amount of
medical expenses it had incurred through Medicaid payment. A
decision was made that one of the Thematic Anchors would be the
loss to the parents of their son. Anthony Ruiz's parents were kept
at the defense table throughout the course of the trial even though
his mother was not a defendant in the case. Opening statement
was constructed so that the loss of Anthony Ruiz's life and the
resultant effect on the parents was woven through the recitation
of the facts which the defense sought to elicit during the trial of
the case. The strategy was risky since the defendant's insurance
carrier put forth less than $5,000 to settle the case despite its
large exposure.

The jury returned a defense verdict in the case. Several of the
women jurors were crying as the verdict was read in open court.
Later, in the hallway outside the courtroom several of the jurors
came up to Anthony Ruiz's parents to console them on the loss of
their child. Hence, it was apparent that the jurors had accepted
one of the Anchors that was put before them.

(continued)

However, there was an additional, but unstated, factor in the case which operated to the advantage of the defense. The State had entered the case to protect its subrogated interest in any award of damages. Plaintiff's counsel had sought to get the State to withdraw from the case in return for an agreement to assign a pro-rata share of any judgement to the State. However, the State was represented by an assistant attorney general who didn't get enough opportunities to take good cases to trial, so the offer of Plaintiff's counsel was rejected. The assistant attorney general not only sat in on the case but took an active role in the trial, examining witnesses and making an opening statement and closing argument. Not only was the jury informed that the State's Medicaid payments had covered all of the medical expenses for Plaintiff, but the clear impression was left that the State would continue to pick up the costs. Thus, the jury could reach its verdict without the guilt of leaving the Plaintiff without the means to meet his future medical expenses—all the while justifying their result in terms of lack of liability on the part of the father or uncle who were the defendants in the case.

James W. Creamer, Jr.
Creamer and Seaman, P.C., Denver

Using Thematic Anchors

When confronted with a large amount of information, jurors will normally attempt to reduce it to what psychologists call implicational molecules. These are sets of statements which, when taken together, are cognitively consistent. When an implicational molecule or set of statements is inconsistent, it is eliminated.

Implicational molecules display three basic characteristics: (1) they tend toward completion; (2) once completed, they are resistant to change; and (3) when there are non-fitting elements, there is pressure to eliminate or correct the inconsistency.

The existence of Thematic Anchors is consistent with the notion of implicational molecules. As the three or four key issues in the trial in the juror's mind, Thematic Anchors work like implicational molecules. They are closely related to basic attitudes, and they afford cognitive consistency.

We can now summarize the ways in which Thematic Anchors work:

1. Thematic Anchors work by linking the issues in the trial to basic attitudes and beliefs in the juror's mind.
2. Thematic Anchors work by enabling jurors to cope with psychological tension and cognitive dissonance.
3. Thematic Anchors work by offering jurors a clear and succinct way of selecting information, organizing information, and making judgements about the case based on anchor points and a frame of reference.

Safety, Not Age

In Iervolino v. Delta Air Lines, Inc., *a senior pilot was seeking to remain in the cockpit after reaching age 60. Most major airlines in the country faced such actions, and most of the cases had resulted in large money verdicts or settlements and reinstatement of older pilots. Such emotionally charged lawsuits were fraught with danger because of strong and rightfully held societal beliefs that people should not be terminated or discriminated against because of their age, gender, race, or religion. So from the outset there was a tendency to favor individuals perceived up front as having been mistreated, making such centrally held beliefs most difficult to dislodge or replace with a countervailing recognition that a company should not be punished if its conduct was justifiable.*

(continued)

(continued)

   To counteract preconceptions and the natural tendency of jurors to sympathize with the plight of people generally fit for continued employment at a time when 60-year-olds are considered in the prime of life with many productive years left, Delta's advocate determined to stress two basic themes to support Delta's motivation and conduct: passenger safety and public welfare versus self interest.

   To achieve that as a means of providing jurors with a sense of completeness and security, Delta's counsel told the jury in the very beginning and throughout the trial that Delta Air Lines' sole and overriding objective was to preserve and perpetuate for its passengers a safety record unequalled in the world; that while 60 year olds may safely serve in the work force in many roles (in banking, law and commerce in general), the decrements of age (from a cardiovascular standpoint, reaction time and similar critical functional needs) would imperil passenger safety; and that the self-interest of senior command pilots who enjoyed bountiful careers and privileges could not outweigh public interest. That position is perhaps best illustrated by the following excerpts from the opening statement:

   May it please the Court, may it please the jury, Delta Air Lines, and Delta's pilots. There are a number of facts and figures in history behind Delta's position that you will hear before this trial is over. And I would like to acquaint you briefly with what I anticipate that evidence will show.

   As I indicated, I'm talking about facts, figures and history. Very briefly, Delta Air Lines started as a crop dusting airline with its headquarters in Macon, Georgia, and

(continued)

(continued)

graduated to the aircraft with which most people are acquainted today. Delta, in its quest for safety, required all three crew members to be pilots. It was the first airline in this country to require that, even though it cost Delta more money to do it. And most other airlines in this country have emulated that policy as they have done with other Delta practices.

Delta has flown over 320 billion revenue passenger miles, transporting almost five million passengers, with the highest safety record of any airline since the invention of the airplane. And it is because of that record which was valiantly fought to be achieved that Delta seeks to protect the integrity of its cockpit. It has over fifteen hundred departures daily system-wide in the country, carrying an average of a hundred thousand passengers a day. It is currently averaging more than 18 hundred hours a day in the air, which is more take-offs and landings than any other airline in the free world, except one.

Why is that material? Delta felt it was material, believes that it's material because of the perpetuation of the practice of operating with the highest safety of which it's capable.

What Mr. Iervolino wants to do is to drop down from the former pilot in command, the captain at Delta, to the second officer seat. Delta said you can't do that. You can't permit a former captain, a man who has reached the pinnacle, to be relegated to a subordinate role and create these role reversal problems, these command authority problems.

That does not mean people this age are basket cases. They may be lawyers, they may be judges, but there are

(continued)

(continued)

> *certain things which they should not be, and one is in charge of five thousand pounds of death defying instrumentalities which can result in catastrophe unless that person is vibrant and has a cognitive functioning power to enable him to perform his responsibilities in the highest interest of safety.*
>
> *And it is for all those reasons and for none other, that Delta Air Lines said to Mr. Iervolino, we cannot let you do that. It is not in the pilot's interest, and it is not in the public's interest. Delta has, as I have demonstrated, the pilot's interest at heart, it's ground personnel's interest at heart. Unequalled maintenance, unequalled morale, unequalled esprit de corps, produced the most enviable safety record in the world by doing these things.*
>
> *So it is not a question of age.*
>
> *What is being sought here is not in the highest and best interest of safety. Based on the evidence, we would expect each of you to return a verdict in favor of Delta Air Lines. The relief Mr. Iervolino seeks for himself is, in reality, public endangerment.*
>
> *Eugene G. Partain*
> *King & Spalding, Atlanta*

The effectiveness of Thematic Anchors is dependent upon presenting them in a highly structured context. Both the message contained in the Anchor, and the context in which it is used, ought to be consistent with the basic attitudinal structure of the jury. Consequently, careful thought must go into positioning Thematic Anchors. In opening statements they should appear as an overt or direct statement rather than in the form of connotation or innuendo. To maximize their effectiveness, Anchors should be articulated as short, easy to remember mnemonics and presented with clarity and specificity. It is also sometimes possible to introduce them this way in voir dire. Anchors should be repeated throughout the trial whenever possible. All the evidence should be introduced in support of the Anchors, and testimony should harmonize with the Anchors and even emphasize their content. In closing arguments, attorneys can then point out how the Anchors provide a coherent view of the case.

The role of Thematic Anchors has been explored in a large number of jury trials. Anchors give a juror a way to organize and integrate the bits and pieces of information introduced and discussed during the trial—information which might otherwise be forgotten. For jurors who are confused, impatient, or fatigued, Anchors can be a useful thread of meaning in a labyrinth of information. For jurors who reason deductively, Anchors can key into preconceptions and provide an avenue to a desired conclusion. Typically, Anchors provide opinion leaders with the means to convert other jurors. Anchors can also give a positively disposed juror the means to hold out against the other jurors when a hung jury might constitute a victory for a litigant. In addition, they provide another important function: for jurors already committed to a verdict decision, Anchors can become ammunition for converting others.

Thematic Anchors: Two Case Studies

We will conclude our discussion of Thematic Anchors with the presentation of two case studies. The first involves a complex commercial dispute involving a high profile business plaintiff. The second relates to the use of Thematic Anchors in an antitrust case.

A Powerful Psychological Anchor: "Too Big Too Fast"

A few years ago there was a dispute between a television shopping program network and a telephone equipment manufacturer. The network claimed that the manufacturer had misrepresented the capabilities of its equipment, which was technically deficient in processing calls from prospective customers. The alleged problems included calls being blocked or dropped before an operator could answer, resulting in millions of dollars in lost sales. There were also reports of equipment malfunctions such as sudden loud noises on the line which hurt operators' ears. The plaintiff was also dissatisfied with the lack of competent service and repair. The network had been very successful and popular and had experienced incredible growth, which seemed to buttress its damage analysis.

The defendant had many potential arguments to make on its behalf. It had a detailed story about the positive relationship it had had with the plaintiff over time. There was a great deal to say about the equipment, its design, development, and use in this and other applications. Of course, to thoroughly understand this technical detail, jurors would have to wade through fairly complex information and unfamiliar concepts and vocabulary. There were also details in the agreements between the two parties that could be positioned to support any number of arguments for either side. However, many of these points were also fairly technical in nature and were not the kind of details that would invigorate a group of non-lawyers. There was also a plethora of financial and economic testimony which each side planned to offer.

An extensive research study was conducted in the venue to determine which case issues jurors would find most salient in constructing a story about the case. Jurors watched each case presentation and were questioned extensively about their perceptions, attitudes, and decisions. Although the research revealed that jurors were split on many of the technical issues (of which the comprehension was moderate to low), there was near consensus on what the case was really about. In the jurors' opinion, this was really a case about a company (the network) which simply grew beyond its capabilities to manage itself. Jurors used the expression "too big too fast" in evaluating the case and in explaining their perception of the plaintiff. This research finding revealed a powerful heuristic (see Chapter 3) which the defense attorney developed into a Thematic Anchor. This Anchor provided jurors with a familiar, efficient, and memorable way to deal with an otherwise complex case. This type of anchor is particularly powerful because it has the effect of allowing jurors to feel psychologically comfortable with their decisions—it could easily account for the problems encountered by the plaintiff.

This discovery opened up many other strategic possibilities. For example, instead of finding ways to offset the plaintiff's success story, the defendant could acknowledge and even applaud the plaintiff's rise to success because it now supported a key thematic element of its story about an otherwise successful business that got in over its head. Not only did the defendant win the case, the jury awarded damages *against* the plaintiff!

One particularly challenging case involving the development of Thematic Anchors occurred in the computer industry. A group of distributors filed suit against manufacturers of computer equipment for conspiring to fix prices in order to keep the costs of accessory components artificially high. Evidence in this case was ambiguous. While there was very little actual evidence of collusion among the defendants, their prices were suspiciously similar. In general, these prices were significantly higher than those charged by other suppliers of similar equipment.

Initial research on behalf of the defendants consisted of a series of small group experimental projects. From this research, the pencil and paper responses of a large number of subjects and later the results of four surrogate juries were available. In the early phases of the research, one issue raised by a large number of subjects was the *process* by which list prices were established. Jurors were curious about the ratio of labor to parts charges, how time was factored into costs, and how markups were employed to establish prices at various levels in the distribution system. As the group was observed wrestling with these issues, it became clear that it would be necessary to provide jurors with a metaphor of an equation or formula. Jurors needed a simple structure as a way of explaining how a complex set of variables were combined to determine a price. In follow-up studies, it was discovered that presenting pricing as a function of formulas or equations was an effective way of simplifying the complex economic issues in this trial. The metaphor permitted jurors to focus on the mechanical aspects of price determination. Consequently, the following Anchor was recommended: "There are three or four commonly used pricing formulas in this industry." This Anchor directly addressed the weakness of the client's case—similar prices among the defendant companies. Moreover, by using the word "formula," the lawyers set up a psychological rationale through which jurors could accept the fact that several companies in the industry could arrive at similar prices without being in collusion with regard to certain product lines and similar equipment.

While the first Anchor was aimed at repairing the defendants' principal vulnerability in this case, the second reinforced their major strength. This strength was the fact that there was no actual evidence of collusion among the three firms involved. In analyzing the handwritten responses of surrogate jurors to open-ended questions, a curious pattern was observed. Plaintiff-oriented jurors tended to deal with the issue of collusion in the abstract.   They were quite willing to believe that corporate executives do indeed get together to further their goals and would certainly do so with respect to price. Defense-oriented jurors were looking for specific indications of collusive behavior. With this finding, the trial team wanted to develop strategies to force plaintiff jurors to deal with the conspiracy issue in the concrete rather than in the abstract. And hence, they needed to focus the notion of conspiracy *definitionally* on specific behaviors. They wanted to force the plaintiff jurors to deal with the fact that there was no evidence of collusion in the case as a definitional condition for a verdict in opposition to their predisposition. At the same time, it was necessary to reinforce defense jurors' perceptions of conspiracy based on concrete behavior. Hence, the Anchor was worded: "People get together to conspire." The real value of this second Anchor was that it served as a constant reminder to the jury that the burden of proof that collusion had taken place was on the plaintiff and that the plaintiff would not be able to produce such proof. Jurors whose judgement would have been based on a conceptual abstraction were forced to confront factual reality.

Structuring the Opening Statement

Pre-trial research consistently reveals that jurors evaluate information presented in opening statements as more probative and salient to their final determination of the case than information they receive at any other time during the trial. To insure that the opening statement given by the attorney is the same one received by the jury, trial lawyers can focus on four important attributes which characterize an effective opening statement:

1.   A direct sense of organization.
2.   Sensitivity to the characteristics of the jurors.
3.   Attention to nonverbal cues.
4.   A commitment to practice and rehearsal.

We all know that the most effective and persuasive presentations are those that draw on emotion, character, and plot. In an opening statement context, this can be accomplished by employing a narrative organizational format.   A narrative presentation is very much like telling a story. Chronology and actors are of prime importance. Juries continually use narratives to "make sense" out of the myriads of facts, conflicting testimony, and difficult or confusing evidence. Without construction of his version of the "story," the attorney faces the danger that the jurors will construct their own. And their version may be inconsistent or even incompatible with the lawyer's!

The appropriate use of a narrative in an opening statement must accomplish two important objectives. First, it must draw on what the attorney knows about the jurors' pre-existing attitudes, values, beliefs, and knowledge; it must fit in with their intellectual and emotional decision-making styles; and it must be incorporated into their belief system. Evidence can and will be compared with the narrative for both consistency and relevancy by the jury. Inconsistent and irrelevant information will often be disbelieved, reinterpreted, distorted, or forgotten, while the underlying story remains essentially the same. Second and equally important, Thematic Anchors must be woven into the narrative for maximum effectiveness. Opening statements based on narratives with these "sign-posts" to guide the jury will provide the prerequisite framework for jurors to interpret what follows during the evidentiary portion of the trial.

Using Thematic Anchors

In addition to identifying the Thematic Anchors in the opening statement, we must be sure that the juror remembers them in order to utilize them throughout the trial. In order to increase the likelihood that the Thematic Anchors are firmly implanted in the juror's mind, a trial lawyer should never overlook the value of repetition. I have found it particularly useful to organize my opening statement in a way which permits me to repeat the important Thematic Anchors so that by the end of the opening statement, all the jurors should be able to recite them by heart. The pattern I usually use is to first identify for the jury three or four important points on which our case rests, by a declarative and easily remembered phrase for each. I then start with the first point and discuss it. When I move to the second, I first repeat the key phrase of the first as an introduction to my second point.

(continued)

(continued)

When I move to the third point, I repeat the key phrases of the first and second, and so forth. By the time I have finished, there is practically a cadence to my articulation of the points which any juror should be able to repeat. I believe in addition to primacy-recency, repetition is the most effective tool to insure that a juror will utilize the Thematic Anchors.

Michael B. Keating
Foley Hoag & Eliot, Boston

Typically, opening statements present arguments in a temporal or linear fashion. A series of events is related chronologically: "On January 3rd, some action took place; on February 15th, there was this response." There are a number of approaches to the problem of organizing an opening statement which may be more effective. First, as we have seen, it may be useful to base the opening statement on a series of major themes in the case. Second, factual topics can be employed as a basis for organizing the statement. Third, previews can be given of key witness testimony to serve as an organizational format. Fourth, critical events can provide a skeleton for the opening statement and for the case as a whole. Finally, it is often possible for constellations of facts, not necessarily related in chronological order, to provide the content of an opening statement.

Two final points relating to effective opening statements are probably gratuitous but are nevertheless frequently forgotten. First, preparation and practicing delivery are two of the most valuable pre-trial activities on which a lawyer can spend his time. Consequently, the opening statement should be rehearsed extensively and before a video camera whenever possible. Notwithstanding comments that practicing an opening statement intrudes upon valuable time that should be allocated to other things, or that the opening will appear rehearsed and lack spontaneity, truly effective speakers thoroughly practice and rehearse before any major presentation. The great communicators of our time, Churchill, Kennedy, and Reagan, were well known for fastidious preparation before any important communication effort.

The second point about effective opening statements is that most of them are too long! When confronted with long opening statements, jurors are likely to become stimulus overloaded, confused, and even possibly bored. Because of the limitation of the human attention span, lawyers simply begin to lose their jury after about 20-30 minutes. Except in rare cases where counsel has deliberately decided to bore the jury (e.g., because more central persuasion methods are deemed ineffective), we have not seen a case that necessitated more of the jury's initial attention than a short 20- to 30-minute opening. This includes cases involving highly sophisticated and complex scientific, technological, and financial issues. As a case in point, Joe Jamail's opening statement in *Penzoil v. Texaco* was approximately 25 minutes long.

Conclusions

In all that we have said thus far about opening statements, sensitivity to the characteristics of the jurors has been implied. Juror profiles are the beginning of this sensitivity. These profiles developed through pre-trial research efforts can be refined by psychological observations made during voir dire. They can also be supplemented by our knowledge of previous juries in the venue. Understanding the psychological and behavioral characteristics of jurors permits the attorney to not only select the components of the opening statement which will be consistent with jurors' cognitions, but also to focus on and fine-tune the most appropriate techniques of persuasion.

CHAPTER 9

The Psychology of Demonstrative Evidence

Psychological Influences

In the previous chapters, we examined the ways in which jurors perceive, process, and make decisions about the information which is presented to them in the courtroom. One important aspect of this sequence which requires closer scrutiny is that of the psychological influence upon perception and in particular upon visual perception.

Current journal articles and books on litigation frequently make reference to the importance of demonstrative exhibits. In most instances these focus on issues of admissibility with little or no attention devoted to the psychological aspects of the topic. For the trial lawyer, it is these psychological attributes that make demonstrative exhibits such a powerful tool in the courtroom.

Jurors learn through all five of their perceptual senses. Chart 1, below, lists each of the five senses along with the percentage of information learned through each.

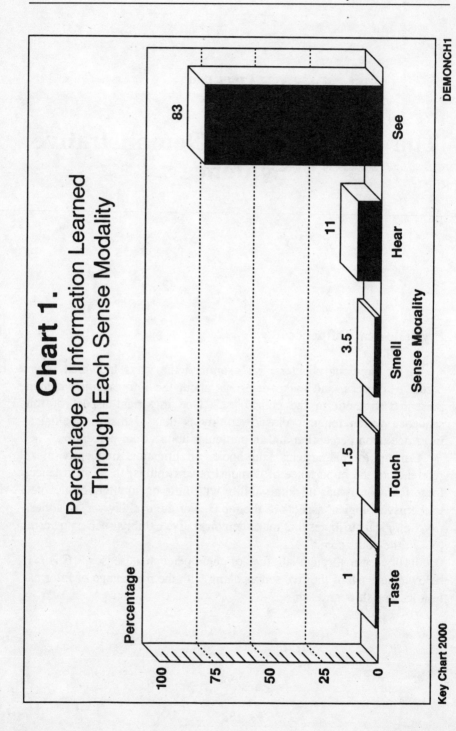

Chart 1.
Percentage of Information Learned
Through Each Sense Modality

Percentage

100

75

50

25

0

83

11

3.5

1.5

1

See

Hear

Smell

Touch

Taste

Sense Modality

Key Chart 2000

DEMONCH1

As illustrated by the chart, most learning occurs visually. In the courtroom, however, a different sense modality is typically employed, almost to the exclusion of the other four: hearing. Verbal testimony has been the mainstay of evidentiary proof in the courtroom for centuries and, in fact, law students are almost exclusively taught by the verbal Socratic method. The lawyer, trained in this method, is naturally comfortable using it.

However, jurors for the most part are not versed in the Socratic method and they do not rely principally upon verbal proofs and dialectics to learn. Of course, the courtroom enlists visual evidence to the extent that the jurors visually observe the witnesses and occasionally are shown substantive exhibits, but generally, the sense of sight is relegated to a minor role in many courtroom proceedings. Given the impact of a visual medium coupled with verbal information it is important to emphasize the enormous importance of visual communication to jurors.

When "One and One" Does Not Equal Two

Educators have for many years utilized a maxim in the educational process: Use as many perceptual senses as possible to get your point across. Merely lecturing to students is not as effective for teaching as is lecturing in addition to employing visual aids in the classroom.   To illustrate the effectiveness of coupling auditory with visual stimuli, the graph below (Chart 2) illustrates retention after "telling" alone, retention after "showing" alone, and retention after both "telling and showing." The combined effect of "telling and showing" together is greater than a simple doubling of their relative contributions.

The Seven Figure Investment

We were defending corporate management in a securities fraud case. Management had purchased all of the stock owned by outside investors, and within days of the sale the corporation was experimenting with a brand new electronic product. Within a few months, the corporation marketed the invention, which caused annual sales to triple.

(continued)

(continued)

We wanted to emphasize to the jury (a) how wealthy these investors were and (b) what a fine return they had gotten from their initial investment in the corporation. We prepared a large poster-board for each investor, showing the amount of this initial investment (usually ten thousand dollars) and we included the total amount received in dividends over the eight to ten-year period of the investment. Then we added the investor's stock sales price to come up with the gross return on his investment. Subtracting the initial cost from the seven-figure gross return left a seven-figure net return on investment for each of them. All words and numbers were black except for the bottom figure (net return) which was much larger, in red.

We showed the jury these boards during opening statement, we cross examined from the boards (asking each investor whether he had ever had a higher return on an investment, and we did not care which way he answered—either way helped us), and based on cross or on later direct testimony, were able to have each board entry authenticated. We were successful in introducing each board into evidence so that the jury members were able to take the boards with them into deliberations. The boards obviously had little to do with the merits of whether management had misled the investors, but they had everything to do with leveling the playing field. We used them in closing argument to reemphasize the wealth, sophistication and good fortune of each investor. During the trial, we made a seven-figure settlement offer, which was rejected by the plaintiff investors. Following a verdict in favor of the defendants, we interviewed jurors and found that indeed they had been influenced by these boards.

Warren B. Lightfoot
Lightfoot Franklin White & Lucas, Birmingham

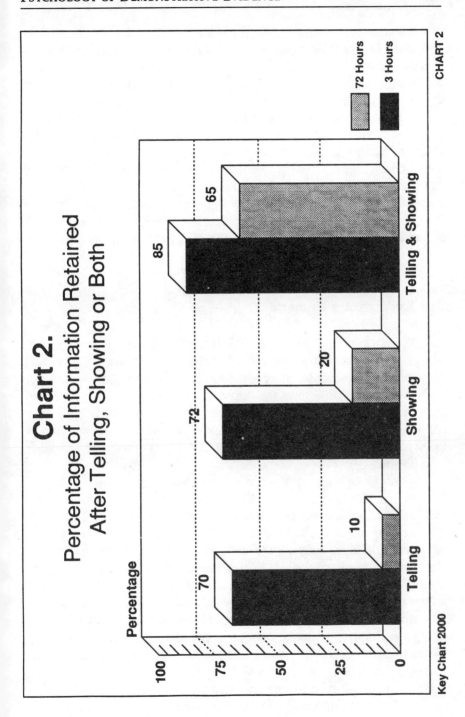

Chart 2.
Percentage of Information Retained
After Telling, Showing or Both

CHART 2

72 Hours
3 Hours

Key Chart 2000

Retention after "telling" was 70% after three hours but dropped to 10% after 72 hours. Retention after "showing" was 72% after three hours and 20% after 72 hours. The largest amount of retention occurs with a combination of both "telling" and "showing": 85% after three hours and 65% after 72 hours.

The courtroom may be appropriately viewed as an educational milieu where both trial teams are attempting to explain, educate, and persuade jurors as well as reinforce already existing beliefs which the jurors may hold. Clearly then, a lawyer who not only tells the jury, for example, that the defendant is an expert marksman with a Mauser rifle, but also shows the jury a target riddled empty in the center by bullets which were fired by the defendant on a practice range, is utilizing the powerful senses of sound and sight to impress upon the jurors the defendant's shooting skills.

The Eye is Not a Camera

The functioning of the human eye has often been compared to that of a camera, however the analogy is less than a perfect one. Physiologically the eye functions differently from a camera in that we are not conscious of the "still" shots that form on the retina. Vision is an active exploratory process. We concentrate our attention on interesting events within a narrow segment of our total field of vision and what determines the narrow segment of our field of vision has more to do with psychology than physiology.

At any given moment, the eye may contain over two million bits of information. The eye is never still—it trembles continuously with what is known as saccadic movements, and thereby constantly shifts information between and among individual cells. To compound the rapid shifting of stimuli within the retina, we constantly "scan" the objects we look at. Our gaze is only fixed for two to eight tenths of a second upon any part of the visual field. So given the tremendous potential for visual information at any given moment, how is it that we ever make "sense" of it? How do we keep from becoming overloaded with stimuli?

Quite simply, we avoid sensory overload by actively picking and choosing from among the visual information which is presented to us. For example, when you use a TV's remote control to flip through the channels, your attention on any one channel may be focused for as little as one second before you switch to the next channel. This means that you were capable of not only viewing an image but of comprehending what you saw and also of deciding whether or not it was worth watching, all in only one second! In order for this complex process to transpire so quickly, an automatic and instantaneous coupling of physiological and psychological processes had to occur.

One assumption which is frequently made about vision is that when someone "sees" something, it is an "objective" process: a physiological one which is fairly invariant from person to person, providing, of course, that the person has adequate vision.   However, research in human perception has demonstrated that seeing something is actually a subjective experience.   We make use both consciously and unconsciously of a "knowledge base" to find, focus on, and identify objects in our visual scene.   The objects in our visual field which are influenced by our knowledge base may be inanimate objects, animals, or people. For example, in one study subjects watched a videotape of a woman. Half the subjects were told that she was a librarian and half were told that she was a waitress. The videotape showed the woman engaged in many day-to-day activities such as listening to classical music, playing the piano, watching television, consuming beverages, and so on. Later the subjects were asked questions regarding what they had seen on the videotape, such as "What kind of music did the woman listen to?" and "What did she drink?" The subjects who were told that the woman was a librarian remembered that she listened to classical music and erroneously "remembered" that she drank wine whereas the subjects who were told she was a waitress recalled that she watched TV and drank beer and so on. The subjects in this study had a knowledge base about librarians and waitresses. This knowledge base consisted of the kinds of activities the subjects thought would coincide with the occupation of waitress or librarian.   This information base caused the subjects to remember information presented on the videotape which was consistent with their knowledge base and to ignore or forget the information which was not consistent with their *prior* knowledge.

This "knowledge base" consists not only of a juror's past formal learning experiences, but also of the attitudes and beliefs which are brought into the courtroom that exist prior to the trial. These attitudes and beliefs actually serve as a "filter" or "lens" (to borrow from the camera analogy), which actively directs the juror's attention. This "filter" allows the juror to see certain things but not others. It allows him to understand new information in terms with which he is familiar and to quickly discard other information which to him makes no coherent sense.

Thus a juror's pre-existing attitudes actually determine which images attract his attention, what he finds interesting and involving, and what he actually "sees."

Demonstrative Evidence: Strategy

When demonstrative evidence is intended to be educational and explanatory, the rationale behind the content of the demonstrative illustration is somewhat different than when it is to be used persuasively. An example from a toxic tort case illustrates one important way demonstrative evidence can educate and inform jurors. One idea which was important to the defense's position and which was vital to juror comprehension of a wide array of evidence in the case was the concept of dose/response. Dose/response is a simple, albeit for many, counter-intuitive, concept: *anything*, be it milk or strychnine, in sufficiently large quantities can be poisonous.

In pre-trial research conducted for this case, an expert witness explained the concept of dose/response to the surrogate jurors. After the witness' explanation, the jurors were questioned to determine how well they understood his testimony. It was found that the jurors did not understand the dose/response explanation which the witness had presented and further, when the surrogate jurors deliberated, the dose/response issue was not utilized as part of their discussions or of their subsequent decision-making.

To address this problem, an exhibit board was designed (see Diagram 1) which pictorially displayed the lethal dosages of several commonly used substances, e.g. coffee, as well as the lethal dosage of the substance in question.

The same expert witness then testified to a new group of surrogate jurors using this exhibit board as an aid. The addition of this simple visual concept resulted in an increase in the juror's understanding of the dose/response concept and became an important element in interpreting a critical set of facts from the defendant's perspective. The exhibit board focused the jurors' visual attention by narrowing their perceptual field. Recall the question previously proposed; how does one make sense of all the visual stimuli the eye is physiologically capable of receiving? In this example, rather than allowing the juror's pre-existing attitudes to dictate where they looked and how they interpreted what they saw, the lawyer picked and chose *for* the jurors. Among the infinite number of possible

Diagram 1

006 Text/Icon

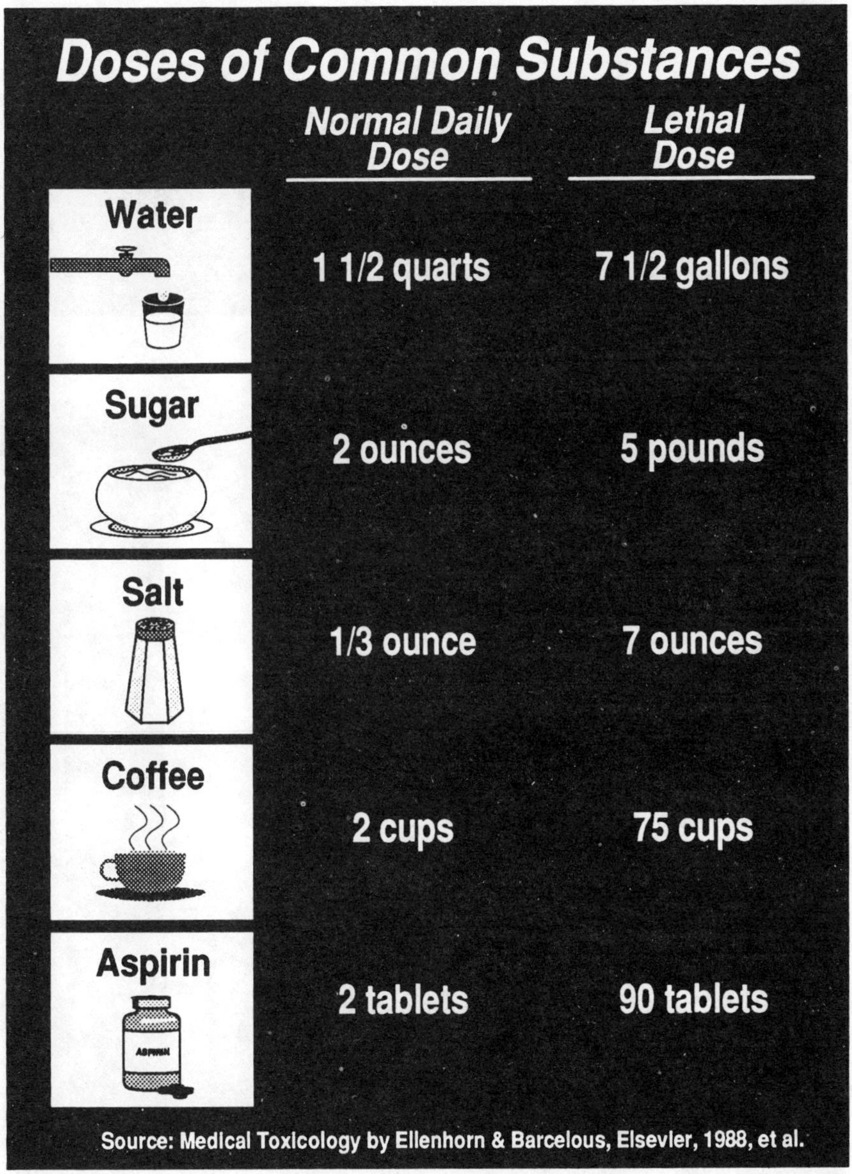

Doses of Common Substances

	Normal Daily Dose	Lethal Dose
Water	1 1/2 quarts	7 1/2 gallons
Sugar	2 ounces	5 pounds
Salt	1/3 ounce	7 ounces
Coffee	2 cups	75 cups
Aspirin	2 tablets	90 tablets

Source: Medical Toxicology by Ellenhorn & Barcelous, Elsevier, 1988, et al.

things to look at during the testimony, the lawyer chose a simple visual image that effectively communicated a difficult verbal idea.   For additional illustrations of similar effective displays, see Diagrams 2 and 3.

Diagram 2

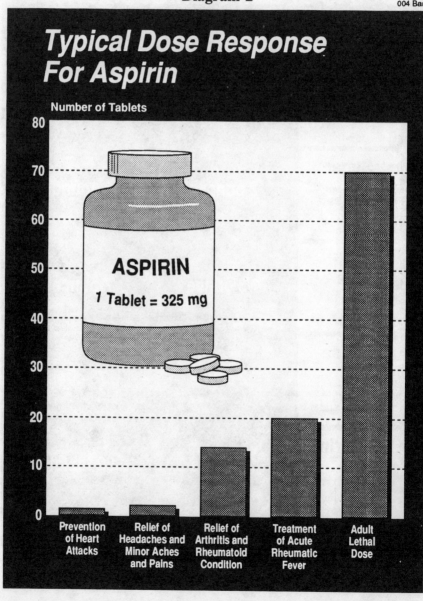

Diagram 3

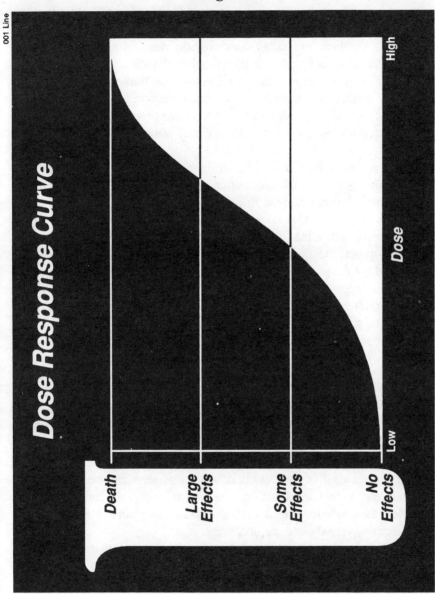

Based upon the results of this pre-trial research, the defense attorney could then proceed with his case, using the expert witness' testimony coupled with the visual aid, confident that his ideas would be communicated effectively.

There are several important elements which should be considered when any demonstrative exhibit is created for educational or explanatory purposes. First, the exhibit must convey a clear and unambiguous message. The visual message must provide meaning rather quickly as it is simultaneously coupled with the verbal explanation. Just as drivers do not back up on freeways to re-read messages on billboards, jurors do not typically ponder, on their own without direction, the visual displays which they see in the courtroom. The lawyer or witness must direct the juror's attention to the visual display and simultaneously provide the verbal explanation.

The aid must be simple and straightforward without presenting an overwhelming amount of information at one time. If the information is too complex, jurors will tend to either tune out the information or attend to only a part of it. The lawyer has no control as to which part of the exhibit jurors will attend to on their own. That is why the lawyer must actively direct the juror's attention.   This active directing can be facilitated by the use of verbal "cues."

Verbal cues can be included in the witness's testimony to create a point or reference for the visual aid. Visual aids by themselves are not likely to be retained in memory without explanation and verbal cues can create simple memory connections for jurors. Think of a verbal cue as a single word or phrase which is repeated several times in reference to the visual exhibit. For example, in the dose/response exhibit board, the witness could have referred to the "hundreds of bottles" necessary for toxicity. The phrase "hundreds of bottles" then becomes a verbal cue to jog visual memory of the exhibit. Refer again to the information on Chart 2, which represents the amount of retention after both "telling" and "showing." There is a brief period of time after seeing something, during which a great deal of the details of what was seen can be recalled, but without the verbal explanation, the visual image is quickly lost in memory. In order to embed the information in jurors' memories more permanently, verbal cues are necessary.

Graphic exhibits must be presented in a context that is free from extraneous and distracting information. Jurors receive much more information than they can attend to and process. Their minds "wander" when they are being talked to or shown something. The critical problem for the lawyer at all times, and especially with regard to a demonstrative exhibit, is to see that the juror's attention is focused where it needs to be for effective communication of the message.   There should be no distractions and the exhibit itself should contain no ambiguous elements or eye-catching effects that are not directly related to the message.

Text Type. The choice of text and type font may enhance a juror's understanding of a visual exhibit. Typographic styles with serifs and Roman type are easier to read than line type or sans serif. Running text should be in lower case letter rather than all capitals. The use of all capital letters significantly reduces reading speed. The text of an exhibit should appear to the jurors about five times larger than the text in a book, so perspective should be considered and prior thought given to the placement of exhibits in the courtroom. Optimum line length should be forty characters and research has shown that for unskilled readers, unjustified text is easier to read than justified text.

The Psychological Center. Recall that seeing is not an objective process, but rather a subjective one. When jurors view a demonstrative exhibit, their visual center is different from the geometric center of the exhibit. (See Table 1.) A juror's eyes tend to focus on the upper one-third of the exhibit initially, and primarily at the upper left quadrant before looking at the rest of the exhibit. Because of this, where possible, critical information should be located within these zones. For this reason, titles and summaries of well-designed exhibits are typically placed in the upper left hand corner.

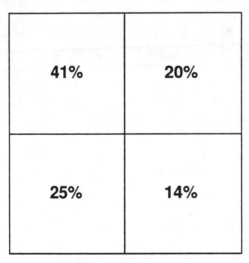

Table 1. Where jurors first look at an exhibit.

The Strategic Use of Exhibits

In addition to advancing knowledge of demonstrative exhibits as vehicles of persuasion, in recent years they have become an ever increasing tool for discussion, particularly when multiple exhibits are used for impeachment. This methodology has become common among more advanced trial practitioners and involves the use of two exhibits dealing with the same subject: one particular and one generalized. Examples are an anatomically correct drawing of part of the human body and a freehand drawing of the same body part, or a scale drawing of the road crash site and an in-court sketch made by one of the witnesses. In this methodology the witness to be discredited is asked to view the generalized exhibit, or even to make a drawing himself. Examination then continues concerning the witness' testimony, and finally the witness is asked to show on the exhibit some critical point, such as the location of a wound on the drawing of the body part. The exhibit will be marked with this location, usually by the witness himself. Later another witness is called by the proponent of these exhibits. He will be shown the anatomically correct diagram and asked to locate the wound. After doing so, he will, based upon the location of the wound on the anatomically correct diagram, be shown the freehand diagram and asked to explain why the first witness' testimony was in error. This explanation will be expansive, making liberal use of the anatomically correct exhibit. By this means the proponent of the exhibits will clearly establish in the jurors' minds the notion that the first witness does not know or does not recall with exactitude the evidence he has given, or, as is often the case with an expert, that he is operating on an incorrect factual understanding in the formation of his opinions.

Another variation of this method is to have the second witness mark the freehand exhibit "in the proper place" and then argue the correctness of his marking with the support of the more particular exhibit. In either case, the effect on the jury is

(continued)

(continued)

significant, since it is treated in the trial as a recognizable mini-issue: did the first witness know what he was talking about or not?

The answer to this ambush by diagram is the making of a motion in limine that if the opposing party has any prepared exhibits or diagrams, he be required to use that exhibit throughout, and be barred from making any freehand exhibits which deal with the same subject matter. This has been fairly effective in limiting such practices. Danger, however, continues to exist where freehand diagrams have been made at the witness' deposition, and acknowledgement of such is requested at trial. Ground can be lost by this means as well as by exhibits created in the courtroom. The same situation can arise even from the use at deposition of photographs which have not been authenticated, but which are marked by the deponent, and later prove not to correctly represent the scene. Counsel for the opponent should resist as far as possible all such practices, for although the witness can explain that he now sees that the exhibit should be marked at a different place, the credibility and certainty of his testimony is invariably weakened in the jury's mind.

Robert A. Clifford
Law Offices of Robert A. Clifford
and Associates, P.C., Chicago

Essentially, we know that jurors process information and hence are subject to persuasion in one of two ways. If a juror is very interested and involved in the topic which is presented to him by the lawyer or witness, he will utilize a "central" route to processing the information. That is, he will attend to the cogent arguments, weigh them, and make a decision. Does this mean that if the juror is uninterested the lawyer cannot persuade him? Not really. Jurors who lack interest in the issues are persuadable. They will be persuaded via a "peripheral" route, a route generally beyond the purview of the verbal argument. There are an infinite number of peripheral cues in the courtroom. The strength of a well-designed demonstrative exhibit is that it can focus jurors' attention on the information the lawyer wants them to retain. Advertisers are adroit in their use of this technique: a billboard which warrants only a glance on the freeway will contain a colorful or sexy image coupled with the product name. Even though the motorist is uninvolved with the actual product, he will have a generally positive reaction to the appeal of the ad. This coupling of a positive visual image in the ad creates a generally positive attitude toward the product.

Gestalt Psychology

Gestalt is a German word for "whole" and the Gestalt School of Psychology, which began in the early part of this century, focused on how people organize visual information and groups of visual elements so that they are perceived as whole. Visual perception is seen as an organized process that operates according to rules which prescribe that the perception of an object or event cannot be broken down into its single component parts.

There are several principles of Gestalt Psychology which predict how a person will perceive a visual image. These are:

1. Area: the smaller the closed portion of an image the more it is apt to "look" like a complete figure.

2. Closedness: Areas with closed boundaries or edges are more likely to be seen as a complete figure.

3. Proximity: Items placed close together are likely to be grouped together in the viewer's mind.

4. Continuation: Arrangements that have few interruptions in a line will be viewed as a complete figure.

5. Symmetry: The more symmetrical an area, the more likely it will be seen as a complete figure.

The utilization of these basic Gestalt principles in the arrangement of the elements in a demonstrative evidence can encourage jurors to see the relationships we want them to see. Additionally, proper arrangement will aid in learning and retention. For example, images presented in close proximity require less memory storage and hence are recalled quickly. Again, instead of relying upon the pre-existing attitudes which the juror brings into the courtroom, a well-designed exhibit can, by using these principles of organization, help direct the jurors' attention to a specific issue, topic, or idea.

Referring back to the toxic tort case discussed earlier, it may important to demonstrate visually for the jury just exactly what "one part per million" of content means. To accomplish this, Gestalt principles can be employed by showing a field of dots in which just one small dot is bright red, while all other dots are blue. The visualization of one dot juxtaposed to a solid field of blue puts into perspective the meaning of this term.

Color. Although there are cultural differences in how people interpret colors, American's preference for the primary colors from most to least is: blue, red, and yellow. Likability of a color is only one dimension that must be considered in designing demonstrative exhibits. High contrast colors are more likely to attract a juror's attention, and for this reason the most important elements of the exhibit should have the brightest colors and the highest contrast. These high contrast colors are white, yellow, and green. Research indicates that the use of more than four or five colors in one exhibit is distracting and should be avoided. The improper use or combination of colors can reduce the impact of the message, or worse, convey the wrong message. Thus, colors must be carefully chosen rather than randomly selected, based upon the preferences of the trial lawyer or paralegal.

Visual Cues. Color coding can enhance and make connections for jurors which are easily understood and readily recalled. These codes or cues can be utilized throughout the trial to create a unity to the visual exhibits. For example, if the jury is to be shown a number of exhibit boards summarizing financial information, the background for the information should be color coded. In this scenario, items dealing with audit, taxation, cash flow, and future projections, for instance, can be separated by assigning each category a distinct color to appear as a band across the top of the exhibit as background to the title. Without this visual cue, all charts in such a complex case would appear merely as "lots of numbers" to jurors. This subtle segregation cues jurors to be alert for different areas of testimony. In this way, although several separate clusters of exhibits are shown, jurors are able to connect them quickly using color as a guide.

Types of Demonstrative Exhibits

There are seven basic types of presentation media which are typically utilized in the courtroom:

1. <u>Still-visual</u>, which consists of still pictures, prints, chalk-talk sketches, still graphics, slide projection, and the printed page.

2. <u>Audio</u>, which consists of tape and disk recordings.

3. <u>Audio combined with the still-visual</u>, for example, a sound film, slide series, or sound-on-slide in which each slide has its own recording, usually on a magnetic band which accompanies the slide.

4. <u>Motion-visual with or without audio</u>, for example, silent motion picture or sound motion picture.

5. <u>Television</u>, which can consist of still-pictures, moving line visuals, or complete video that has motion and sound.

6. <u>Physical models</u>, which may be scale models or life-size replicas.

7. <u>Computer graphics</u>, which may consist of computer printouts produced in the courtroom or simulation models either produced in the courtroom after entering data into a computer which is programmed with a model or scenario of the physical world, or produced prior to the trial and displayed in high resolution graphics mode.

The Laser Disk

The laser disk provides the lawyer with one medium for the instant presentation of evidence on the TV screen. It is one of the newest courtroom technologies and it allows instantaneous access to tangible evidence in the form of both still and moving images. One laser disk can store over 54,000 images on each side. These images can be documents, videotapes, photographs, diagrams, drawings, charts and graphs, or virtually anything tangible. Using an electronic device that resembles a VCR player, the information can be instantly retrieved and displayed to the jurors via high resolution television monitors in the courtroom. This alleviates the fumbling and searching for exhibits which can occur, especially as the number of exhibits and documents used at trial increases.

One advantage the laser disk technology provides is that the exhibits may be included on the disk in several different formats, e.g., with or without labeling, enlarged as well as reduced, with color and without color. This allows for instant last minute "changes" in the format of the exhibit which might be necessary due to opposing counsel's objections.

Additionally, the laser disk allows the use of videotapes with a relative ease of access which is not available on conventional VCR. Freeze-frames may be performed without loss of resolution, due to the digital nature of the laser disk versus the VCR format.

Laser Disk vs. Conventional Presentation. Both state and federal courts have allowed optically stored digital images to be used as evidence in trials and they may in the future replace the use of conventional physical documents. However, one word of caution is warranted. There are times when the full impact of a large exhibit which may remain in the courtroom during the entire trial is desirable: Careful consideration must be given to the overall objective of the exhibit and the trade-off of choosing the laser disk medium over other forms of presenting this evidence. Professionally trained graphics consultants working closely with the lawyer can advise more specifically whether or not the laser disk is an appropriate medium for use in a particular case.

Some lawyers are hesitant to use the laser disk technology because they believe it might alienate the jury or be perceived as too "high tech" or too "slick." In post-trial interviews conducted with jurors who were presented with evidence via the laser disk medium, the general response has been a positive one. While jurors feel favorably predisposed toward the images they had seen on the TV, they were unaware of the actual laser disk equipment or of the sophistication involved in its use. After all, TV is a comfortable communication medium for most people. Sixty-eight percent of the US population report that watching TV is their main source of pleasure. The typical American watches two to three hours of TV a day (the set is turned on an average of seven hours a day in US households) and TV has come to be accepted as a legitimate source of information. At the mall, there are TV screens to help shoppers find the location of stores; in understaffed classrooms students learn from TV lecturers; and the TV screen brings Nintendo and entertainment games to hundreds of thousands of young people every day. Due to its familiarity, the presence of the TV in a courtroom has become a singularly unremarkable event to jurors.

One case involving the use of the laser disk illustrates how the TV medium is accepted by jurors. The defendant was a large corporation. The plaintiff was an individual and the venue was a small rural community. Most of the demonstrative evidence presented during the trial was shown on TV monitors. In post-trial interviews, none of the jurors mentioned the laser disk until they were prompted to comment on it. There were no negative comments and the jurors were appreciative of how the lawyers and witnesses had saved time, contributed to their interest in the evidence, and held their attention.

The Design of Good Exhibits

Persuasion or education are always significant goals in communicating information to the jury. However, lawyers may also wish to reinforce and confirm beliefs which the jurors already retain. How can demonstrative exhibits be used to reinforce and confirm beliefs which the jurors already hold?

Visual displays can be made more accessible to jurors by using everyday experiences to convey a difficult concept. If the material in a graphic display is recognizable to jurors, they will more quickly grasp the message and remember it. For example, referring to the exhibit in the tort case presented in Diagram 1, designers used coffee cups to illustrate the idea of dose/response for "harmless" substances. It was extremely effective because everyone has had some experience with coffee drinking. The impact would have been lessened significantly had the exhibit board displayed only medications. A well-designed exhibit will contain visual images consistent with important concepts from the case in addition to verbiage, numbers, or other graphic representations that are attracting and appealing that convey instantaneous meaning. These images can be presented in shapes such as bars or pie charts.

For reasons having to do with control, money, and time, lawyers and expert witnesses may prefer to produce their own courtroom graphics. In practice, the results of these efforts frequently result in exhibits that are too complex and visually unappealing. Most importantly, these graphics typically fail to leave the jurors with the lasting images the lawyer wants to instill; images which will be recalled later in the case and during the deliberations.   Any money saved and any conveniences gained are quickly forgotten when it becomes clear that the jury failed to recognize or understand a key piece of testimony due to an ineffective graphic presentation.

A clear case in point was illustrated in a recent criminal trial. The lawyers for the State presented well constructed and well thought arguments and the evidence was compelling. One element, however, which the prosecution felt was critical for their case was the unusual, out-of-the-ordinary behavior which the defendant had displayed prior to the crime. Rather than using demonstrative exhibits to impress this idea upon the jurors, the prosecution utilized verbal eye-witness testimony. From post-trial interviews, the lawyers were astounded to find that during deliberations, no mention of this very important fact was made by a single juror. Had the lawyers introduced a time-line exhibit graphically depicting the defendant's activities before, during, and after the crime, this idea might have been attended to by the jurors and addressed in the deliberation.

If used correctly, professionally prepared graphic evidence can be a valuable asset to the trial team.   The preparation of exhibits can be guided by pre-trial research which can reveal areas of confusion and vulnerability. This effort can assure that the demonstrative exhibits will have their intended effect upon jurors.   A graphic expert's objective should be to work closely with the trial team to ensure that the lawyer's communication objectives are met while satisfying the juror's need for simple and appealing graphic images.   For obvious reasons, it is very important for the trial lawyers to be involved in the development of all of their demonstrative evidence.   However, the graphics expert provides an impartial and invaluable perspective on what is most important to communicate to the jury and the best ways to present this information. They also have the time and talent to devote to the project, freeing lawyers to focus on what they do best.

Conclusions

In this chapter we have examined why visual communication is so powerful. Not only do jurors learn best when a combination of perceptual senses are engaged, especially hearing and sight, but jurors enter the courtroom with preconceived attitudes, ideas, and beliefs which will determine what the juror sees and hears. The challenge for the lawyer is to make sure jurors see and hear what the lawyer wants them to see and hear.

Lawyers are typically very comfortable in narrowing a juror's auditory focus: the lawyer is an expert at communicating verbally. A recent questionnaire was sent to lawyers across the nation which asked the question, "What qualities do you believe make for an outstanding trial lawyer?" The most frequent response was, to paraphrase, "An outstanding ability to simplify extremely complex facts and ideas and communicate them to a jury." This is the ultimate purpose behind demonstrative exhibits: to simplify and communicate.

The design of good courtroom graphics requires a great deal of thought, expertise, and preparation which most lawyers cannot or will not devote during the trial preparation process. As a result, all too frequently graphics are hastily produced at the last minute and the message the lawyer wants to communicate is not adequately delivered.

CHAPTER 10

Understanding Punitive
Damages

A national publication recently commented that for many cases, the jury verdict is only a point of negotiation between parties and that high awards set the stage for high settlement. Fear of a large jury verdict sometimes can force defendants into paying far more than they think the case is worth, just to avoid facing a jury.

The fear of large verdicts and punitive damages in particular have long been a fascination and practical consideration for trial lawyers everywhere. In many instances, jurors dismiss and/or blend the distinction between "actual" and "exemplary" monetary awards, making the task of analyzing behavior and motivation of these trials even more difficult.

Calculating Punitive Damages

There often are motivations which cannot be determined from the verdict form alone. An example is a Tennessee case in which the jury returned a compensatory award of $1,171,000 and a very specific punitive damage award of $466,465. There was nothing in the evidence which even hinted at such a number. Furthermore, it was not an even percent nor a multiple of the compensatory amount. Adding to the puzzle was the fact the compensatory award represented less than 30% of the damages plaintiffs' expert testified had been suffered. Juror interviews solved the puzzle. The jurors believed their function was to make the plaintiffs whole with respect to the injuries caused by the defendant's acts. They were of the opinion there were other causative factors in the case. Thus, they had to decide what portion of the total damages were attributable to the defendant. Using the damage evidence presented by the plaintiffs' expert, the jurors determined $1,171,000 was so attributable. However, they recognized attorneys' fees and court costs would mean plaintiffs would receive something less than this amount, which the jury viewed as complete recovery. To resolve this problem, the jury made its own estimate of costs incurred by plaintiffs, as well as the amount which would go to the attorneys. The total was $466,465. Of course, there was absolutely no evidence from which either component of the total could be determined. As there was a perceived need to state two awards and there was no other place to identify the amount of costs and fees to be reimbursed, the punitive damage characterization was employed.

Donald D. Eckhardt
A.O. Smith Corporation, Milwaukee

The legal world is replete with examples of jurors and juries awarding large and often unexpected and unexplainable (from a defendant's vantage) levels of compensation to individual and corporate victims. Some instances, like the various Ford Pinto verdicts of the early eighties, or the *Penzoil v. Texaco* verdict have been analyzed and re-analyzed, with numerous explanations of the juror's behavior offered by various observers. Other cases, though noted, are less studied and present an even greater mystery to companies and defense lawyers involved with them. In recent years, a pharmaceutical manufacturer was found liable for its failure to warn against certain opthamologic uses of one of its products even though evidence indicated that the treating physician was negligent in misapplying the drug to the plaintiff's eye. The company was ordered to pay $3 million in compensatory damages and $124 million in punitive damages.

In California, the employee of an oil company sued for the second time, over lack of promotional opportunities due to gender. The jury awarded $17 million including $15 million for punitive damages which taken together was many times more than the person could have earned in any capacity over a lifetime at the company. Also in California, plaintiffs had sold their business to another entity, and were then sued for conspiracy by a minority shareholder. The plaintiffs asked their firm's insurer to finance the defense and were refused. In a bad faith claim, the jury awarded the plaintiffs, who sued the insurance carrier, $62 million of which $60 million represented punitive damages.

All of this jury behavior came into sharp focus from the perspective of many trial lawyers when the Supreme Court essentially ruled punitive damages are here to stay by suggesting that jurors have wide latitude over the appropriate amount and proportion of a punitive award in relationship to a compensatory finding (*Pacific Mutual v. Haslip*). From both the plaintiff and defendants' basic perspective, there are many possible interpretations of the *Haslip* decision which range from the continuum that the constitutionality of punitive damages has been affirmed, to the council on competitiveness, which seeks to restrict a plaintiff's ability to recover punitive or even large compensatory damage awards. In either case, trial lawyers everywhere are preoccupied with the notion of punitive damages.

Fred Morris[*] relates a typical concern. He participated in a case that was tried in a very small community in Northeastern Iowa. The community has a population of about 1500 people, was surrounded by miles upon miles of corn, soybeans, dairy farms, etc., and was the plaintiffs' "home town." The community was not thought to be, and indeed was by all appearances not, a liberal or extravagant area.

---

[*] Frederick W. Morris, *Leonard Street & Deinard, Minneapolis.*

Nonetheless, the jury awarded the plaintiff over $1 million in damages and $2.5 million in punitive damages. Moreover, the jury deliberated only a few hours. In this case, it was undisputed that the plaintiffs' economic situation had *improved* rather than deteriorated over the years since purchasing the defendant's product in question. However, the plaintiffs' claim was that production would have been higher but for the poor quality of the product in question.

According to Morris, the verdict in this case may indeed have been "conservative" in comparison to what a more liberal jurisdiction might have awarded. Nonetheless, given the facts of the case, he now derives no special comfort as a defense lawyer when someone refers to a jurisdiction as "conservative."

Identifying Punitive Jurors

Attempts to identify the characteristics of punitive jurors have been frustrating at best. Traditionally, lawyers have tended to focus on surface traits or observable characteristics of jurors which were thought to be stereotypically associated with punitive jurors. The characteristics most frequently employed are demographically based; that is, characteristics of jurors associated with their age, race, sex, level of education, and occupation. All of the research that has been conducted reveals that, once again, demographic characteristics are exceedingly poor predictors of verdict predisposition in general and for the propensity to award punitive damages in particular. This finding is really not surprising. As we have discussed in preceding chapters of this book, the decisions that people make in any environment are a function of behavioral constructs rather that the demographic make-up of the individual. In a juror context, what people believe to be and the personal experiences that they have had are obviously more important in helping them form opinions and conclusions about the character of litigants, matters of fact, or issues of evaluation than are, for example, their weight, their age, or their sex.

When Demographics Failed to Predict

In a commercial fraud case a jury was selected from residents who primarily lived in Rochester, Minnesota. Rochester, Minnesota is the home of the Mayo Clinic and has a well educated population. In addition, Southeastern Minnesota and Rochester are known within the state as conservative and Republican.

With the aid of consultants, we thought we had successfully selected a jury that was not punitive. Notwithstanding the educational level of the jury, the conservative nature of the regional area, and our best sense of the jury, the jury returned a verdict of $1 million in compensatory damages and $3 million in punitive damages. Following the trial, we learned that two of the jurors lobbied to award over $10 million in punitive damages. It also should be noted that this jury asked the judge during deliberations whether or not any award of punitive damages could be given to an independent organization, i.e., to someone other than the plaintiff. The jury, having decided to compensate the plaintiffs for their actual losses, was initially moved to award punitive damages but to give them to a neutral organization rather than to the plaintiff. Of course, the judge's instruction was not to concern themselves with that issue but simply to arrive at a number, if they were to award punitive damages.

My "take away" from the case was, in part, that jurors have a thin skin for what they believe to be misrepresentations. In addition, I agree with the comment this chapter that jurors are more likely to award punitive damages in commercial fraud cases than personal injury cases.

Frederick W. Morris
Leonard Street & Deinard, Minneapolis

If demographic variables are unreliable predictors of punitive jurors, are there any other measures or characteristics of these people that can be employed to assist the trial attorney in jury selection? Clearly, we know that these people exist; can they be identified by observable characteristics? Fortunately, the answer to this question is yes! In fact, jury research on this issue has revealed that there are several highly reliable indicia of punitive damage predispositions, and these have been successfully employed in simulated research environments as well as used in actual court cases. These characteristics are behavioral in nature and relate to the psychological and sociological characteristics of people who sit on juries.

The Psychology of Punitive Jurors

One psychological variable which has been found to have strong associations with punitive damages is the emotional state of depression. There are numerous examples of punitive jurors manifesting indications of depression. To accurately diagnose depression from a medical or clinical perspective requires very specialized training and experience. Nevertheless, there are signs or traits that trial lawyers can use. These include facial expressions, posture, eye contact, and responsiveness to questions from either the attorney or the judge.

In extreme cases, all of us are capable of observing people who could be defined as psychologically or emotionally depressed. In those extreme cases where a depressed individual is easily observed and recognized, there is a high probability of that person awarding punitive damages should the jury find against the defendant. What about instances where depression is latent and not observable without the assistance of trained specialists? Fortunately, behavioral scientists have learned that there are specific instances in the lives of most people which normally result in depression or anxiety. Some of these are psychological in nature, and others are more sociological in nature.

Death and Dying. Most human beings faced with the death or imminent loss of a loved one or close friend experience depression. In fact, most psychologists agree that otherwise normal and psychologically healthy people require about two years to recover from the death of a loved one. Hence, where appropriate, voir dire questions should be addressed to this area of the juror's personal life whenever possible. This is particularly critical in personal injury or death cases. If a juror indicates that he or she has suffered any sort of personal or family tragedy, or social trauma, the juror should be scrutinized with great care and caution.

Divorce/Separation. Jurors who reveal that they have recently been divorced or are in the process of obtaining a divorce or separation, represent a punitive threat. Interestingly enough, this is particularly important in the case of middle-aged men. Dissolution of a long-term marriage and family structure is very difficult for most people. This situation can be particularly devastating when the male partner has not initiated the termination of the marriage relationship. When placed in a position to make judgements or evaluations, these jurors frequently possess feelings of resentment or bitterness and are willing to lash out at other people when provided an opportunity to do so.

Trial lawyers are well-advised to exercise great caution with middle-aged people who are recently divorced or separated if punitive damages are a significant threat in the litigation.

Professional or Occupational Trauma. People who have suffered severe emotional experiences relating to their job, occupation, or profession are potentially dangerous jurors. Not unlike jurors described in the divorce scenario above, these people are typically angry, frustrated, and oftentimes experience deep feelings of inner humiliation and embarrassment. If the trial attorney discovers during voir dire that a particular juror is unemployed, it is very important to explore this issue. Obviously, this must be done with sensitivity to avoid exacerbating the underlying cause of potential antagonism and hostility.

Frequently, the spouse of an individual who has lost his or her job may experience even greater feelings of anxiety and depression than the individual who has actually been fired or displaced. The wife of a middle-age executive who has lost his job may possess feelings of guilt over her repressed anger at her husband and his predicament. Once again, post-trial interviews have revealed that these people are often strong proponents for the awarding of punitive damages.

Sociological Variables

In addition to these psychological characteristics frequently associated with punitive damages, there are three significant sociological predictors of people predisposed to award punitive damages. These conditions are referred to as anomie, locus of control, and occupational underemployment.

Anomie. Sociologists define anomie as a condition existing in a society where people experience a sense of normlessness. That is, people are confused as to "the rules of the game" and their roles as individuals in society. When people lose a sense of understanding as to where they fit in or how their personal role relates to the overall social structure, they often experience feelings of frustration and anxiety. When people feel, for example, that "life has passed them by," "that they've been left behind or left out," "that they played by the rules but haven't been rewarded," they may experience a generalized and non-specific hostility referred to as anomie. A post-trial interview with a 60-year old male juror who was singularly responsible for convincing the jury to impose a huge punitive award against a major pharmaceutical company revealed precisely this phenomenon. This life-long blue collar worker expressed criticism, antagonism, and hostility toward the defendant, and yet he could not accurately be described as "anti-corporation." In fact, he displayed intense antagonism and frustration not only with large corporations, but also with the government, politicians, labor unions, teenagers, blacks, and Jews. This particular juror felt that he had worked hard all of his life, had followed the rules, and had failed to receive any of the attendant rewards he associated with the prescribed social norms of society. This man's generalized frustrations with significant social institutions were clearly focused on the defendant in the lawsuit. Serving on the jury permitted him an opportunity to vent his frustrations and antagonisms on a clearly defined social entity.

Can a lawyer detect the existence of anomie during voir dire? There are indeed a number of question areas which will sensitize lawyers to the existence of anomie. These include questions relating to life satisfaction in general, that is, questions designed to ascertain the individual's general description of his feelings of satisfaction and happiness with his personal, social, work, and family life.

To illustrate this point, Charles Faruki* provides the following example. Asking the question, "in your job how closely and frequently do your supervisors or management play by the rules?" is an open-ended question that can yield interesting responses. In an age discrimination case that he tried, that question elicited a response from a potential juror who had previously indicated that he had not lost his job or had any employment problems, but that he did feel that management was arbitrary because they were not evenhanded in the treatment of employees. Further questioning resulted in that juror being removed for cause, saving a valuable peremptory challenge.

Locus of Control. A second important sociological variable found to be associated with punitive damage verdicts is a concept referred to as locus of control. Locus of control defines the extent to which people perceive the nature and extent of control that they possess in their own lives. Some people feel that they can conquer any objective and possess a confidence in their own ability to master adversity and pursue opportunities. These people are referred to as having a high internal locus of control. On the other hand, there are people who feel that external events shape their lives and their significant events. These people frequently explain that "luck or fate" was responsible for serious negative or positive events in their lives and that "things just happen to the individual." These people are described as having a high external locus of control.

When a juror perceives that his or her life has been characterized by external events (frequently bad luck), he or she becomes a good candidate for awarding punitive damages. Voir dire questions relating to locus of control can be formulated in terms of: (1) job stability; (2) the relationship between the juror's education and current occupation or employment; (3) the juror's level of contentment or satisfaction with his or her current life situation; and, (4) general expectations about the future.

---

* Charles J. Faruki, *Faruki Gilliam & Ireland, Dayton.*

Expectations About the Future

The juror questionnaires made available to counsel in different jurisdictions vary widely in the extent of information available about potential jurors. Although some questionnaires are quite brief, most contain age, education, and job information. Any time a job does not appear to "match" or correspond with the educational level (i.e. any time the potential juror's education could in his or her mind "justify" a higher or better job in the mind of the juror), I ask the following question, prospectively, to inquire as to how the juror feels about the future of his or her job (in terms of its stability or security). I ask whether he expects to hold the same job in several years, or, if he is elderly, until retirement. Thus, in a product liability action, I asked a potential juror who had a factory job but had a college education if he expected to hold the same job in several years. The juror replied, "unfortunately yes; the companies have not created jobs for all graduates," revealing much about this juror's attitude toward corporations. Do not ask if the juror expects a promotion, because that tends to embarrass him; ask rather, if he expects to hold the same job in several years' time.

Charles J. Faruki
Faruki Gilliam & Ireland, Dayton

Occupational Underemployment. Occupational underemployment can exist at two levels. The first is represented by a juror's current occupation or job being inconsistent with that individual's level of education or training. As an example, an individual with a master's degree in art history who is working as a clerk in a grocery store or as a cab driver would be defined as underemployed. Another example might be a juror who majored in elementary education in college and is unable to secure employment as a teacher. Research has demonstrated that when placed in a jury environment, these people frequently become punitive jurors.

The second classification of occupational underemployment can be described as job or occupational inconsistency within the mind of the individual. That is, these people believe in their own minds that they ought to have a better job, a higher position, or more authority. The reality of many cases is that these people are already at a level of maximum capability or performance.

Jurors who perceive that they are underemployed are the Archie Bunkers of the world. They frequently dominate their family and close personal and social relationships but fail to receive the external social reward and reinforcement to which they feel they are entitled. In many instances, these people proceed through life with feelings of generalized frustration and antagonism that can be leveled at a defendant in a law suit. This is particularly the case when the defendant represents a large company or some other entity with which the juror can associate his perceived lack of social reward, external gratification, and recognition.

Juror Expectations and Punitive Damages

The profile of the punitive damage-prone juror is only half of the assessment which the trial lawyer must make. The lawyer must also assess the facts to gauge how far a juror's perception of the behavior at issue may differ from his or her expectations (regardless of legal standards) of how firms or individuals should act. Thoughts of punitive damage awards will grow in any gap between these preconceived expectations and the defendant's failure to deal with them, and certain personalities may be particularly influenced by the disparity. For example, in a franchise relationship setting, we believe that jurors see major franchising companies as being extremely competent business organizations (to the point of always knowing "the answer") and as having major emphases on standards and policies. Jurors often see franchisees as individuals who are in need of standards and unable to succeed without following someone else's rules. Evidence of franchisor incompetence, or of a failure to observe policies, or a franchisor's failure to provide clear directions to the franchisee in need of direction may be viewed as a departure from the expected relationship perceived by the juror. A

(continued)

(continued)

trial attorney must also look at developing materials and a mode of presentation which will help close this gap. For example, if the expectation is that the defendant is so competent that every one of its products will be "successful" and the claim is that distributors were induced to invest in a new product because success was promised, portrayal of the defendant as <u>incompetent</u> will be a direct challenge to preconceived notions and increase the risk. The defendant must attempt to support the proposition that competent *companies engage in experimentation; that uncertainties relating to the product were known; and that the project moved forward because the distributors wanted the opportunity to secure potential benefits for themselves. Receptivity to evidence of this type must be integrated into the juror profile. Jurors who look at problems in a narrow or concrete way may find it difficult to accept this evidence. They will be left with a significant gap between their perceptions of what should be and what they believe should have occurred and what they believe actually occurred and the risk of a punitive damage award will be heightened.*

Alan H. Silberman
Sonnenschein Carlin Nath & Rosenthal, Chicago

In addition to individual characteristics of punitive, damage-oriented jurors, there are several definable situations in which either the case facts and setting, or the overall composition of the jury ultimately affects the likelihood of punitive damages being awarded.

Other Factors

Frequently the very nature of the parties involved in litigation has an impact on jurors' willingness to award punitive damages. Recent studies by various reporting services have shown material differences in punitive damage awards based upon type of case. For example, a study of 25,000 civil jury verdicts from many locations around the country revealed that jurors were more likely to award punitive damages in financial and property damage cases, and least likely to award such damages in cases involving personal injuries. These included both medical negligence and product liability situations. While this might run contrary to expectations, one explanation focuses on juror's perceptions of control. For example, in most personal injury related cases, jurors look at the extent to which plaintiffs controlled, contributed to, or had some overall impact upon the outcome of the case. Damages may be mitigated to the extent they are perceived to have some influence on the injury producing situation. On the other hand, jurors will focus upon the defendant's control in most commercial cases and as a result, be extremely unforgiving in terms of damages when they believe an error in judgment by the corporate citizen has been made.

Charles Faruki suggests that it is frequently useful in opening statement and in closing argument to point out to the jury what facts the defendant had at the time a decision in question was made, precisely what the decision was, and what factors supported it. An error in judgment is less likely to be punished by a jury if the actions of the defendant seem reasonable, given what was known at the time. Faruki provides an example from a breach of contract and tort suit against a manufacturer that had terminated the plaintiff as a distributor of its products. The opening statement broke down the facts that were undisputed as to plaintiff's poor performance and failures of payment; exactly what decision was made (i.e. non-renewal; not a unilateral cutoff but a decision to allow the distributorship agreement to expire at the end of its term without renewal), and what the evidence would show as to why that decision was taken (with reference back to the undisputed facts, as well as to what the testimony from the defendant would show).

The geography of a court case and the related sociology of the venue can have a material impact upon the likelihood of punitive damages. For years, trial lawyers have debated the impact of geography. In one camp, some trial lawyers are convinced that the facts win the case and as such, the case can be tried anywhere with similar results. Research on this issue provides results contrary to this belief. Specific studies presenting the same case to similar demographically constructed juries in venues such as San Francisco, Boston, Miami, and Nashville yield dramatically different results. This can be in part explained by the sociology of an area and the extent to which social conditions significantly impact individual behavior. To use one extreme example, juries in Beaumont,

Texas, very frequently award large damages irrespective of jury composition. In part, Beaumont as a community, has taken on many characteristics found in individual jurors such as feelings of frustration and betrayal by large corporations. Overall, it is important not to underestimate the impact that aggregate community values can have upon the jury thought process.

Donald Eckhardt* notes that jurors frequently misunderstand their role in the deliberation process. Nine jurors must concur in a verdict in Missouri civil actions. In a hotly contested case, the jurors were evenly divided when the jury began its deliberations. During three days of deliberating, the six jury members favoring a plaintiff's verdict were able to persuade three of the defense jurors to change their view. Once the third defense juror had swung to the plaintiff's side, the three hold-out defense jurors withdrew from further participation in the deliberations; specifically the damage determination. It was their view the defendant had not committed any unlawful acts, thus, the plaintiff had not been damaged as a result of anything done by the defendant. Consequently, it was inappropriate for them to express any opinion with respect to damages, except to reiterate the amount ought to be zero. To say the least, there was little discipline imposed upon the other jurors in deciding upon the amount to award.

Jury dynamics can have a profound impact upon the propensity of the jury to award punitive damages. While there are many subtleties involved in the dynamics of the jury's verdicts, the one overriding factor which should be focused upon is the dichotomy of perceived knowledge by some jurors and total lack of knowledge by other jurors with respect to courtroom procedures and the deliberation process.

In looking at cases in which punitive damages have been awarded, post trial interviews often times demonstrate that a minority of jurors set the deliberation tone and/or provided fabricated facts for fellow jurors.

In a recent contractual case between two oil companies, the jury awarded $22 million in punitive damages when only $4 million in compensatory damages were being sought by plaintiff. Post trial interviews indicated that one juror was in favor of awarding punitive damages, but that juror was insistent on awarding $100 million and provided many contrived facts and opinions to his fellow jurors as to why this made sense. As an example, this juror convinced or at least gave

---

* Donald D. Eckhardt, *A.O. Smith Corporation, Milwaukee.*

fellow jurors reason to believe the defendant oil company earned $100 million **every hour** of its existence. More significantly to the example, defense oriented jurors reported after the fact that they had done an extremely good job by fighting for days during deliberations with the one plaintiff juror and as a result, held down damages to "only" $22 million. In this instance, even if pre-trial research had not been undertaken to help identify punitive damage oriented jurors, the trial team should have been able to identify the areas in which jurors needed greater education regarding the defendant's financial position.

As one final point, it should be noted that jurors frequently report tremendous confusion about damage award concepts. It is common for jurors to be unable to articulate the distinction between compensatory and punitive damages, why one type versus the other should be awarded, or even who ends up being the recipient of punitive awards. Similarly, there is often great discussion and debate, even when instructed by the court to the contrary, regarding insurance coverage and the manner in which the attorneys will be compensated. It is not uncommon for jurors to decide on the dollar amount of an award for a plaintiff, and to then increase that number by a factor of 50 to 100 percent or more to cover attorney fees. Perceived long term economic conditions can also play a roll. There have been cases in which jurors have reported in post trial interviews that they decided what the appropriate amount of the award should have been and then multiplied that number by some factor to account for inflation.

Donald Eckhardt reports that in at least two cases in different jurisdictions, but involving long running litigation with respect to the same product line, a defense juror, frustrated by an inability to persuade the plaintiff oriented jurors of the error of their ways, angrily suggested it was illogical to find an intentional misrepresentation without awarding punitive damages. In both cases the plaintiff jurors had not intended to enter a punitive damage verdict. However, at the urging of the defense juror, an award was made in each case. With friends like this, says Eckhardt, who needs enemies!

Conclusion

Punitive damages frustrate defendants but they should rarely be surprising. Effective pre-trial research can identify the propensity for punitive damage awards as well as the factors driving these juror predispositions. Punitive damages are not always the result of the jury being mad or vindictive. In many instances however, people are included on juries who are predisposed to award punitive damages against certain defendants irrespective of the facts or merits of the case. As we have seen, these jurors are frequently associated with identifiable characteristics which can be examined during voir dire.

## CHAPTER 11

Jury Research for Effective Trial Strategy

Commenting upon the importance of jury research in preparing for trial, John Martel[*] describes a case where a major bank had to cope with a $40 million dollar lender liability claim. The plaintiff, a long term customer, characterized the bank as his business partner and blamed his near collapse on the bank for calling his loans and refusing him further credit. A number of similar cases had been tried in various parts of the country with devastating results to bank defendants. Martel called upon his consultants to find ways to deal with the David and Goliath theme he knew the plaintiff would exploit. Using focus groups and a variety of other small group research techniques to analyze the myriad of facts and potential defenses, the following major Thematic Anchors (see Chapter 8) evolved:

1. Loans should be repaid.
2. A bank may be a corporation, but it owes a duty to its depositors—people just like you—to protect their money by calling bad loans from bad risks.
3. The plaintiff was a borrower, not a (fiduciary) partner, and he caused his own financial problems.

---

[*] John S. Martel, *Farella Braun and Martel, San Francisco.*

Focusing on these themes accomplished more than all the available experts and statistics to destroy plaintiff's case without payment of a nickel. In this case, effective jury research was a key element in achieving a successful result for the client.

The key to the effective utilization of the concepts and principles offered in this book is valid and reliable information about prospective jurors. If, for example, a trial lawyer suspects that certain types of jurors may hold negative attitudes toward his client, he needs to know with as much specificity as possible: (1) whether or not these suspicions are correct; and (2) the nature of these negative attitudes and the intensity with which they are held. This chapter will be concerned with an overview of how juror research provides valid and reliable answers to these kinds of questions.

The Need for Scientific Rigor

The behavioral sciences bring with them a complex and sophisticated method of research and analysis. These disciplines deal in information called data, experimental facts, or statistics. This information comes in a language of its own and in many instances is different from that of everyday discourse. For those not trained in social science methodology, this language requires interpretation, and in many instances translation, before it can be successfully incorporated into trial strategy.

The use of scientific methods of data collection, measurement, and analysis are not novel. Detailed and rigorous behavioral research has long been employed by advertisers and communications experts. Not only do they recognize the importance of this research, but they also make full use of its findings prior to making significant decisions. No responsible corporate executive would consider expending or placing at risk millions of dollars solely on the basis of prior experience, instinct, or advice from a colleague. Today, there are very few advertising or marketing executives who "read consumers" or know "what sells" without a great deal of pre-market research. This is particularly true for companies like Procter & Gamble, Microsoft, General Foods, and others with a reputation for continual success in the marketplace.

The Need to Know

One of the fascinating things about the practice of trial law is coming to the realization that in order to be successful, you must "unlearn" much of what you were taught—and therefore thought was important—in law school. Seasoned trial lawyers know, for example (sometimes having learned it the hard way), that juries rarely decide cases based on which side has presented the most and/or the most logical evidence on the issues that the lawyer considered to be important. Indeed, when one thinks about it, it really is extraordinarily presumptuous for an attorney to believe that he/she can persuasively present his or her client's case to a jury without the faintest empirical notion of what issues are likely to be important to the jury and what pre-existing attitudes the jurors may have about the litigants and the factual circumstances of the case. (As a profession, we really should take a lesson from consumer product companies, which invest substantial time and money on market research to determine public interest in, and demand for, a new product before bringing it to market.)

While the conventional wisdom in years gone by was that this critical information could be obtained by means of a thorough voir dire examination of the prospective jury panel, most trial lawyers now realize that information gained in this fashion is, for the most part, "too little and too late." It is too little largely for the reason discussed somewhat in the text, namely that because jurors want to avoid any social disapproval, they will "readily offer acceptable voir dire answers that do not accurately reflect their underlying values." Moreover, information obtained during voir dire is generally "too late" because it comes at the start of the trial, long after most critical decisions have already been made about what issues will be important to the jury and which testimony or other proof will be most persuasive on those issues. In contrast, it has been my experience that pre-trial jury research can be a valuable tool in developing in a timely fashion the kind of information needed to successfully present a case to a jury.

Robert A. Boas
The Coca-Cola Company, Atlanta

The quality and integrity of juror research is dependent upon the use of scientific procedures involving measurement, data collection, and analysis. Without the proper application of these procedures, we may be correct in what we predict about a jury, or we may be wrong. We won't know until jurors return their verdict. The point is, no legitimate social scientist would hazard a guess as to what a jury might do were he to merely walk into a courtroom and impressionistically "pick a jury." Frequently, we see jury consultants with inadequate training label jurors with certain traits, characteristics, or propensities. There are even those who will, after "reading the jury," provide the lawyer with assessments of the panel's ultimate verdict and level of damages! While there is an abundance of these self-styled experts who will provide attorneys with ad hoc, on-the-spot advice, this guidance is, in reality, not at all superior to what an untrained secretary or paralegal might provide. Social scientists who have devoted their professional lives to understanding how people behave will not engage in speculation or guesswork of this nature. Subjective guesswork made in the courtroom is not a valid and reliable basis for the development of strategies based on attitude theory, causal attribution, perception, learning, and the range of other topics considered in this book. These concepts, and their use, require the development of information about jurors based on scientific methods.

The Use of Jury Experts

There are no nationally recognized standards that prescribe the education and experience which are necessary to practice the art of "jury consultant." Therefore, anyone can hold himself or herself out as qualified to practice this profession. Training ranges from a Ph.D. in Psychology on the one hand to a degree in business administration on the other.

Several years ago we defended the manufacturer of a birth control device and tried cases in many jurisdictions. We experimented with "jury consultants" with a range of qualifications. One consultant was sure that potentially adverse jurors could be identified by simply watching their eyes during voir dire. We

(continued)

(continued)

were persuaded to use a peremptory challenge because, according to the consultant, the venireman had the "eyes of a psychotic."

In retrospect, we wasted a peremptory challenge. The instincts of a jury consultant will be correct about 50 percent of the time. The lawyer and other laymen have about the same chance of being correct. The only way to increase the chances of identifying a potentially adverse venireman is to employ the scientific methods discussed in this chapter.

Of course, extensive use of these methods cannot be justified in every case. The trial lawyer should know about each of these methods so that they can be used where appropriate.

When extensive research is not justified, other less comprehensive techniques can be employed in cases which have a probability of going to trial. Under the supervision of a qualified jury consultant, meaningful data can be collected by presentation of a version of the facts of a similar case to a panel of carefully selected individuals who are likely to have the same characteristics of a jury selected from that venue.

Without feedback from these laymen and a qualified jury consultant, the lawyer can only speculate about the best way to present the case to a particular audience.

Franklin M. Tatum, III
Wright Robinson McCammon Osthimer & Tatum, Richmond

Validity and Reliability in Juror Research

When conclusions are reached about jurors, it is important to know how valid these conclusions are. How do we know what we think about jurors is in fact correct? Suppose someone tells us that jurors will find a particular witness convincing. Is this a valid statement? Upon what is it based? How can its validity be tested? Suppose it is suggested that blue collar workers will be good jurors for the defense because they proved to be defense jurors some years ago in a slightly related case. Is this a reliable supposition? Was it really the fact that because jurors were predominantly blue collar workers the attorney received a defense verdict in the first trial? Or was it a more complex set of interacting factors? Is it reliable to generalize from one trial experience to another? How similar are the two trials, and are the same issues going to be employed by jurors as a basis for their decision?

When social scientists talk about validity, they mean the following: Is something we believe to be true, actually true? For example, is it valid to suppose that by observing a juror's age, race, sex, or employment history we can accurately predict how that juror will respond to specific witnesses, learn evidence, comprehend instructions, or ultimately vote?

In addition to concerns about validity, jury research must be reliable. Reliability relates to the consistency of what we know to be. Will attitudes which are highly salient in one case remain so in another? Is it reliable to use the same trial strategies in a series of "similar" cases? What may have been a valid approach in one case may not be reliable in another.

Obtaining validity and reliability in this sense is only possible through the use of scientific methodologies. Social scientists are very concerned about the concepts of validity and reliability any time they attempt to predict or explain human behavior.

To insure the validity and reliability of pre-trial research, data about jurors must be carefully collected and measured. The analysis of these data must proceed along the lines set by established statistical models. Sampling procedures must be adhered to with rigor, and typical errors of measurement and analysis, which have been studied and catalogued by experts in methodology, must be avoided.

In order to be certain that research results are valid and reliable and can be successfully applied to a given case, it is necessary to make juror research highly specific. Knowledge that certain kinds of jurors were good for a case in Denver some years ago will not be an adequate basis for decisions regarding a new case in Boston. Specific witnesses must be tested, as well as specific demonstrative exhibits, opening arguments, and prospective juror types.

The Need to Retest Attitudes and Themes in Different Geographic Areas

In one series of recent cases involving claims of fraud in the inducement of equipment supply contracts, and breach of those agreements, pre-trial research disclosed startlingly different juror attitudes and verdict preferences in different geographic areas. Despite the fact that the same pre-contract representations and documentary evidence were involved in all venues, focus groups and practice trial jurors in New York exhibited a much greater willingness to excuse misrepresentations in a commercial context than did their counterparts in Ohio and Nebraska. Unlike practice jurors in the midwest, who had expressed an initial moral concern over the representations, and only came over to defendants' position after careful review of the evidence and intensive parsing of the legal prerequisites for fraud, the New York participants consistently expressed cynical surprise that a purchaser would actually rely on a seller's representations. Thus, the "defense in depth" trial strategy previously adopted in the Midwest—to demonstrate in detail the truth of each representation, and to carefully explain the context in which each was made —gave way to a more aggressive, attacking defense—blaming the plaintiff purchaser himself for casually relying upon the defendant's representations, rather than undertaking an independent review and appraisal.

With regard to the contract claims, however, the situation was somewhat reversed. Here, the midwest focus groups, with marked consistency, concluded that "a contract is a contract," and were not receptive to the plaintiffs' efforts to avoid the effect of contractual language limiting liability. The New York jurors, on the other hand, seemed far more willing to disregard "boilerplate" clauses, and were inclined to award more comprehensive compensation for the perceived loss. While the contract claim was dismissed on motion, a major strategy change would have

(continued)

> *(continued)*
>
> *been required had it proceeded to trial in New York, with a greater emphasis on the negotiating history of the specific clauses in question, and detailed evidence of industry-wide reliance on those claims.*
>
> *William A. Gordon*
> *Mayer Brown & Platt, Chicago*

The Concept of Causality in Juror Research

Statements that one thing has caused another are commonplace. It is often alleged during a trial that some injury has a direct and specific cause. Attorneys frequently attempt to teach jurors that the alleged causality is grounded on casual and impressionistic assumptions rather than scientific assessments of fact. In juror research, the concept of causality must be employed in a highly restrictive manner. When it is said that a plaintiff verdict was caused by the jurors' conviction that the pharmaceutical product in question had been inadequately tested by the defendant, did the corporate testing program really cause the jurors to decide the case against the defendant? Could there have been another cause? Or more likely, could there have been a number of contributing factors ranging from other important facts to the trial lawyer's presentation of the case to the jury? While it may sound simplistic and naive, we are frequently told that "a company witness lost the case," or that "the jury didn't understand the judge's instructions."

Since lawyers often exercise considerable efforts to educate jurors to the real meaning of causality, it is interesting that the concept is difficult to apply in the case of understanding jurors and the decisions they make. Social science experts do not lightly assume that a given trait or set of traits can "cause" jurors to look for probable associations between a verdict on the one hand and some set of attitudes, traits, or demographic characteristics in the jury. In juror research, a search takes place for the way in which jurors display certain cognitions and behavioral intentions with regard to the facts in the case, the litigants themselves, or even the legal counsel involved. What jurors say about how they feel and what they think they will do is a complex tapestry. It must be studied very closely. Correlations and associations can be discovered which will be useful in predicting verdicts with a certain stated probability. This is far different from saying that one thing has caused or will cause another.

Data Collection

Data are information we seek about jurors. They consist of juror demographic traits, such as education, occupation, residence, sex, age, and religion. They also include information about juror attitudes and beliefs, juror verdict preferences, biases, and stated behavioral intentions with regard to the specific case under consideration. There are consequently many different kinds of data which take many different forms.

Data are collected to be measured, analyzed, and interpreted. The types of measurement, analysis, and interpretation which social scientists employ require that the data be collected in highly specific ways using what are referred to as measurement scales.

Measurement Scales

Much of the data collection in jury research is a matter of asking surrogate jurors (people matched to the general characteristics of the anticipated panel) questions or observing their behavior. These questions are designed to yield specific structured responses so that the resulting data will be valid and reliable. Data are generally numbers or verbal responses translated into numbers. It is important to be able to put these responses into numerical forms so that statistical analysis can be employed to interpret their meaning.

In our everyday lives, we tend to think about measurement in the sense of well-defined scales having a natural zero point and constant unit of measurement. At one time or another, we have found it useful or necessary to use measuring instruments such as yardsticks, gasoline gauges, and weighing scales to determine such things as height, volume, and weight.

In behavioral research, there are various types of scales which are based on the underlying assumptions regarding the correspondence of numbers to the properties of behavior and the ability to perform mathematical and statistical operations on these numbers. While there are many data classifications schemes, the most appropriate for our discussion in this book are referred to as *nominal, ordinal, interval*, and *ratio* scales. Each of these possess very specific properties and is related to specific standards of empirical analysis.

Nominal scales consist simply of classifying objects, events, individuals, or behaviors into categories. Each category is given a name or assigned a number. These names or numbers are used merely as designations or labels. Nothing else is inferred; there is no implied relationship among the numbered categories. With respect to religion, for example, jurors could be classified as:

1 = Protestant
2 = Catholic
3 = Jew
4 = Other.

With nominal scales, there is no qualitative or quantitative assessment given to the scaled categories. In this example, the Protestant rating is not "higher" or "lower" than any of the other classifications. Because the numbers assigned to categories making up a nominal scale serve only as tags or labels, arithmetic calculations performed on nominal data have no meaning whatsoever. For example, one cannot calculate a mean average of nominal data. Hence, there are severe limitations associated with the statistical analysis of classification scales.

Another kind of useful scale is called an *ordinal scale*. Ordinal scales place categories in some order with respect to the degree to which each category possesses some characteristic or trait. Yet we cannot say in numerical form how much this is. An example will make this clear. Suppose we wish to know how believable prospective jurors consider certain product testing organizations. We might ask jurors to use an ordinal scale to rank a number of different organizations and then obtain data in this form:

Most believable	1.	Consumer product testing agencies.
	2.	University Research Centers.
	3.	Independent testing laboratories.
Least believable	4.	Manufacturers' testing programs.

Hence, an ordinal scale, or ranking scale, has been employed to indicate the extent to which these agencies possess an intangible quality called believability. The categories are placed in order or rank according to the central characteristic which is being tested. Ordinal data present more information than data from a nominal scale but still do not allow meaningful use of arithmetic operations.

Interval scales are another form in which behavioral data are frequently collected. An interval scale has all the characteristics of ordinal measures, and, in addition, the units or intervals between successive positions are equal. For this reason, these scales or attempts at creating them are particularly important in juror research. Many of the constructs discussed in this book such as attitudes, learning, and perception are measured with scales containing equal-appearing psychological intervals. As an example, the perceived competence of an expert witness can be measured on an interval scale from +5 (very competent) to -5 (very incompetent). Because a mean average and standard deviation can be calculated from interval data, a very sophisticated statistical analysis can be performed.

Finally, *ratio scales* may be used in juror research. With these scales, a ratio of numbers is used to express the degree to which some attribute is possessed. Ratio scales are often very useful in presenting data. Suppose that in a given venue, 80 percent of the prospective jurors have a direct economic interest in the outcome of a public utilities case. It might be useful to state that the ratio of potentially biased jurors in this case is 4 to 1. Ratios can also be used to indicate rates. It might be important to note that the accident rate at a particular intersection is 612 per hundred thousand vehicles and that the average for ten other intersections in the same part of town is only 52. Thus, there is an almost 12-1 greater chance of having an accident in the first intersection than in any of the others. All parametric and non-parametric statistical procedures may be undertaken with ratio-scaled data, and hence ratio data provide maximum flexibility in data analysis.

Ratio scales are found more commonly in the physical sciences than in the behavioral sciences. Measures of weight, length, time intervals, velocity, etc., all conform to ratio scales. In the social sciences, we do find some variables such as money, age, and years of education, which can be ratio scaled.

The Likert Scale

One commonly used form of questioning in jury research is referred to as a modified Likert Scale. A Likert Scale is a rating scale with response categories ordered to represent the degree of a respondent's agreement or disagreement with a statement. This can be illustrated by the following:

"How do you feel about radial tires?"					
	Strongly Agree	Agree	Neither agree nor disagree	Disagree	Strongly Disagree
Bias ply tires are not as safe as radial tires					
Radial tires should be required by law					
People who do not use radial tires should pay higher insurance premiums					

People can be asked to indicate the extent to which they agree or disagree with these statements. There are other ways to ask these questions, but the use of a Likert Scale has the advantage of measuring not only agreement versus disagreement but the intensity with which an opinion is held.

Questions Based on Semantic Differential Scales

Another useful question form is the Semantic Differential Scale. Semantic Differential Scales are rating scales in which responses are ordered to evaluate an object on the basis of some bipolar attribute. Here is an example:

Please indicate the degree to which you think the corporation is characterized by the following traits:

Good Employer . . . . Bad Employer
Large Company . . . . Small Company
Responsible Firm . . . . Irresponsible Firm.

These bipolar adjectives or statements can be used to investigate the image of the plaintiff or the defendant, the salient attributes of a case presentation, or even to assess the characteristics of witnesses or demonstrative exhibits. Defending a large oil company in a price discrimination action, Diann Kim[*] found that Semantic Scales of "Power/Not Powerful" and "Good/Bad" revealed that—without any knowledge of the specific dispute—prospective jurors perceived oil companies as powerful and bad, and dealers as powerless and neutral as to good and bad. Further research indicated that, in this case, the oil company's "power" translated into a perceived ability to treat the dealer unfairly and discriminatorily. With these comparative attributes in mind, the oil company took pains to demonstrate at several points in the trial that the dealer had greater discretion and control over his own operations and fortune than the oil company, which was required to apply its policies uniformly to all dealers. By shifting some of the bipolar "power" attributes, the oil company was able to level the playing field with the dealer.

---

[*] Diann H. Kim, *Tuttle & Taylor, Los Angeles.*

Obviously, the design of questionnaires and the questions they contain is both a subtle and an important aspect of jury research. One important application of this art is the design of questions for voir dire. Of course, research into juror attitudes and verdict preferences remains the primary and fundamental application of test instruments.

Techniques of Data Collection

There are a number of techniques which are useful in collecting juror research data. These include the use of either structured or unstructured interviewing procedures and a mix of direct and indirect approaches.

A structured interview is an interview made up of a series of highly specific questions to which there can only be one of a selected number of given responses. If a prospective juror is asked to classify himself as a liberal, moderate, or conservative, the question is specific, and the responses are structured as a series of three possible choices. It is also possible to inquire into political attitudes and preferences through the use of unstructured questions. A prospective juror could be asked: "What are your political preferences?" Now, the answer would probably be somewhat rambling and much less precise. Such an answer might, however, yield information which was not obtained through the use of a structured question.

Questioning procedures can be either direct or indirect. Usually, juror research uses a combination of both approaches. Direct questions inquire directly into the matter about which information is sought. If it is desirable to know what a prospective juror thinks about a particular corporation, a direct inquiry can be employed. The obvious problem in doing so is that the respondent may identify the interviewer as someone who has a special interest in the matter, either pro-company or anti-company, and give a biased response. Indirect questions, about a category of companies or companies with certain traits, will appear more objective to respondents. Thus, the information gained from indirect questioning may be more reliable. The point is that there are times when structured or unstructured interviews should be used and times when questioning should be either direct or indirect. The choice of data collection technique will have a significant impact on the quality of the data.

In many jury research applications, a test instrument or questionnaire is used. This will enable the investigators to treat each respondent exactly the same way and to accurately compare, for example, verdict preference with attitudes toward specific issues. By treating each respondent in precisely the same way, reliability can be assured.

Since the data collected through the use of the test instruments can be subjected to sophisticated statistical analysis, it is helpful to gather these data in some convenient numerical form. This means that questions must be structured in such a way that the response leads logically to the assignment of a numerical value. The simplest way to do this will be to ask questions which have two-valued answers such as: Are you married? The answer will be "yes" or "no." Such an answer can be readily given a numerical form such as 1 for "yes" and 0 for "no."

A major limitation which must be taken into consideration when data collection procedures are used is that the questioning process itself may bias the response. Unskilled and untrained interviewers often obtain unreliable and invalid data because they are unaware of problems associated with validity and reliability. If a correct answer is embarrassing to a respondent, the response is likely to be disingenuous. Under some circumstances, respondents will give answers because they think such answers will be pleasing or acceptable to the person conducting the research, not because the answers represent the true state of their opinions. Data may also be unreliable because respondents are being asked for information they do not possess. Prospective jurors may have been told too little about a case, or given misleading information about it. If this occurs, their responses will not provide a reliable guide to the way in which they would actually behave if asked to serve on the jury.

Juror Profiling

Juror Profiling uses a method of investigation called survey research, which is one of the most important means of data collection and analysis employed in the application of social science concepts to litigation. Survey research has been employed as a way of testing hypotheses in economics, sociology, political science, and marketing. It has been made possible by the development of procedures for selecting probability samples from large populations. It also requires techniques like the ones discussed above for obtaining valid and reliable information from a test population. Finally, survey research rests upon procedures of statistical analysis which can only be carried out in a cost efficient manner through the use of advanced computers.

In practice, survey research is the investigation of some area of concern in which people hold distinctive attitudes and beliefs. These attitudes and beliefs are ascertained through the development of carefully composed questions which constitute the survey instrument. Usually the number of questions is a compromise between the scope of the survey and the need to deal with respondent fatigue. The survey is then administered in person, through the mail, or by telephone. In jury research, telephone surveys may be the most efficient and reliable. The survey will include questions about who the respondents are and the attitudes, experiences, and associations they have in relation to the case.

Question Criteria

The purpose of any questionnaire is to gather information. However, the way in which a questionnaire is designed will have a determining effect on the reliability of the data which are obtained. The way in which questions are asked can have a tremendous impact on the ultimate findings of the study. There are a number of criteria which must be employed in the construction of questions for Juror Profiling. When these criteria are properly implemented, the quality of the information gathered in the survey is greatly enhanced. For any research instrument, considerations of economy should govern the asking of questions. Only questions which have direct value within the context of the survey's overall objective should be asked. Respondents will display only a limited amount of patience and cooperation in answering questions; this generally will not exceed 20 minutes.

Another criterion which must be employed is formulating questions concerning whether or not the items will actually elicit the desired information. A problem frequently encountered in jury research is that respondents have the information we want but they will not reveal it. For example, it may be important to know whether or not prospective jurors have used contraceptive products, have had cosmetic surgery, have ever defaulted on a loan, or have been responsible for the death or injury of another person. Yet these subjects are of such a nature that prospective jurors may be reluctant to disclose this information in the context of a survey. Nevertheless, these and other sensitive subject areas can be successfully explored when questions are properly framed and presented to the respondent. The design and formulation of research instruments dealing with these kinds of issues require a great deal of experience and sophisticated training in an area of psychology called psychometrics. Psychometrics involves the measurement of human responses utilizing advanced statistics and mathematics.

In the case of Juror Profiling, the content of the questions will be determined in large part by a process of applying common sense, intuition, and the appropriate social science theory. The matter of appropriate theory is very important. The content of questions regarding attitudes and behavior must be predicated on certain expectations regarding attitudes and behavior in the general population for us to discover. In the case of jury behavior, we must have some hypotheses about relevant behavior constructs and make these hypotheses part of our questions. These hypotheses will depend on past data, our experience with juror research in general, and our theoretical knowledge about how jurors work.

Independent and Dependent Variables in Surveys

Any research effort must specify what are called independent and dependent variables. Independent variables, as the name implies, are independent of the characteristics or quality we are attempting to explain, predict, or estimate. In jury research, independent variables are the characteristics jurors possess at the beginning of the trial, like age, income, educational level, sex, occupation, personal experiences relevant to the issues in the case, and experience as consumers and members of society in general. Relatively immutable attitudes possessed by jurors are also independent variables.

Dependent variables are the specific behavior or reactions we want to predict or explain. Because juror research represents an effort to provide these assessments in a valid and reliable way, it is important to find out what kind of linkages exist between independent and dependent variables. It is important to gain clean and unambiguous information about both independent and dependent variables so that an analysis of potential juror perceptions, reactions, and verdict decisions can be undertaken.

Basing Trial Strategy on Survey Research

Numerous trial strategies can be based on survey research. The most obvious of these is juror selection *per se*. Attitude surveys can also be used to discover and confirm Thematic Anchors, or to evaluate the desirability of possible Thematic Anchors for use in the case presentation. In one antitrust case, for example, the lawyers felt that there were more than four hundred issues which could have been presented to a jury to prove that the defendant did indeed violate the antitrust laws. Research with small groups was employed to reduce this number to about ten. At this stage of the research program, survey research was then conducted to carry out a precise investigation into potential juror attitudes toward these ten issues. Based on the results of the survey, a relatively small number of issues were seen as most central to the case. In this manner, it was possible to learn not only how jurors responded to these issues but also to evaluate the intensity of their relevance.

In an important antitrust case, Diann Kim employed survey research to identify facts that jurors believed so fundamentally that they could not and would not be shifted. Pre-trial survey research indicated that prospective jurors believed plaintiff's gasoline station competed with a second station, and that none of the arguments raised by defense counsel could defeat this belief. At the same time, the prospective jurors seemed amenable to the argument that those two gasoline stations did not compete with a third station at issue. Accordingly, while the defense challenged the notion of competition between plaintiff's station and the second station, it shifted the focus of its attack to competition with the third station. With the help of a carefully crafted special verdict form, the defense was able to obtain a verdict based largely on the lack of competition between plaintiff and the third station.

Other Considerations

Voir Dire Questionnaires. As Chuck Preuss[*] suggests, a well-crafted jury questionnaire can be invaluable in ascertaining critical juror motivations. Jurors will often answer written questions of a private nature to which they would avoid a direct response in an oral setting

---

[*] Charles F. Preuss, *Bronson Bronson & McKinnon, San Francisco.*

before their peers. Moreover, personal but crucial questions can be asked in a jury questionnaire which counsel could not risk posing to a single juror in the presence of the panel. Such questionnaires should seek to elicit viewpoints which can assist counsel in determining how the juror will likely respond to thematic issues in the case. Elaboration or refinements of sensitive written responses can often be obtained in chambers out of the presence of the other panel members. Answers to questions of a less sensitive nature can serve as the basis for asking other questions as part of the normal voir dire process.

Change of Venue. At times, the lawyer's judgement or pre-trial research demonstrates the need to enter a motion for change of venue. Survey research into the sample of potential jurors may reveal such an existence of intractable bias and a tendency to prejudge the case among such a large number of potential jurors that a cogent argument for moving the trial to another locale can be advanced. As Bill Gordon* points out, survey research has been successfully used in a number of cases involving allegedly defective nuclear power plants. Potential bias against nuclear power, demonstrated through telephone surveys, has been relied upon by two courts as a basis for transfer of trial venue. The impact of a verdict on electric rates perceived by potential jurors, again demonstrated by telephone surveys, has also resulted in transfer of trial venue to a site outside the plaintiff utilities' service area.

Post-Trial Analysis. Post-trial analysis, including in-depth interviews with jurors, can often determine why a jury reached its verdict. The resulting information can then be applied to similar cases in the future and can assist with multi-district litigation.

Qualitative and Small Group Research

We have focused in this chapter on the use of jury research techniques that produce reliable and valid results. We have emphasized the necessity of using proper sampling procedures, question construction, and analytical methods. Most of the approaches we have discussed depend upon collecting data that can be converted directly into numbers and statistically analyzed. One possible drawback of this approach is that the robustness of the data may be somewhat limited. It is possible to ask 2,000 scientifically selected people 1,000 scientifically designed questions on a questionnaire and still not have a proper sense of the depth and nature of their feelings about a particular issue.

Simply observing people as they interact or engaging them in in-depth open ended interviews can offer enormously rich data that could not otherwise be obtained. In jury research we are particularly interested in how jurors interact with each other in order to make sense of the evidence they have heard and to persuade each other. Videotaping surrogate jurors and observing them as they deliberate in front of two way mirrors can be extremely fruitful. Among the things we would be interested in observing and analyzing are the following: How do jurors make sense of what they have heard; what is more or less salient; what arguments are successful and which are less successful; what issues seem to evoke emotional responses; how well are jurors able to articulate what they have absorbed; what personal experiences and analogies do they draw on in creating meaning; and, what errors in reasoning do they make.

All of these pieces of data may be somewhat difficult to obtain using questionnaires. Yet, there is an important caveat. In obtaining richness we may have to sacrifice some reliability. Unless we employ multiple groups and analyze reactions to the same stimulus across groups, we should be very wary about making generalizations from this type of small group research.

Small group research has a number of applications in the development of trial strategy. These include the identification of salient dependent and independent variables, the assessment of key witnesses, exhibits and documents, and the opportunity to evaluate competitive strategies and tactical alternatives. It can even be used to stimulate the trial itself through extensive multi-day exercises. Small group analysis is, however, more sophisticated than simply throwing a group of people into a room to watch them talk. To be used correctly, it requires a great deal of in-depth training in sub-specialties of sociology referred to as phenomenology, ethnomethodology, and participant-observer research.

Experimental Designs

The research product attorneys use in devising trial strategy can also be based on carefully thought out experiments. Experiments consist of forming hypotheses about some course of action and setting up a means of testing these hypotheses. Experimental designs have been employed to test chemical substances, ideas or concepts, and products from pharmaceuticals to automobiles. They can also be used to test aspects of an attorney's case. It might be hypothesized that opening statement A is superior to opening statement B. This hypothesis can then be tested in an experimental setting utilizing surrogate jurors as subjects. Experimental designs can also be employed to assist with decisions regarding alternative approaches to the use of demonstrative exhibits.

In a recent case, a manufacturer of light airplanes was alleged to have designed and built a defective plane that was not airworthy in certain take-off and landing conditions. The defense had at their disposal a number of ways of demonstrating to the jury that the aircraft was airworthy and could not have been defective in the way plaintiff asserted. There was an available film of the aircraft showing it taking off, performing in the air, and landing. Second, the defense had access to various models of the airplane which could be shown to jurors. Finally, the judge in this case was willing to permit jurors to go to a local airport to inspect and become acquainted with actual aircraft of the type in question.

It was important to know which of these kinds of evidence would be most useful, if useful at all, to the defendant. The defendant variable in this case was the jurors' reactions to each of these different kinds of evidence. In order to ascertain what these reactions would be, an experiment was devised using what is called an after-only experimental design. In such a study, the jurors' reactions to the different kinds of evidence would be measured one time only, after their initial exposure to the treatment or independent variables. Matched groups of jurors were shown the film, shown the model, and taken to the hangar to look at the actual plane. The reactions of the jurors to the defense claim that the plane was safe were then carefully measured. Those who had seen the film had relatively neutral reactions. The film didn't seem to hurt the defense, nor to help very much. The trip to the airport, however, proved very damaging to the defense. Jurors saw a washer on the ground beneath the plane, oil and grease stains on the tarmac, and other subtle things that actually heightened their level of flying apprehension. The airplane did not seem as substantial and solid to jurors as they had anticipated. In fact, the visit to the airport stimulated negative attitudes toward safety, small airplanes, and the airworthiness of this particular aircraft. The model, however, proved to be very positive and useful in supporting the claims of the defendant concerning the safety. The model was used in court and contributed significantly to a verdict for the defense.

In practice, the use of experimental methods can be rather complicated. Factorial designs, for example, are designs in which two or more variables are tested at the same time and in interaction with each other. Such a procedure can be used in juror selection research in which it is necessary to study the effects of many independent variables upon a potential juror's verdict preference. With factorial designs, it is possible to study what are called the "main effects" of a variable, as well as the effects of that variable interacting with others. The analysis of these designs can be highly complicated and dependent upon advanced training in mathematics and statistics.

There are many ways in which experimental designs can be misused. If, for example, the same group of jurors were shown each of the kinds of evidence considered in the airplane products case noted above, no valid research results could be obtained. The lack of validity in such a procedure would come from what is called the pretest effect. Having seen the film, study subjects would be sensitized to the topic of the lawsuit, and their reactions to the model would not be the same as if they were viewing the airplane for the first time. This is a matter of what is called internal validity, that is, measuring in fact what we think we are measuring. In Ph.D. seminars in the behavioral sciences, graduate students are taught to recognize the various threats to validity and the mathematical processes by which these threats can be controlled or eliminated.

Generalizing Experimental Results

In order to generalize from an experiment involving a number of potential jurors to the juror population as a whole, experiments must have what is called external validity. Jury research is aimed at providing reliable generalizations about all of the jurors who may be called in a given case. As such, the jurors used in the research must be representative of this larger population. This quality of representativeness is what gives an experiment external validity.

Reliability in Experimental Designs

Finally, in order to insure reliability, an experiment needs to be repeated on different occasions and the results compared. If the research result can be replicated and the results do not vary across experiments, the findings can be taken to be reliable. Thus, although a design like the after-only design used in the airplane case may sound simple when summarized, this design must be employed with caution and knowledge for proper experimental research procedures. Otherwise an invalid and unreliable research result can be obtained.

Statistical Analysis

In a number of places in this chapter, the concept of statistical analysis has been raised. Statistical analysis is designed to portray the relationships which exist among variables. These relationships are of several types, and various techniques of statistical analysis are needed to describe and discover each of these relationships. While there is a wide variety of statistical procedures available to help analyze juror research data, the method by which the data were collected and the form in which presented is of critical importance. In fact, untrained people frequently write questionnaires and collect data which are incompatible with meaningful analysis.

Types of Statistical Analysis and the Form of the Data

The topic of statistical analysis obviously exceeds the scope and intent of this book. In fact, people can devote their entire careers to the mathematical sophistication associated with research methodology. Hence, the intent here is to present the reader with an overview of some of the most frequently employed analysis procedures. These include:

Analysis of variance is a technique for showing the dependence of one or more metric variables upon one or more treatments or independent variables which are nominally scaled. By metric data, in this case, we mean interval scaled or numerical data.

Regression is a technique of statistical analysis for showing that the presence of one variable can be used to predict the presence of another. In order to use regression, all the variables must be metric, or intervally scaled. Using regression, it is possible to predict a juror's verdict on the basis of several characteristics. This prediction can be made with a stated probability.

Correlation analysis is a way of showing the strength of association between metric variables. The measure of association is summarized in a single number, and the magnitude of this number is a measure of the strength of this association. Thus, using correlation analysis, it is possible, for example, to state how strongly a juror's attitude on a certain subject will predict the juror's verdict.

Discriminant analysis is still another useful technique of statistical analysis. Discriminant analysis can be used when there are nominally scaled dependent variables like verdict preference, which is dichotomous or has two values—preference for the plaintiff or for the defendant. With this procedure, variables like juror age, level of education, and level of income must be metrically scaled. Discriminant analysis permits the grouping or clustering of those independent variables which best discriminate between jurors who favor the plaintiff and those who favor the defendant.

In addition to these procedures, there are a number of additional statistical analysis techniques which are frequently used in jury research. These include factor analysis, canonical correlation, multiple regression, cluster analysis, automatic interaction detection, log-linear regression, and multidimensional scaling. Each requires a specific kind of data, and each can be used to show specific kinds of relationships among variables.

Univariate, Bivariate, and Multivariate Techniques

In addition to the desirability of a specific kind of analysis, statistical techniques also depend upon the number of variables to be considered. When the analysis consists of only a single variable, these univariate techniques are referred to as descriptive statistics. Descriptive statistics are employed to demonstrate the distribution of a variable (the ages or sex of a jury panel) or to provide measures of central tendency—the average age of the panel, the median level of income, etc.

Bivariate analysis refers to statistical analysis of two variables. This type of analysis would be infrequently encountered in research due to the complexity of juror decision making. It is difficult to envision a situation in which an attorney would be concerned about the impact of only one independent variable, say, juror sex, and a dependent variable such as the credibility of a particular witness. Correlation and regression techniques are the primary types of statistical analysis used in bivariate models. When many variables are under consideration, it is customary to speak of multivariate analysis. Multiple regression and correlation, analysis of variance, multiple analysis of variance, discriminant analysis, and factor analysis are among the statistical techniques used in multivariate models.

With these procedures, it is possible to analyze any number of independent and dependent variables simultaneously.

Sampling

A thorough knowledge of sampling and sampling techniques is essential for the meaningful use of juror research in the development of trial strategy. Without adequate sampling procedures, research cannot be considered valid or reliable. It is, therefore, extremely hazardous to base any juror selection decision or trial strategy consideration upon research for which sampling procedures were not carefully designed and evaluated.

In jury research, prospective jurors in the venue are considered the basic population or sampling frame. To define this population, some list, like a list of registered voters or the names of licensed drivers, in some jurisdictions, can be used. The premise of any sampling procedure is that the population can be sampled in such a way that the people chosen, although relatively small in number, will exhibit the same characteristics found in the entire population.

Characteristics of the Anticipated Panel

Sometimes, of course, it is not possible to recruit surrogate jurors or conduct jury research in the ideal venue. A major oil company, facing charges of illegal price discrimination between its gasoline stations in three towns spread many miles apart along the same rural highway, wanted to know if local jurors believed any of the stations competed with one another. Research could not be conducted in two towns primarily at issue because of the possibility that, in those small and close-knit communities, prospective surrogate jurors had either heard of the lawsuit or would spread word of the jury research. Researchers rejected the notion of recruiting a panel from towns located along a different highway, since the highway at issue was distinctive in that it ran between Los Angeles and a major tourist ski area. Ultimately,

(continued)

(continued)

the jury research was conducted in, and with surrogate jurors drawn from, the third, most distant, town. To compensate for any distortions of the results due to the unavoidable focus on the third town, the researchers collected additional demographic data on the surrogate jurors' familiarity with the other two towns and the highway at issue, as opposed to a second highway that also crossed the third town. By integrating this additional data in the analysis, researchers were able to make valid findings even though they were unable to conduct research in the preferred venue.

Diann H. Kim
Tuttle & Taylor, Los Angeles

Sampling is really a common sense procedure. Suppose a new film is opening and the producers wish to know if the ending is effective. Investigators can be hired to ask each person leaving the theater how he or she liked the ending. Using this procedure, not everyone in the theater will be sampled, however. Those who did not like the film and have left early would not have been encountered by the interviewers. Shy people may also avoid the investigators. Even though a sample will have been taken, how reliable will it be? And even if it is a reliable indicator of how the film plays before this particular audience, will its response be representative of an audience in another city? Obviously, this approach will not suffice for more than an initial, and not very reliable, impression.

In order to insure that the statistics of the sample have a high probability of actually representing the population, it is necessary to take a random sample. A random sample means that each member of the population has a chance of being included in the sample which is equal to its proportional membership in the population. If half the population is Catholic, then Catholics should have a 50-50 probability of being included in the sample. If 1 in 5 people in the population is a married woman, then every married woman should have a 20 percent chance of being included in the sample. If the sample is made up in such a way that 75 percent of those interviewed are Catholic and 50 percent are married women, it is not a random sample and the statistics provided by the sample will not be reliably representative of the population as a whole.

The laws of statistics tell us that if a sample is randomly selected and of sufficient size, the statistics in the sample will reflect the actual characteristics of the population. In practice, there will be some error in any statistical procedure, most of which will be sampling error. However, the rules of statistical sampling will tell us how great this error is. Statisticians use the term confidence interval to describe how likely our statistics represent actual population parameters. A 95 percent confidence interval should be the goal. This means that it is 95 percent certain that sample statistics represent the population parameters or characteristics.

Choosing the correct sample size in jury research depends upon several factors. These are the confidence level we wish to achieve, and some reasonable estimate of what we expect the population parameters to be. With complex research designs, calculating these factors properly is a task for expert statisticians.

Advanced knowledge of statistics becomes even more essential in research involving small groups. Here, non-probability samples must be utilized. The technical reason for this is that the law of large numbers does not apply to small samples, and it cannot be assumed that all the traits under study are normally distributed in the population. While it would be beyond the scope of this book to explain these concepts, this area of statistics is referred to as non-parametric statistics. The point to be made is that statistical analysis is often valuable in small group research, but it is difficult to do and can easily generate totally meaningless results if the proper techniques and safeguards are not employed.

Conclusions

It has been said at the outset of this chapter that jury research is the key to effective jury trial strategy. Furthermore, effective trial strategy does not require just any kind of jury research, but jury research which is valid and reliable and conducted according to the canons of rigorous scientific method. Throughout this book, the terms research and pre-trial research have occurred a good deal. It has been repeatedly emphasized that research and the way it is carried out is as important to the utilization of social science concepts as the concepts themselves. When an attorney is provided recommendations for trial strategy, the lawyer must have the confidence that he is getting what he is told he is getting. This confidence will be justified when there is reason to believe that the recommendations are based upon sound applications of methodology.

CHAPTER 12

The United States of America v. Lee Harvey Oswald:

An Exercise in Psychological Strategies and Trial Techniques

Introduction

Ornate Louis XV frescoes, which adorned the walls of the Gold Room in the Fairmont Hotel in San Francisco, were partially obscured by a dozen large screen video monitors and a courtroom stage. This juxtaposition of eighteenth century art and twentieth century technology greeted over 500 lawyers who crowded into the Gold Room to watch the ABA's "Trial of the Century." The trial was the Litigation Section's Showcase program for 1992. It was a two-day trial which prosecuted Lee Harvey Oswald for the assassination of John F. Kennedy.

The program was designed with several objectives in mind. First, it was an opportunity for trial lawyers to observe two teams of the country's most prominent trial advocates in a high profile and emotionally charged case. Second, it provided a forum in which to present a sophisticated reanalysis of selected evidence gathered by the Warren Commission and the House Select Committee, utilizing advanced scientific techniques that were unavailable at the time of the original investigations. And third, it gave the trial lawyers in the audience a chance to observe state-of-the-art visual technology and to learn, first hand, how laser disc, computer animation, and event reconstruction could be effectively presented to a jury in a complex and emotionally charged case.

Members of the courtroom cast consisted of James J. Brosnahan, John W. Keker and Joseph Cotchett from San Francisco, representing the U.S. government. The defendant, Lee Harvey Oswald, was represented by Thomas D. Barr, David Boies and Evan R. Chesler from Cravath, Swaine & Moore in New York.

The fact witnesses for the trial were actors and volunteers who had been given portions of actual transcripts or affidavits to learn. They were prepared for direct and cross examinations by the lawyers as they would have been prepared for a real trial. Questions asked during direct and cross examinations were primarily based upon previous questions asked of the actual witnesses during the Warren Commission and the House Select Committee's investigations. The witnesses were then rehearsed until they could play their parts convincingly and accurately. The experts called by each side were, in reality, the country's leading specialists in their fields: Dr. Roger McCarthy and Dr. Robert Piziali of Failure Analysis Associates, and medical experts Dr. Martin Fackler and Dr. Cyril Wecht.

The Jury Panel

A panel of seventeen people was recruited from the actual pool of eligible jurors in San Francisco and represented a cross section of the citizens in the community. They were paid for their participation and knew nothing of the specifics of the trial prior to their first "question-naire" session the day before the trial began. At that time, the jurors were administered a series of questionnaires that measured their attitude, opinions, and beliefs, not only as they related to the assassination and the attendant publicity that surrounded it, but also about seemingly unrelated topics, such as their TV viewing habits, their reading preferences, and their religious beliefs. These seventeen people, then, comprised the panel of jurors for the trial. The lawyers were allowed to strike a total of five: three for the prosecution and two for the defense. After voir dire, the remaining twelve jurors comprised the actual jury. They were treated as any jury would be in a similar trial. They were instructed not to discuss the case among themselves or with anyone else during the course of the trial.

Voir Dire

Voir dire was limited to 15 minutes for each side. However, the lawyers were provided with typically available background information (Table 1) on all of the potential jurors prior to the commencement of the trial and they relied heavily upon this information in determining their strikes. The prosecution was allowed three strikes and the defense permitted two.

Both teams had a general idea of what constituted a "risky" juror for its side. Age was considered a factor for both the prosecution and the defense. From the prosecution's perspective, younger jurors would not remember Kennedy and would be less inclined to share a sympathetic view of the fallen President. The defense, on the other hand, believed older jurors might be more cynical and less sympathetic to their position.

Trial lawyers, even successful ones, believe in their accuracy during voir dire; that is, accuracy in identifying those jurors who would be antagonistic to their positions during the course of the trial. This belief is self-perpetuating and difficult to confirm or disconfirm. An opportunity seldom presents itself in which to verify, one way or the other, the accuracy of voir dire strikes. Lawyers rarely have the opportunity to actually observe the jury deliberation process, nor do they have the opportunity to learn how the "struck" jurors would have reacted to the trial. Until San Francisco, that is.

Immediately prior to the trial, members of the audience were polled regarding how accurate they perceived themselves to be in voir dire. All respondents felt they were "moderately" to "extremely accurate" in voir dire. The audience was also asked to mark its choices of jurors to strike. Half the audience was asked to mark its strikes for the prosecution and half was asked to mark its strikes for the defense. Based upon the information in Table 1, which was available to the lawyers trying this case, the reader may wish to decide which jurors would be appropriate for the defense to strike and which would be appropriate for the prosecution. Later in this chapter, we will revisit this issue and return to a discussion of the jurors and their verdict.

The five jurors from the pool who were struck by the defense and the prosecution played a very special role in this trial. They comprised the five member "alternate jury." The alternate jurors were present at the

Table 1. — Juror's Biographical Information

#/AGE/SEX	POL. PARTY	ETHNICITY	EDUCATION	INCOME	OCCUPATION
#1. 42 F	Democrat	Black	2-4 yrs. college	60-75K	Sales rep. for real estate
#2. 51 F	Democrat	Black	2-4 yrs. college	20-40K	Secretary
#3. 43 F	Democrat	Asian	Post graduate	25-40K	School Teacher
#4. 29 M	Democrat	Asian	2-4 yrs. college	25-40K	Manager in Medical Industry
#5. 70 M	Democrat	Black	2-4 yrs. college	40-60K	Bank Auditor
#6. 54 M	Democrat	White	2-4 yrs. college	40-60K	Retired Executive
#7. 42 M	Democrat	White	2-4 yrs. college	25-40K	Photographer
#8. 51 F	Democrat	White	< 1 yr. college	over 75K	Secretary/Benefits Cons.

Table 1 — Juror's Biographical Information (continued)

#/AGE/SEX	POL. PARTY	ETHNICITY	EDUCATION	INCOME	OCCUPATION
#9. 30 M	Democrat	Asian	2-4 yrs. college	< 25K	Artist
#10. 34 M	Republican	Latino	< 1 yr. college	< 25K	Freelance Printer
#11. 34 M	Republican	White	< 1 yr. college	25-40K	Meat Cutter
#12. 26 M	Democrat	White	2-4 yrs. college	25-40K	Computer Programmer
#13. 52 F	Republican	White	2-4 yrs. college	over 75K	Homemaker (previous Nurse)
#14. 34 M	Democrat	White	Graduate degree	over 75K	VP Bank
#15. 42 F	Democrat	Black	< 1 yr. college	25-40K	Student
#16. 44 F	Democrat	White	< 1 yr. college	25-40K	Owner antique business
#17. 45 M	Democrat	White	< 1 yr. college	25-40K	Wallpaper Hanger

trial and evidence was presented to them in precisely the same way as it was presented to the twelve actual jurors, however, the alternate jurors did not participate in the jury's final deliberations.

At various times during the trial, after the twelve jury members had left the courtroom, Dr. Anthony asked the alternate jury members probing questions in order to illuminate, for the audience, what might have been transpiring in the minds of the actual jury members. In order to determine what impact the lawyer's arguments or specific evidence might have had upon the jury, the alternate jurors also completed short questionnaires at specific intervals during the course of the trial. Among the questions asked of the alternate jurors at these intervals was, "At this point, what is your verdict?" And, "On a scale of one to seven, how certain are you, at this time, of your verdict?" By using this data, it was possible to determine their verdict orientation at given times and to note when and if changes in their verdict dispositions occurred. It was also possible to ascertain, at the end of the trial, the accuracy of the trial team's strikes.

How accurate were the lawyers with their peremptory challenges? The prosecution was correct on two out of their three strikes and the defense on two out of their two. One of the prosecution's strikes, who became an alternate juror, voted for conviction twice during the trial prior to finally rendering a not guilty verdict. He was the only alternate juror to change his verdict over the course of the trial. Something a little out of the ordinary occurred with this particular juror.

"JFK" The Movie

On the evening after the first day of testimony, this alternate juror, contrary to Judge Byrne's instructions which admonished the jurors from conducting any further research on their own, went to see the movie "JFK." In the film, Oliver Stone presents several conspiracy theories regarding Kennedy's assassination and he raises doubts about Oswald being the lone assassin.

The next morning, prior to closing arguments, this alternate juror confided that he had seen the movie, not because he had any special desire to see that particular film, but because he was curious about it due to all the references which had been made to it during the trial. But he said that in spite of having seen it, the movie did not make an impact on him one way or another. He still maintained that Oswald was guilty and he said that he didn't understand why there was such a "big deal" about the movie. His adamant guilty position was taken prior to closing arguments. After closing arguments, he had changed his mind and his verdict was "not guilty."

It would appear to be a reasonable assumption that the movie did in fact have an influence upon this individual's verdict. Perhaps what had transpired was the influence of the phenomenon discussed earlier called the "sleeper effect" (see Chapter 3). It may have occurred in this case when our juror heard information presented by a non-credible source— Oliver Stone's movie. The juror may have discounted the information as non-factual at the time. Later, when his memory was jogged, this individual then recalled some of the "evidence," while its source was forgotten.

The evidence which was presented in the movie and the recapitulation of the evidence which was presented by the defense in the closing arguments were very similar thematically. It is possible that the two sources of evidence became enmeshed in this juror's mind, reinforcing one another until he became convinced that the defense was correct and, forgetting the non-credible source where he heard the information outside of the courtroom, he changed his verdict.

In light of what we know about the "sleeper effect," it is also very likely that this juror would not credit the movie with his change of view. In fact, ten weeks after the trial, this juror was interviewed again and asked about the impetus for his change of verdict. He gave several very cogent reasons. For example, he felt that he just could not believe that Oswald could have fired the shot, hid the gun, and run down several flights of stairs in the time it was alleged he did. However, among his reasons, he did not include the fact that he had seen "JFK: The Movie."

What of the other jurors? Had any others seen the movie "JFK"? This was one of the questions asked of the seventeen jurors prior to the trial. Of the seventeen potential jurors, not a single juror or alternate juror who would later render a "guilty" verdict had seen the movie, while five out of the seven who rendered "not guilty" verdicts had seen the movie.

In order to determine whether jurors who had seen the movie had sought it out to confirm already existing beliefs about conspiracy theories, they were also asked on the questionnaire prior to the trial, "Do you believe that Oswald killed President Kennedy?" and "Do you believe there may have been a conspiracy?" None of the seventeen admitted that they believed a conspiracy occurred. Some believed that Oswald was guilty and some said that they just did not know. A few said they went into the trial hoping to hear evidence which would convince them that a conspiracy had occurred, but these few were unanimously disappointed. They rendered guilty verdicts. So it appears that prior to the trial, defense jurors who had seen the movie had no stronger beliefs about Oswald's guilt or innocence than jurors who had not seen the film.

Opening Statements

Opening statements were limited to thirty minutes for each side. Joseph Cotchett delivered the prosecution's opening statement. He emphasized the three "simple points" which the prosecution would establish that: (1) Oswald shot the weapon at President Kennedy; (2) the shot he fired killed the President; and (3) he did it with deliberation and intent.

He then went on to describe Oswald as a fanatic, a disturbed man, a man with a love of weapons and Castro. He outlined Oswald's aberrant behavior the day of the assassination: how he had taken off his wedding band and left it at home; how Oswald had acquired his weapons under an alias "Alex James Hidell"; how Oswald had run away from the scene of the shooting while everyone else ran to see what had happened.

Cotchett later indicated to the audience that "My job is to inflame and prejudice the jury in the opening statement. I opt for inflaming from the outset." The media he used to inflame them were his own animated manner and the laser disc replay of the Zapruder film that showed graphically, in slow motion, frame by frame, the "kill shot." The laser disc medium which he used was especially effective. The disc froze the image on the crucial frame: the moment the President was shot in the head. A conventional video cannot freeze the action and still maintain a clear image. The image was very graphic. Cotchett speculated, "Too graphic? Let's see how the jury votes. I think the 'kill shot' will stick in their minds. I wanted them to be sick at what they saw."

Did he succeed? On the questionnaire which the jurors answered after the trial, one question asked, "When you close your eyes and think about the trial, what is the first thing that comes to your mind?" The most frequent answer given by the jurors was the "kill shot" in the Zapruder film.

Thomas Barr delivered the opening statement for the defense. His primary purpose was to "poke, poke, poke holes in the prosecution's arguments." He wanted to raise questions and lots of them. After all, he said, "We had to win only one juror to our side." In order to poke holes in the prosecution's arguments he had to rely on facts, not emotions. There were no witnesses who could account for Oswald's behavior. No one knew why, for example, he used a false name to purchase his rifle. No one knew why he had acted in an uncharacteristic manner in the days preceding the assassination. The defense's position was to "press for reasonable doubt." This involved raising the specter of other possible shooters and other scenarios. Barr's strategy was not to present a single theory which could explain all the facts, but rather to raise reasonable doubts about the theory the prosecution had presented.

In his opening, Barr stated "After twenty-six volumes of the Warren Commission and twelve volumes of the House report, you would believe that the government by now would have all the facts clear and undisputed. After the most massive series of investigations in the entire world, there should not be the slightest doubt of any kind as to what the facts are. Every fact should fit very clearly. And yet every single fact of any significance in this case is open to serious doubt." Barr went on to raise many questions: Where was Lee Oswald when the shots were fired? Where did they come from? How many shots were fired? Who fired them? How many shooters? Why wasn't the shot made earlier on Elm Street, when there was a head-on vantage for a shooter on the sixth floor?

Barr did not use the laser disc technology which the prosecution had used, but perhaps more consistent with his appeal to facts rather than emotion, he used an exhibit board which displayed the questions stated. He said that he wanted to plant those issues in the jury's head and that technology would not help.

Technology

Spectus Technologies, Inc., a firm specializing in scientific and engineering visualization services and video presentation systems for the courtroom, provided the demonstrative evidence for both the prosecution and defense. Engineering visualizations were used throughout the trial, from opening statements to closing arguments. In accordance with the theme of the event, newer methods of presenting demonstrative evidence in today's courtrooms were used in concert with the traditional methods. The presentations included text retrieval, foam boards, graphics, photography, an 8 x 8 foot mural of Dealey Plaza, video production, and three dimensional computer animation.

Most of the prosecution's exhibits were displayed on TV monitors. All images were produced, stored, and accessed by laser disc media and displayed on ten large screen monitors for viewing from any position in the mock courtroom and in the auditorium. The laser disc medium assisted the lawyers by rapidly presenting evidence and significantly reducing the number of assistants needed to coordinate tangible evidence. One laser disc can store over 54,000 images on each side. Images can be documents, videotapes, photographs, diagrams, drawings, charts and graphs, virtually anything tangible. Using an electronic device that resembles a VCR player, the exhibits are instantly accessed via a bar code scanner and displayed to the audience and jurors on high resolution television monitors positioned in the courtroom.

Computer simulation was employed extensively by the prosecution in presenting their theories of the events that transpired at Dealey Plaza on November 22, 1963. This technology has been used predominantly in civil cases over the past few years, and is increasingly being used in criminal proceedings. In computer simulation, a model is constructed based upon known physical laws. The physical evidence which the trial teams had available, such as bullet angles, bone beveling results, etc., were plugged into the model so that a complete "picture" of reality could be reconstructed. This "picture of reality" was then animated and displayed to observers via high resolution TV monitors.

The prosecution's presentation revolved heavily around the expert testimony of Dr. Robert Piziali. He is a specialist in the biomechanics of human injury and accident reconstruction at Failure Analysis Associates in Menlo Park, California. After a thorough investigation of the information available from the Warren Commission and the House Select Committee, he focused on the evidence which related to the number of shots that were fired, where the shots were fired from, and whether or not Oswald was capable of firing the shots in the time available. Utilizing trajectory analysis and the Zapruder film to recreate the event at Dealey Plaza, Piziali developed a geometric representation of the Plaza. Employing a procedure called texture mapping, the computer images that were developed provided a correct visual representation of the area. He then had his team at Failure Analysis build an exact replica of the limousine, placing people in the car in the same position as the President and Governor Connally. With his mathematical analysis and the information from the autopsy reports of the bullets' paths through the bodies of the President and Governor Connally, Dr. Piziali was able to generate a working computer model of the entire event. The resulting animation was able to demonstrate the geometry and timing of the theorized three shots. He was then able to trace the bullet's trajectory backwards to its most likely origin. That point was the sixth floor of the Texas School Book Depository, where the prosecution had placed Lee Harvey Oswald at the time of the murder. Dr. Piziali's opinion was that there were three shots and they all came from the sixth floor. He testified that there was no physical evidence that a shot was made from the grassy knoll. Martin L. Fackler, M.D., a ballistics expert and president of the International Wound Ballistic Association, supported the prosecution's contention that a single shot had wounded both Kennedy and Connally.

In post-trial interviews, the jury indicated that Dr. Piziali's testimony and demonstrations were very interesting as well as convincing. Both prosecution and defense jurors were asked to cite the evidence which they liked most. The computer analysis and event reconstruction visualizations presented on the TV screens were their choices.

Dr. Roger McCarthy was the principal expert witness for the defense. As an internationally recognized expert in engineering analysis, event reconstruction, and ballistics, he analyzed the motivations and choices an assassin would have made if he were attempting to shoot the President. McCarthy's testimony focused on Oswald's marksmanship, the weapon used, and the selection of shots which Oswald was alleged to have chosen. Using computer animation, Dr. McCarthy explained the view and shot selections available to Oswald from the sixth floor of the school book depository. This bird's-eye view of Dealey Plaza showed the effective zone which a gunman would have had firing at the President. In order to recreate the scene, the characteristics of the rifle and scope were measured. Dr. McCarthy performed a field test using an exact replica of Oswald's rifle in order to determine the speed at which the rifle could be operated and to measure the motion of the rifle through the fire-reload sequence. The data for the timing and motion of the rifle was then entered into the computer and synchronized with the timing and motion of the Presidential motorcade. Using a three dimensional representation of Dealey Plaza, the computer model of the Caracano rifle was placed in the sixth floor window of the school book depository on the television screen. Finally, by simulating the view through the rifle scope and adding the audio track of the recorded rifle shots, the reenactment could be created. In McCarthy's opinion, the Mannlicher Caracano rifle was an inferior weapon and Oswald would not have selected it if he truly intended to kill President Kennedy. The gun was the wrong choice, the bullets were also the wrong choice, and the vantage point for the shots was clearly wrong. The defense alleged that more than one gunman was involved—which would have increased the effective "kill" zone. Several fact witnesses located on the grassy knoll at the time of the shooting testified in support of this proposition. Dr. Cyril H. Wecht, a pathologist who had served on the House Select Committee, was intensely critical of the prosecution's "magic bullet" theory and contributed skepticism of the prosecution's lone assassin contention.

Moment-by-Moment Response Analysis

In addition to the evidence and courtroom proceedings, TV monitors were also used to display DecisionQuest Inc.'s moment-by-moment response analysis. This technique allowed the lawyers in the audience to observe immediate evaluations made by selected participants in the ongoing events in the courtroom. Prior to the trial, the alternate jurors, a panel of lawyers, and six prominent judges were trained in the use of cordless hand-held electronic monitoring devices. By operating the devices, the participants registered their immediate reactions during the trial by indicating the extent to which events were "convincing" or "not convincing."

The participants were responding continuously to lawyer arguments, witness testimony, and courtroom exhibits, and their responses were instantly aggregated and displayed on TV monitors as an overlay of color-coded lines resembling a graph. The audience saw the actual trial events, as well as the overlay, on a single screen.

For example, during the opening arguments, Mr. Cotchett held the Mannlicher Caracano rifle as he described in detail how the assassin aimed and fired the rifle. His voice and manner of presentation were extremely compelling and convincing and this was reflected by the immediate increase in "convincing" responses observed in the moment-by-moment analysis on the TV screen.

One of the more educational aspects of the moment-by-moment analysis in this trial was its use to observe the discrepancies among the lawyers', judges' and alternate jurors' reactions. For example, the judges and jurors responded differently to the reference in the opening statement that Oswald had murdered Officer Tippitt only a few minutes after the assassination of President Kennedy. The judge's responses dropped dramatically, to "not convincing" while the alternate juror's responses rose dramatically to "very convincing." During the discussion session after the opening statements, the panel of judges and the alternate jurors were asked to discuss their responses. The judges in general explained that they reacted negatively to the idea of "trying a case within a case." The jurors on the other hand, stated that the news of the Tippitt murder was something new and that they had not been aware of it. This caused them to reason that the two murders could have been a "chain of events" and that it made Oswald appear to be "more desperate."

Another example of the variance displayed in the DecisionQuest moment-by-moment analysis came about with the prosecution's reference to Oswald's use of an alias: Alex James Hiddell. The alternate juror's ratings dropped to "not convincing" while the judge's ratings rose to "very convincing." The jurors later explained that they really hadn't seen the relevance of his possessing a driver's license with another name on it. The judges on the other hand, felt it was very important. As one judge stated, "When someone uses a false name to obtain a weapon, it is circumstantial evidence that he intends to do something with it he wants to hide." While this fact was obviously incriminating to the legal professionals, the same piece of information was evaluated in very different ways by the lay jury.

The Verdict

The jury deliberations were broadcast to the audience via closed circuit TV. For most of the lawyers in the audience, the opportunity to view a jury deliberation process is a rare event. The members of the trial teams intently watched and listened to the closed circuit monitors, undoubtedly noting whether their arguments had been received and understood by the jurors. After several ballots, it became clear that the jury members were split on the verdict: seven "guilty," five "not guilty." The alternate jurors were also polled regarding their final verdict, even though they did not participate in the actual deliberation process. The five-member alternate jury rendered three "guilty" verdicts and two "not guilty" verdicts. The ratio of "guilty" to "not guilty" ballots is virtually the same for both the actual jury members and the alternate jury members. Table 2 displays a list of the seventeen jurors with their respective numbers, along with their verdicts, and Table 3 displays the alternate jurors' verdicts, which they marked on the questionnaire three separate times during the trial. Interviews with the jury immediately after their deliberations and again ten weeks later revealed that the jury was hopelessly deadlocked, and irrespective of time, it would have remained hung.

Table 2.

Jurors and Their Verdicts

JUROR #	ROLE	VERDICT
# 1.	Actual Juror	Guilty
# 2.	Actual Juror	Guilty
# 3.	Actual Juror	Guilty
# 4.	Actual Juror	Guilty
# 5.	Defense Strike/Alternate Juror	Guilty
# 6.	Actual Juror	Guilty
# 7.	Prosecution Strike/Alternate Juror	Not Guilty
# 8.	Actual Juror	Not Guilty
# 9.	Actual Juror	Not Guilty
# 10.	Defense Strike/Alternate Juror	Guilty
# 11.	Actual Juror	Guilty
# 12.	Prosecution Strike/Alternate Juror	Guilty
# 13.	Actual Juror	Guilty
# 14.	Prosecution Strike/Alternate Juror	Not Guilty
# 15.	Actual Juror	Not Guilty
# 16.	Actual Juror	Not Guilty
# 17.	Actual Juror	Not Guilty

Table 3.

Alternate Jurors' Verdicts

	Juror Number				
	# 5	# 7	# 10	# 12	# 14
Verdict After Opening Arguments	Guilty	Guilty	Guilty	Guilty	Not Guilty
Certainty of Verdict *	4	5	5	4	3
Verdict After First Day	Guilty	Guilty	Guilty	Guilty	Not Guilty
Certainty of Verdict *	6	5	4	6	2
Final Verdict	Guilty	Not Guilty	Guilty	Guilty	Not Guilty
Certainty of Verdict *	6	3	4	6	3

* Certainty of verdict was measured on a scale from 1 to 7, with 7 representing "Very Certain" and 1 representing "Very Uncertain."

What juror characteristics were related to the verdict? The audience and the defense team had different perspectives in the use of their peremptory challenges. Of the audience members who were asked to strike for the defense, 83% struck juror #13, the female homemaker who had been a nurse at one time, and 58% struck juror # 1, the black female sales representative. Both of these jurors would have been correct defense strikes and ultimately rendered "guilty" verdicts. However, the defense team struck juror #5, the older gentleman who was a bank auditor and juror #10, the male Latino printer, both of which also proved to be correct strikes for the defense, in that their verdicts, given on a post-trial questionnaire, were "guilty." The audience and the defense team had different ideas about what constituted a "risky" juror for the defense. However, both the audience and the defense teams were accurate in their choices of jurors to strike; all four ultimately rendered a verdict of "guilty."

The audience members who struck for the prosecution, agreed with only one of the prosecution's actual strikes; a majority of the audience (64%) and the prosecution struck juror #7, the male photographer. His final verdict would have been "not guilty," as he stated on the post-trial questionnaire. However, the remaining strikes made by the audience for the prosecution displayed no consensus. The prosecution, in addition to juror #7, struck juror #12, the male computer programmer and juror #14, the male bank vice president. The prosecution was correct in peremptorily challenging juror #14, as his final verdict as an alternate juror was "not guilty"; however, juror #12 rendered a final verdict on the post-trail questionnaire of "guilty" and hence represented a prosecution error.

In spite of the overall accuracy of their peremptory challenges for this trial, there appeared to be no firm consensus among the audience and the trial teams as to *which* jurors to strike. Traditionally, lawyers attempt to identify surface traits or demographic characteristics of jurors which are believed to be predictive of juror bias. Generally these demographic characteristics are sex, level of education, race, income, and occupation. However, as we had discussed earlier, research conducted on alternate and actual jurors confirms again and again that demographic characteristics are generally poor predictors of a juror's verdict, and we found this to be true once again in the analysis of the jurors for this trial.

The trial teams thought a number of personal characteristics would be related to a juror's verdict. *Age* was deemed important by both the prosecution and the defense; the younger the juror, the more favorable to the defense; and the older the juror, the more favorable to the prosecution. The reasoning here is simply that the younger jurors would not remember the events which transpired in November of 1963. Juror's *gender* was also considered important by the prosecution; they felt that women tended to be more sympathetic in general. Of particular importance for the prosecution was two *occupations*: computer programmer and artist/photographer. These occupations were considered especially consequential for the prosecution, because many of their weighty exhibits were extremely "high-tech" in nature, consisting of computer simulations and enhanced graphics. The prosecution felt that an artistic person, as well as one knowledgeable in computers, would think too creatively while viewing these exhibits and would interpret them, not as something factual, but as "art" and as evidence which the prosecution had "created."

Of these three demographic traits—age, sex, and occupation—only occupation as an artist/photographer was relevant for the final verdict. Neither age nor sex were predictors of the final verdict. The youngest juror, who was ostensibly a double-threat for the prosecution because he was also a computer programmer (a triple-threat if you consider gender), rendered a verdict of "guilty." By the prosecution's voir dire reasoning, he should have been anti-prosecution as well as anti-computer-generated evidence, but as it turned out he was not. Nor was jurors' sex associated with the final verdict. Virtually the same percentage of the women as of the men (57% and 60% respectively) rendered a "guilty" verdict, and, likewise, essentially the same percentages of women and men (42% and 40% respectively) rendered a "not guilty" verdict. Thus, women were no more or less likely than men to render a "not guilty" verdict: knowing a juror's gender, in this trial, did not help in predicting that juror's verdict.

As discussed earlier, the artist/photographer was an accurate peremptory challenge by the prosecution, but for the wrong reasons. He was the juror who went to see the movie "JFK" and was the only "struck" juror to change his verdict; the other four rendered consistent verdicts at all three measurement times.

There *was* an artist in the actual jury. He was either overlooked by the prosecution during voir dire or the prosecution felt that one of the other jurors was more of a threat to their case. At any rate, this artist, juror #9, reacted *precisely* as the prosecution had predicted an artist would react to the "high tech" evidence. Throughout the deliberations, he was vocally critical of the computer generated animation and questioned the assumptions and the methods used as the basis for the angle analysis and recreation of Dealey Plaza. He continued to express his skepticism in a post-trial questionnaire, stating that there was an "oversimplification of the case with visuals" by the prosecution, yet criticizing the defense's presentation by stating that their "case lacked visual substance." His verdict was "not guilty," precisely how the prosecution had predicted an artist would react.

Race is often viewed as an important demographic characteristic, and it was for this trial. However, its importance was counterintuitive. Stereotypically, minorities are thought to be more sympathetic to a criminal defendant. In actuality for this case it was just the opposite; of the jurors who were minority group members (i.e., black, Hispanic or Asian), 75% rendered "guilty" verdicts (as opposed to 40% of the white jurors who rendered "guilty" verdicts). Again, the stereotype of a sympathetic minority group member would have lead to an erroneous prediction.

To summarize then, the only demographic variable which was predicted by the trial teams to be associated with the verdict and was in fact associated with the verdict, was the occupation artist/photographer. We had the luxury in this case of requiring our jurors to complete a number of extensive questionnaires prior to the trial that the lawyers didn't have an opportunity to see. Let's examine some other juror characteristics and their relationship to the verdict in the case.

Behavior as an Alternate Measure for Cognition

As we have suggested throughout this book, behavioral characteristics can frequently be reliable indicia of verdict disposition. We found, in this case for example, that religious affiliation and church attendance were related to the final verdict, but the juror's perceptions about how religious a person he/she is, was not related to the verdict. We asked three questions pertaining to religion: 1. "Do you consider yourself a religious person?" 2. "What is your religious affiliation?" and 3. "How often do you attend church?" Knowing whether a juror considered himself to be *religious* did not aid in predicting that juror's final verdict; approximately 65% of all the jurors, regardless of their verdict, considered themselves to be "not religious." However, a juror's responses to the second and third questions which pertained to religious affiliation and church attendance did provide information which was significantly correlated with the final verdict. Seventy-one percent of the jurors who answered that their religious affiliation was "none," ultimately rendered a verdict of "not guilty" while 80% of those jurors who answered that they had a specific religious affiliation (e.g., Catholic, Protestant, Baptist), rendered a final verdict of "guilty." Thus knowing whether a juror had a religious affiliation was a strong predictor of the juror's final verdict in this trial. Similar percentages were found when a juror stated that he or she "never" attended church; 62% of these jurors rendered a "not guilty" verdict, whereas only 30% of the jurors who stated that they did attend church found for the defense. This appears to be a fine distinction regarding religiosity, but it points to the subtleties of behavioral data—a great deal depends upon how you ask the questions.

In a similar vein, political preference mattered, but how liberal or conservative a juror viewed him/herself to be, did not. We asked two questions regarding political preference: 1. "How did you vote in the last Presidential election?" and 2. "How politically liberal or conservative do you consider yourself to be?" There were only three jurors who voted a Republican ticket in the last Presidential election, and they *all* rendered a "guilty" verdict. But in answer to the question of how liberal or conservative they considered themselves to be, the jurors who voted the Republican ticket considered themselves to be no more or less conservative than did the jurors who voted a Democratic ticket. On a 7-point scale with higher ratings meaning more liberal and lower ratings meaning more conservative, the mean rating for the "not guilty" jurors was 5.2 and the mean rating for the "guilty" group of jurors was 5.1. The difference of a .1 scale point is negligible and the means for the two groups are essentially equal. Thus, had a lawyer asked a juror how liberal or conservative he considered himself to be, the juror's answer would not have helped predict that juror's verdict. But, had the lawyer understood the relevance of the information regarding past voting behavior, he could have accurately predicted the verdict for the Republican jurors as "guilty." What emerged here, then, is a seeming lack of consistency between what a person actually does or is and how he views himself. Overt behavior then, rather than self-perception or self-disclosure, appears to be more predictive of how a juror is predisposed to ultimately vote.

Personality

One set of questions on the pre-trial questionnaires measured personality structures on thirty different traits. Comparing the results of this analysis with each juror's ultimate verdict produced some interesting associations. For example, defense jurors scored very high on an "open-mindedness" trait while the prosecution jurors scored in the average range. However, defense jurors were not open-minded about everything; they were particularly open-minded about *ideas* and about *activities.*

The picture that emerged regarding the defense jurors' decision-making process was that these were individuals who were willing to consider new or even unconventional ideas. They also enjoyed speculating about philosophical issues and puzzle solving activities. From a behavioral perspective, the defense jurors tended to engage in more novel experiences and consistently varied their environment more than the prosecution jurors. How did the openness trait manifest in the deliberations? The defense's goal throughout the trial was to raise doubts and to propose alternative scenarios and possibilities for the jurors to consider. Defense jurors, throughout the deliberations, expressed their doubts about the prosecution's theory and how it did not adequately explain all of the details of the crime. The issues raised by the defense made sense in that there were just too many unaccounted possibilities to allow these jurors to convict.

We would expect defense jurors to be more analytic than the prosecution jurors based upon their elevated openness scores. In fact, when they were asked on a separate question what their best subject in school had been, math was their most frequent choice. Only one prosecution juror rated math as his favorite while the majority of the others indicated that more descriptive subjects such as English were their preference.

In this trial, there were really two sources of evidence. One was the trial evidence which was presented by the lawyers. The second source was never admitted during the trial. It was the movie "JFK." Pre-trial publicity surrounding this case has reached monumental proportions over the past 29 years. Not only have countless books been written regarding the assassination, but even the neighborhood comic-book stores sell "Conspiracy Comics," which present young readers with conspiracy and cover-up theories of the assassination. Perhaps more than any other trial, jurors in this case had been exposed to information, theories, and speculation prior to the official proceedings. How much of this information did jurors bring with them into the courtroom and what was its impact? Prior to the trial, we asked jurors how familiar they were with the conclusions of the Warren Commission. Only two prosecution jurors said they had any familiarity with the Warren Commission's findings. The defense jurors, on the other hand, professed knowledge about the Warren Commission findings. Hence, the primary source of information regarding the assassination for prosecution jurors was the evidence which was presented in the trial. Defense jurors, on the other hand, entered the trial with other sources of "evidence" through the movie and media coverage of the Warren Commission.

Predispositions

Past research on specific political attitudes and verdict indicates that jurors who favor capital punishment are more likely to convict in a murder trial. This was also found to be true for the jurors in this trial. As measured on the pre-trial questionnaire, of those jurors who favored the use of the death penalty, 67% rendered a "guilty" verdict whereas only 40% of those jurors who did not favor the death penalty rendered a "guilty" verdict. A second attitude was also identified which followed this same pattern—those jurors who favored gun control legislation were more likely to render a "guilty" verdict.

It is a common belief among judges and lawyers that jurors are capable of suspending these predispositions and weighing the evidence impartially as it is presented. As we have seen throughout this book, this is not necessarily the case. In fact, much of the process involved in weighing new information vis-à-vis an attitude is not a conscious one. Further, we cannot discount the impact a visual medium like film can have on a person's attitudes. *Entertainment Weekly* observed, "when it comes to dramatizing those theories, his (Stone's) filmmaking is so supple and alive that "JFK" practically roots itself in your imagination." This is exactly what it appears to have done to those jurors who saw it.

The "sleeper effect" can also help explain the other juror's verdicts of "not guilty." Prior to the trial, all the potential jurors were asked two questions: 1. "How much do you agree that Lee Harvey Oswald assassinated John F. Kennedy?" and 2. "How much do you agree that he acted alone?" Sixteen of the seventeen potential jurors, at that time, were either neutral or agreed that Lee Harvey Oswald was the assassin, likewise they were either neutral or agreed that he had acted alone, even though some of them had seen the movie which strongly suggested the opposite. In this instance, those four who had seen "JFK" prior to the trial had in fact dismissed it as merely "film" and "not factual," as they had indicated on the pre-trial questionnaire. This is the second finding which casts doubt on the possible alternative hypothesis that the jurors believed the conspiracy theories beforehand and sought out the film to verify their beliefs. Not one of the jurors who had seen the film stated prior to the trial that he believed Oswald was innocent. Clearly something potent intervened to cause those particular jurors to resist the prosecution's arguments and to believe that there was a reasonable doubt about Oswald's guilt. The defense presented arguments and theories similar to those presented in the movie. Thus, this was the second time the jurors had been presented with these conspiracy theories. The prior visual information which was presented in the film reinforced the information which was presented by the defense, making the information doubly weighty for those jurors who had seen the film.

The second attitude which was particularly salient for this trial and of particular importance for the prosecution's case, was the jurors' attitudes about video technology. The lawyers in this trial, especially the prosecution's, were particularly innovative in their use of "high tech" evidence. They relied heavily upon state-of-the-art technology to present their case, and exactly how the enhanced visuals and computer graphics would affect jurors, no one knew. No precedents had been established regarding their effects. However, to the untrained eye, the exhibits bore a strong similarity to video games and computer graphics. The jurors' past experience with video games and computer graphics might have provided them a level of comfort and receptivity regarding what they perceived to be a similar medium. The question was asked of the potential jurors prior to the trial, "How much do you like or dislike Nintendo and/or video games?" All but one of the jurors who rendered a "not guilty" verdict, reported on the pre-trial questionnaire that they strongly disliked Nintendo and/or video games. This dislike was carried over into the way they viewed the prosecution's "high tech" evidence presentation; if the jurors had a previously negative experience with this medium, this predisposed them to feel uncomfortable with the information which was presented in a similar medium. Their negative attitude effectively filtered out the full impact of the video evidence which was so heavily utilized by the prosecution. The prosecution had not "reached" these jurors due to the nature of the medium. This negative attitude toward video technology would have been important to ferret out in the voir dire process, allowing at the very least for the prosecution's peremptory strikes of those jurors and at the most, recognition that a secondary or supplemental medium must be used to present the evidence should those jurors remain in the jury.

Deliberations

While the deliberations provided fascinating insights about the impact of the lawyers' trial strategies and tactics, two particularly interesting observations deserve comment. The first related to a specific reference made in the prosecution's opening statement. The jurors were told that Oswald's widow would testify that he practiced the bolt action of his rifle daily while sitting on his porch. In actuality, the promise of this witness providing testimony was made in error. Pre-trial stipulations precluded Mrs. Oswald's testimony. In the ordinary course of events, opposition counsel would take delight in having the other side placed in the position of failing to meet an opening statement promise of proof. In this case however, even though the widow's observation was never delivered in court, it was talked about and "remembered" by jurors as trial testimony during deliberations.

A second interesting finding related to the use of the high technology visual evidence. In the questionnaires completed by jurors after the trial, they identified the advanced technology that supported the expert testimony as critically important in influencing the verdict of prosecution jurors.   Interestingly enough, while the computer animations and simulations involved extremely sophisticated technology to produce, to the jurors, these visual representations were not very different from many of their day-to-day visual experiences outside the courtroom.

Rather than being seen as "slick," too complicated, fancy, or inappropriately unique, jurors saw the video as personally accessible. The lawyers in this case brought the contemporary media of the shopping mall's video location maps, Nintendo, automatic ticketing machines, and twentieth century teaching tools into the courtroom. Not only were these jurors comfortable with this method of presenting evidence, they also found it interesting, appealing, and an enormously helpful method of translating verbal testimony from abstract to concrete reality.

Conclusion

The ABA's "Trial of the Century" provided trial lawyers with an opportunity to observe unparalleled courtroom skills. Additionally, it was a rare opportunity to dissect the voir dire process, to get inside the jurors' heads and determine what attitudes they brought with them and how those attitudes affected their verdict.

The results of the analyses performed on the juror's responses to the questionnaires administered before and after the trial, supports previous findings; surface traits and demographics were poor predictors of a juror's verdict. Much more relevant to the final verdict were juror's attitudes as they related to specific salient issues in the trial.

One of the most compelling questions of our time continues to be who fired the shots that killed John F. Kennedy? For almost 30 years a passionate debate has intensified. On one side, the Warren Commission found that Lee Harvey Oswald acted alone in killing the President. However, in 1978 the House Select Committee concluded that there may have been more than one gunman involved in the shooting. While this trial provided an examination of many critical elements of the case utilizing sophisticated state-of-the-art science and technology, and employed the talents of prominent trial advocates, many questions remain unanswered.

Did Lee Harvey Oswald kill President Kennedy? Like the jury in San Francisco, the author and editors of this book have arrived at different verdicts based upon the evidence presented in the "Trial of the Century."

Suggestions for Additional Reading

Anderson, K.E. *Persuasion: Theory and Practice.* Boston: Allyn & Bacon, 1971.

Argyle, Michael. *Bodily Communication.* (2nd Ed.) Methuen, London, 1988.

Berger, Charles R., and Stephen H. Chaffee (Eds.). *Handbook of Communication Science.* Newbury Park, CA: Sage Publications, Inc., 1987.

Brehm, Sharon S., and Saul M. Kassin. *Social Psychology.* Boston: Houghton Mifflin Co., 1990.

Cialdini, Robert B. *Influence: How and Why People Agree on Things.* New York: William Morrow & Co., Inc., 1984.

Cronkhite, G. *Persuasion, Speech and Behavioral Change.* New York: Bobbs-Merrill Co., 1969.

Dichter, Ernest. *Consumer Motivation.* New York: McGraw-Hill, 1964.

Forsyth, D.R. *Social Psychology.* Monterey, CA: Brooks/Cole, 1987.

Hovland, Carl. *The Order of Presentation in Persuasion.* New Haven, CT: Yale University Press, 1957.

Hovland, Carl I., and Irving L. Janis (Eds.) *Personality and Persuasibility*. New Haven, CT: Yale University Press, 1959.

Karlins, M., and H.I. Abelson. *Persuasion: How Opinions and Attitudes are Changed*. New York: Springer Publishing, 1970.

Knapp, Mark L., and Gerald R. Miller, (Eds.) *Handbook of Interpersonal Communication*. Beverly, Hills, CA: Sage Publications, Inc., 1985.

Mation, Ronald, J. *Communication in the Legal Process*. San Francisco: Holt, Rinehart & Winston, Inc., 1988.

Milburn, Michael A. *Persuasion and Politics: The Social Psychology of Public Opinion*. Pacific Grove, CA: Brooks/Cole Publishing Co., 1991.

O'Keefe, Daniel J. *Persuasion: Theory and Research*. Newbury Park, CA: Sage Publications, Inc., 1990.

Oskamp, S. *Applied Social Psychology*. Englewood Cliffs, NJ: Prentice Hall, 1984.

Petty, Richard E., et. al. "Multiple Roles for Affect in Persuasion," *Emotion and Social Judgments*. Oxford, England: Pergamon Press, Inc., 1991.

Pratkanis, Anthony R., and Elliot Aronson. *Age of Propaganda: The Everyday Use and Abuse of Persuasion*. New York: W.H. Freeman & Co., 1992.

Reardon, Kathleen Kelly. *Persuasion in Practice*. Newbury Park, CA: Sage Publications, Inc., 1991.

Reardon, Kathleen Kelly. *Persuasion: Theory and Context*. Beverly Hills, CA: Sage Publications, Inc., 1981.

Schumaker, John F. (Ed.) *Human Suggestibility: Advances in Theory, Research, and Application*. New York: Routledge, 1991.

Shaver, Kelly G. *Principles of Social Psychology (3rd Ed.)* Hillsdale, NJ: Lawrence Erlbaum Associates, Inc., 1987.

Smith, Mary John. *Persuasion and Human Action.* Belmont, CA: Wadsworth Publishing Co., 1982.

Vinson, Donald E. "How to Persuade Jurors," Abbott's *Surrogate Juries.* American Law Institute-American Bar Association Committee on Continuing Professional Education, 1990.

Vinson, Donald E. "Psychological Anchors: Influencing the Jury," Abbott's *Surrogate Juries.* American Law Institute-American Bar Association Committee on Continuing Professional Education, 1990.

Vinson, Donald E. "The Shadow Jury: An Experiment in Litigation Science," Abbott's *Surrogate Juries.* American Law Institute-American Bar Association Committee on Continuing Professional Education, 1990.

Vinson, Donald E. "Social Science Research Methods for Litigation," Abbott's *Surrogate Juries.* American Law Institute-American Bar Association Committee on Continuing Professsional Education, 1990.

Vinson, Donald E. and Philip K. Anthony. *Social Science Research Methods for Litigation.* Richmond, VA: The Michie Company, 1985.

Vinson, Donald E. and Philip K. Anthony. "Strategies & Techniques of Psychology in Jury Trials," Masterson's *Civil Trial Practice.* Practicing Law Institute, 1986.

Zinbardo, P., and E.B. Ebbesen. *Influencing Attitudes and Changing Behavior.* Reading, MA: Addison-Wesley, 1970.

Zimbardo, Philip G., and Michael R. Leippe. *The Psychology of Attitude Change and Social Influence.* New York: McGraw-Hill Book Company, 1991.

Contributing Lawyers Index

Subject Index

A

Actor-Observer effect, 95
Affective jurors, 60-61
Ambiguous information, 70
Analysis of variance, 244
Anomie, 212
Anti-business jurors, 105-106
Aristotle, 5-6, 7
Attitude change, 25-28
Attitude components, 20-21
Attitude formation, 21-23
Attitude salience, 29-32
Attitudes, 17-20
Attitudes and behavior, 24
Attributes of persuasion, 36-37
Attributions, 92-108
Attributional biases, 94-100

B

Barr, Thomas, 250, 256
Base rate frequency, 63-64
Belief systems, 15-17
Bias, 114
Boies, David, 250

Brosnahan, James, 250

C

Causal schema, 90-94
Causality, 228
Change of venue, 239
Chestler, Evan, 250
Cicero, 6
Cotchett, Joseph, 250, 256
Cognitions, 13-15
Cognitive dissonance, 167-168
Cognitive jurors, 61-62
Color, 199
"Compliance with Standards"
    defense, 103-106
Confirmatory evidence, 69
Correlation analysis, 244
Counter-factual thinking, 72-74
Credibility, 37-39

D

Data collection, 228
Defensive attribution, 97-102